EQUIPPING THE SAINTS

Equipping the Saints

Ordination
in Anglicanism Today

<small>PAPERS FROM THE SIXTH INTERNATIONAL ANGLICAN LITURGICAL
CONSULTATION</small>

Editors:
Ronald L. Dowling
David R. Holeton

the columba press

First published in 2006 by
the columba press
55A Spruce Avenue, Stillorgan Industrial Park,
Blackrock, Co Dublin

Cover by Bill Bolger
Prepared for publication by Brian Mayne
Origination by The Columba Press
Printed in Ireland by ColourBooks Ltd, Dublin

ISBN 1 85607 543 5

Table of Contents

Introduction

With the conclusion of the International Anglican Liturgical Consultation's work on Christian Initiation (Toronto Statement – IALC IV, 1991) and the Eucharist (Dublin Statement – IALC V, 1995), it seemed a natural step for the IALC to turn it's attention to the matter of ordination. The IALC had agreed that its work would reflect the WCC Paper *Baptism, Eucharist and Ministry*. This it did over a series of three meetings. A preparatory conference held at Järvenpää in 1997 with the intention of concluding the work at a full consultation planned in conjunction with the Congress of Societas Liturgica to be held in Kottayam (India) in 1999. An unfortunate misunderstanding between the Local Committee of Societas Liturgica and government officials resulted in permission for the Consultation not being granted after most of the participants had already arrived in Kottayam, with a number refused entrance visas and therefore unable to attend. In the light of that, the Steering Committee decided that the meeting did not constitute a full Consultation and that the IALC's work on ordination would be brought to its conclusion in two years when it met in Berkeley, California.

The 1997 Järvenpää Conference divided its work into three major areas: i) the nature of order in the church; ii) imparting ministry within the church; and iii) ecumenical questions for the future of the church. The work of the Conference along with a number of preparatory papers and essays commissioned as a result of the Conference appeared as *Anglican Orders and Ordinations: Essays and Reports from the Interim Conference at Järvenpää, Finland of the International Anglican Liturgical Consultatioin, 4-9 August 1997* [Alcuin/GROW Joint Liturgical Study 39] (Cambridge, 1997).

While the planned 1999 Indian Consultation could not meet as such, those present divided into three working groups to discuss: i) the structure of ordination liturgies; ii) theological issues, and iii) the processes of discernment of vocation and preparation for ordination. By the end of the meeting, it was clear that further work needed to be done before there could be any statement on the question of ordination. The group leaders proposed the formation of an editorial committee who would work on the material produced by the working groups and refine it in the light of the plenary discussions. That work was then circulated to IALC members present in India for further comment. It was that material that became the working draft for IALC-VI when it met at Berkeley in August 2001. The Berkeley Statement – *To Equip the Saints* – is thus the result of at least five years' work. It represents the reflected opinion of the over seventy members of the Consultation, coming from twenty-nine Provinces and Member Churches of the Anglican Communion.

It was clear that the reception of *To Equip the Saints* would require a series of essays and Provincial reflections to draw out the many ramifications of the statement, as had been the case for both the Toronto and Dublin Statements. This volume adheres to the pattern set in *Growing in Newness of Life* (Toronto, 1993) and *Our Thanks and Praise* (Toronto, 1998), a pattern which has been positively received around the Anglican Communion with its combination of theoretical and practical essays.

The matter of order and ordination has been much more marked by controversy among Anglicans in recent years than have been either Christian Initiation or the Eucharist. The question of the ordination of women to the diaconate, presbyterate and episcopate has stirred great emotion in some parts of the communion over the past thirty years while, in other parts, it has been accepted as a natural consequence of the implications of the baptismal ecclesiology which has come to take a place for many Anglicans at the heart of their self-understanding of who they are as church. Currently, the question of the ordination of homosexual men and women is eliciting similar emotion. It is, perhaps, salutary to remember that, over the past century-and-a-half, debates over baptismal regeneration and the ceremonial (and, consequently theological) expression of the eucharist elicited similar emotion and threat of schism.

Since the first time a small Anglican Liturgical Consultation gathered in Boston (1985) to discuss the question of children and the eucharist, successive IALCs have affirmed a baptismal ecclesiology as the foundation for their work. Noting that 'the church is the whole body of the faithful ... created through baptism into the death and resurrection of Jesus Christ, which is the sign of faith and of participation in God's act of redemption', the Consultation made it clear that baptism is constitutive of the life of the church and is the sole act required to admit to the eucharist. The life of the church flows from God's act in baptism.

From the time of the conference in Järvenpää (which affirmed 'Baptism as the foundation in which a theology of the ministry of the whole people of God is rooted'), a baptismal ecclesiology has been the foundation on which the IALC's discussions on orders and ordinations have been built. The articles by William Crockett and Louis Weil in this collection treat this question in greater detail. The practical implications of a baptismal ecclesiology for Anglican ordination rites themselves are also addressed, in part, within these pages. Much reflection, however, still needs to take place on what may seem to be a cognitive dissonance between the theology of the renewed rites and some of the ritual acts that have begun to appear in Anglican ordinals.

As Paul Bradshaw reminds us, there is a widespread consensus both within Anglicanism and among a broad spectrum of churches that ordination is through the laying-on-of-hands with prayer. The imposition of hands must be visibly central at an ordination. The first Anglican Ordinal (1550) clearly broke with the medieval tradition in which anointings, the giving of implements of office and vesting had clearly come to overshadow the central act of ordinations – to the extent that there was an ongoing debate among theologians as to which act, in fact, constituted ordination. Among the scholars of the time, only the minority appear to have maintained that it was the imposition of hands! In the end, Cranmer retained only the giving of the Bible. The vesting, the anointing, the giving of the implements (chalice and paten for presbyters, the pastoral staff for bishops) were all eliminated from the Ordinal. Slowly, they have returned to Anglican use; at first unofficially and now officially in many new Anglican ordination rites. In addition to this, the presentation of other presents from the parish, friends and family of the ordinand have come in some places to assume a place within the ordination rite itself. Other ceremonies, some without either historical precedent or any convincing theological rationale (like the washing of the feet of the newly ordained deacon), have come to have a permissive place within some new Anglican ordinals. The central act of ordination, the imposition of hands, is again in danger of being so overwhelmed by ancillary rites that its centrality is obscured.

Non-scripted commentary on the sign-acts increases this danger. While these are clearly pastoral in their intent, they can often do considerable damage to the theology of the rites them-selves. One bishop was known to present copies of his church's new prayer book instead of a Bible, an act which was accompa-nied by the words: 'Receive the word of God in a form usable by the people.' Similarly, allegorical explanations of the vestments, now a common practice in some dioceses, give them attention which they do not merit at that moment and militate in favour of the restoration of the more ancient practice of vesting the candi-dates according to the order to which they are to be ordained *before* the liturgy begins.

A perhaps more important consideration is that these sign-acts risk giving the impression that ordination is admission to a clerical caste set apart from the people of God as a whole. Acts that perpetuate clericalism, whether intentional or not, need to be re-thought. When anointing at baptism has found a place in many Anglican baptismal rites, do we really wish to risk confusing it by officially introducing anointings at ordinations which are easily seen as being 'better' than the anointing received at baptism?

While, from the very outset of the process that led to the Berkeley Statement, there was strong support for the restoration of the diaconate as a full and equal order, there are still serious questions that must be dealt with before this becomes a reality. Some of these are questions for the churches in general, others are specific to Anglicanism. It is easy, for example, to affirm the vocational diaconate in theory, but dioceses which actually en-courage parishes to find men and women in their midst who may have this vocation are still a minority. In many places, dea-cons are still seen as anomalies and the presbyterate remains the 'normative' vocation for Anglicans.

This will only begin to change when Anglicans address the question of direct ordination to the presbyterate, a question which John Gibaut pursues further. While *To Equip the Saints* in-vites Provinces to consider the possibility of direct ordination to both the episcopate and presbyterate, the idea has met with fierce resistance from some within the communion. The objec-tions raised appear to deny the historicity of the practice both in the pre-reformation church in the East and West as well as with-in Anglicanism itself. The question is an actual one; as the Porvöö Churches and the Lutheran Churches of North America which have entered into full communion with the Anglican Churches of North America do not and have never observed the *cursus honorum* of ordination to the diaconate before ordination to the presbyterate. Nor have we asked them to do so in our ecumenical dialogues.

While a resolution of this question will likely take some time, there are other matters which Anglicans can address immediately. One is the question of dressing in an order which is not one's own. Of this practice, Louis Weil remarks: 'This strikes me as an example of an appalling trivialization of an outward symbol (a vestment) which does not correspond to the interior reality. It would be wise to remember that both the Orthodox and Roman Catholic Churches canonically inhibit a minister of one order from wearing the vesture of another order. Since we claim to share with those two traditions a concern for the maintenance of the three-fold pattern of ministry, even a slight degree of humility would suggest that these traditions understand vesture not merely as a surface decoration, but rather as corresponding to the reality of the person's place in the community. This is not a liturgical charade.'[1]

Should one ask a presbyter why s/he is dressed as a deacon for the liturgy, the answer is usually 'but I'm still a deacon'. This is neither the theology of the early church nor of classic Anglicanism. It appears to have entered Anglican thinking during the nineteenth century as a part of the Catholic Revival and was, perhaps, a reflection on the medieval custom (revived by some Anglo-Catholics) of bishops wearing 'full pontificals' which included wearing the dalmatic and tunicle (the vestments of the deacon and the sub-deacon respectively) under the chasuble. While the practice may have been originally intended to signal that the bishop represented the fullness of order, it could not have represented the bishop remaining in each order – in part because until the rigorous observance of the *cursus honorum* in the West, most bishops had not been ordained to each of the orders in the *cursus*.

There are other issues related directly or indirectly to the question of orders and ordination that are presently seen as more pressing by some Provinces. The two that are most divisive in the communion are those of the ordination of women (at all, in some provinces, to the presbyterate and episcopate in others,

---

1. Louis Weil, 'Should the Episcopal Church Permit Direct Ordination?' in: Edwin F. Hallenbeck ed., *The Orders of Ministry: Reflections on Direct Ordination*, 1996, (Providence RI, 1996) 62.

and to the episcopate in still others) and the ordination of homo-sexual men and women. Put in the context of a baptismal theolo-gy, particularly the biblical claim that baptism levels what are otherwise seen as unassailable distinctions of gender, race and social class, these issues ought to be seen in a new light. Both is-sues, however, raise the question of episcopal pastoral care for those who dissent from the synodical resolution of one issue or the other by the legally responsible jurisdiction. The case of the Church of England is outlined by Colin Buchanan. Oddly, the suggestion that there be 'extended' episcopal care is a novelty in the life of the church and a great puzzlement to those who look at Anglicans from the outside. It does beg the question of what other issues there are where the clergy and, following them, the communities to which they belong, can take issue with the local church and seek pastoral care elsewhere. The ecclesiological im-plications of these 'solutions' seems to need far more theological reflection than they have received to date.

The so-called question of lay presidency at the Eucharist has somewhat fallen into the shadows of these other debates but is one for which some way forward may be made in the light of the understanding of the relationship between the ministry of ser-vice to the community and presidency at the eucharistic assem-bly found in *To Equip the Saints*.

It is the hope of all the members of the IALC who participated in the series of meetings that eventually led to the Berkeley Statement, *To Equip the Saints*, that its findings, along with the essays found in this book, will contribute to the ongoing life of the Anglican Communion. Both the Toronto Statement on Christian Initiation and the Dublin Statement on the Eucharist have found a place in the life of a number of Provinces, it is our hope that the Berkeley Statement will be given a similar place.

Ronald L. Dowling
David R. Holeton
Editors

The Contributors

PAUL F. BRADSHAW is Professor of Liturgy at the University of Notre Dame, Indiana, USA and Director of the Notre Dame London Program. He is also the current Chair of the International Anglican Liturgical Consultation.

COLIN O. BUCHANAN retired in 2004 as Bishop of Woolwich in the Church of England. He was a founding member of IALC and has served on its Steering Committee. He is a prolific writer and commentator on liturgical subjects.

GEORGE CONNOR is Bishop of Dunedin, New Zealand, Convenor of the Common Life Liturgical Commission, Anglican Church in Aotearoa New Zealand and Polynesia and Convenor of the Joint Liturgical Group (New Zealand).

WILLIAM CROCKETT is Professor Emeritus of Systematic Theology at the Vancouver School of Theology, Canada. He is also a member of the Inter Anglican Standing Commission on Ecumenical Relations (IASCER).

IAN DARBY is Rector of Prestbury, Pietermaritzburg, South Africa. He is an Anglican representative on his country's Church Unity Commission and convenor of its liturgical committee. He is also a member of his church's liturgical commission.

CAROL DORAN is Professor of Music and Liturgy at the Virginia Theological Seminary, Alexandria, Virginia.

RONALD DOWLING is Rector of St Mary Magdalene's Parish, Adelaide, South Australia, a member of the Liturgy Commission of the Anglican Church of Australia and was the second Chair of IALC.

JOHN ST.H. GIBAUT is Associate Professor of Church History at Saint Paul University, Ottawa, Canada. He is also a member of the International Commission for Anglican-Orthodox Theological Dialogue and the Inter Anglican Standing Commission on Ecumenical Relations (IASCER), and is Canon Theologian of the Diocese of Ottawa.

PAUL GIBSON is Co-ordinator for Liturgy for the Anglican Consultative Council and Secretary of the International Anglican Liturgical Consultation.

DAVID HOLETON is Professor of Liturgy at the Hussite Theological Faculty of the Charles University in Prague, Czech Republic, and was the first Chair of the IALC. He is currently President of Societas Liturgica.

LIZETTE LARSON-MILLER is the Nancy and Michael Kaehr Professor of Liturgy and Dean of Chapel at the Church Divinity School of the Pacific, Berkeley, California.

RICHARD LEGGETT is Professor of Liturgical Studies at the Vancouver School of Theology, Canada.

TOMAS MADDELA is Dean of St Andrew's Theological Seminary, Manila, The Philippines, and has served on the Steering Committee of IALC.

BRIAN MAYNE was Chancellor of Down Cathedral until his retirement in 2001. He was Secretary of the Church of Ireland Liturgical Advisory Committee 1989-99 and editor of the 2004 edition of the Church of Ireland *Book of Common Prayer*.

WILLIAM H. PETERSEN is Provost and Professor of Ecclesiastical and Ecumenical History at Bexley Hall an accredited seminary of the Episcopal Church in partnership with Trinity Lutheran Seminary, Columbus, Ohio.

CHARLES SHERLOCK is Registrar and Director of Ministry Studies, Melbourne College of Divinity, Executive Secretary of the Liturgy Commission, Anglican Church of Australia, and a member of ARCIC.

ELIZABETH SMITH is the Vicar of St John's Parish, Bentleigh, Melbourne, Australia and a member of the Liturgy Commission of the Anglican Church of Australia.

PHILLIP TOVEY is Director of Reader Training, Diocese of Oxford, and Liturgy Tutor, Ripon College, Cuddesdon, England.

GILLIAN VARCOE is Rector of the Parish of St Mary-in-the-Valley, Canberra, Australia and was Editor of *A Prayer Book for Australia* (1995). She is sessional lecturer in liturgy in the School of Theology, Charles Sturt University and a member of the Australian Liturgy Commission.

LOUIS WEIL is the James F. Hodges and Harold and Rita Haynes Professor of Liturgics at the Church Divinity School of the Pacific, Berkeley, California.

Abbreviations

Anglican-Lutheran
Agreements
Anglican-Lutheran Agreements, Regional and International Agreements 1972-2002. Sven Oppegaard and Gregory Cameron eds. (Geneva, 2004).

BEM
Baptism, Eucharist and Ministry. [Faith and Order Paper no 111] (Geneva, 1982).

Bradshaw 1971
Paul F. Bradshaw, *The Anglican Ordinal: Its History and Development from the Reformation to the Present Day.* [Alcuin Club Collections no 53] (London, 1971).

Bradshaw 1990
Paul F. Bradshaw, *Ordination Rites of the Ancient Churches of East and West.* (New York, 1990).

Bradshaw 2002
Paul F. Bradshaw, *The Search for the Origins of Christian Worship: Sources and Methods for the Study of Early Liturgy.* (New York, 20022).

Called to Common
Mission
Called to Common Mission: A Lutheran Proposal for a Revision of the Concordat of Agreement (Chicago, 1999) and in *Anglican-Lutheran Agreements* 231-242.

Diaconate as
Ecumenical
Opportunity
The Diaconate as Ecumenical Opportunity: The Hanover Report of the Anglican-Lutheran International Commission. (London, 1996) and in *Anglican-Lutheran Agreements* 177-200.

Down to Earth
Worship
The York Statement in: *Liturgical Inculturation in the Anglican Communion: Including the York Statement 'Down to Earth Worship.'* David R. Holeton ed. [Alcuin/GROW Liturgical Study 15] (Bramcote, Notts., 1990).

First ... BCP
The First and Second Prayer Books of King Edward VI (London, 1910/1965).

Final Report
Anglican-Roman Catholic International Commission. *The Final Report.* Cincinnati, OH (Washington, DC, 1982).

15

Growth in Communion	*Growth in Communion: Report of the Anglican-Lutheran International Working Group 2000-2002.* (Geneva, 2003) and in *Anglican-Lutheran Agreements* 275-337.
Järvenpää	*Anglican Orders and Ordinations: Essays and Reports from the Interim Conference at Järvenpää, Finland, of the International Anglican Liturgical Consultation, 4-9 August 1997.* David R. Holeton ed., [Alcuin/GROW Liturgical Study 39] (Cambridge,1997).
Nature and Purpose	*The Nature and Purpose of the Church: A Stage on the Way to a Common Statement* [Faith and Order Paper no 181] (Geneva, 1998).
Niagara Report	*Anglican-Lutheran International Continuation Committee. The Niagara Report: Report of the Anglican-Lutheran Consultation on Episcope, Niagara Falls, September 1987.* (London, 1988) and in *Anglican-Lutheran Agreements* 87-128.
Porvoo	*Together in Mission and Ministry: The Porvoo Common Statement (Conversations between British & Irish Anglican Churches and Nordic & Baltic Lutheran Churches)* (London, 1993) and in *Anglican-Lutheran Agreements* 145-176.
To Equip the Saints	The Berkeley Statement. Herein, XXX and in *Anglican Ordination Rites: The Berkeley Statement: 'To Equip the Saints'; Findings of the Sixth International Anglican Liturgical Consultation, Berkeley, California, 2001.* Paul Gibson ed. [Grove Worship Series 168] (Cambridge, 2002).
Virginia Report	Inter-Anglican Theological and Doctrinal Commission. *The Virginia Report.* (Harrisburg, PA, 1999).
Walk in Newness of Life	*The Toronto Statement in: Growing in newness of life: Christian initiation in Anglicanism today: papers from the fourth International Anglican Liturgical Consultation, Toronto, 1991.* David R. Holeton, ed. (Toronto, 1993) and in *Christian Initiation in the Anglican Communion: The Toronto Statement 'Walk in Newness of Life'; the Findings of the Fourth*

International Anglican Liturgical Consultation.
David R. Holeton ed. [Grove Worship Series 119]
(Bramcote, Notts., 1991).

Waterloo Declaration   *Called to Full Communion: The Waterloo Declaration*
(Toronto, 1999) and in *Anglican-Lutheran*
Agreements 243-248.

Baptismal Ecclesiology: Uncovering a Paradigm

Louis Weil

The words we use are not cast in marble. Words are slippery. Their meanings change, often so subtly that we do not notice. Then we recognise that others are using a word in a sense quite different from our own meaning. And so the same words may carry quite different implications for different people. T. S. Eliot expresses this fragility of language quite vividly in his poem *Burnt Norton*:

> Words strain,
> Crack and sometimes break, under the burden,
> Under the tension, slip, slide, perish,
> Decay with imprecision, will not stay in place,
> Will not stay still.

My sense of how words may connote different things to different people was re-awakened at the meeting of the International Anglican Liturgical Consultation (IALC) at Cuddesdon College, Oxford, in August, 2003. For several years I had been advocating, both in my teaching and writing, what I called 'a baptismal ecclesiology'. Through my ecumenical work I had become aware that the divisions between the various major traditions of Christianity correlate with the diverse models of ordained leadership in these traditions. Whereas agreements on baptism and eucharist had proven relatively easy to achieve through the work of various ecumenical dialogues, the real difficulties surfaced when the differing models of ordained ministry were addressed. It was in this latter context that issues of authority and power came into focus and proved to be the most difficult barriers to resolve.

In this essay I am seeking to explore the comprehensive character of a baptismal ecclesiology in offering the most adequate context in which to consider other fundamental aspects of the church's nature. For many centuries the various models of hierarchical ecclesiology have led the various Christian traditions into an adversarial mode of mutual engagement embodied in a breakdown of the common sharing of the eucharistic gifts. We

---

1. T.S. Eliot, 'Burnt Norton,' V, in *Four Quartets* (London, 1944) 19.

shall begin with a consideration of the characteristics of certain major hierarchical ecclesiologies.

The primary characteristic shared by the various hierarchical modes of interpreting the church's life is that they view the church through the prism of its ordained leadership. This may be recognised most easily in a tradition's polity, that is, the pattern of church government by its ordained leaders. Often it becomes a descriptive term for the particular tradition; for example, our own Anglican tradition is grounded in an episcopal polity. 'Episcopal' appears in the official name of the church in certain provinces of the Anglican Communion. Episcopal polity is also fundamental in the ecclesiology of the Eastern Orthodox Churches, which also speak at times of their ecclesiology as 'eucharistic' in that the unity of the episcopate is expressed most fully in their role as chief pastors, especially in their pastoral presidency of their eucharistic communities.

Another model of ecclesiology is the presbyteral polity of the Reformed Church tradition, which is associated most notably with the ecclesiology of John Calvin. Within this model the leadership of the church rests in the hands of the *collegium* of the 'elders' or 'presbyters'. In the sixteenth century, the rejection of papal authority and debates over the theology of ordained leadership led to an overlap between episcopal and presbyteral models of church government. A Reformed exegesis of certain New Testament texts generated ambivalence with regard to the parity of these two models.[2] The adherence of the Church of England to episcopal polity did not inhibit the occasional authorisation of ministers not ordained by a bishop to serve in English parishes. The principle invoked in these cases was that where episcopal ordination was not available, the ordinations of those clergy (legitimately ordained according to another model) should be recognised. This principle, however, did not apply to non-conformists in England who refused to accept episcopal polity established as normative in the Church of England.

In the teaching of Richard Hooker, the episcopal model, al-

---

2. See Norman Sykes, *Old Priest and New Presbyter: Episcopacy and Presbyterianism since the Reformation with especial relation to the Churches of England and Scotland* (Cambridge, 1956) esp. Ch. III, 'An Imparity of Ministers Defended,' 58-84. See also the discussion of this debate with regard to the Ordinal in, G. J. Cuming, *A History of Anglican Liturgy* (London, 1969) 163-4.

though not defended as absolutely essential for the life of the church, nevertheless assumes that it is the normative model within the whole Christian tradition.[3] At the same time, Hooker does not invalidate those traditions which have not maintained episcopal order because of the accidents of geography and/or history. He does not, however, place presbyteral polity on a parity with episcopal polity, but teaches that the episcopate is the providential model for ordering the church's life.

We see in such historical debates about church polity how much theological energy was spent on conflict over the proper ordering of the church's ministry. In advocating the paradigm of baptismal ecclesiology, my intention is to place the ecumenical issues within a different frame of reference. After all, since we acknowledge a common baptism, are we not suggesting that what unifies Christians is greater and more fundamental than the issues which divided us? I realise full well that patterns of ordained leadership and issues of hierarchical authority continue to loom large on the ecumenical horizon. But if we frame and debate those issues within the context of the underlying baptismal unity, might this not offer us a 'larger room' in which to reconsider the bases of division between our traditions?

Further clarification is needed with regard to the scope of the term 'baptismal ecclesiology'. The question has been raised as to whether this term is adequate without specific reference to the significance of the Eucharist as a fundamental aspect of ecclesiology. This is an example of how our terminology can 'slip, slide … not stay in place'. In a thoughtful essay included in this collection, Paul Gibson raises this concern. Gibson writes:

> I do not believe we may ground a theology of ministry on a baptismal ecclesiology because I do not believe baptism is about the structure of the church. Baptism is the door; the table is where structure and order are defined.[4]

Gibson's view must be seriously considered. Certainly if baptism is isolated from the eucharist, as has been the case for centuries, then baptismal ecclesiology can only be viewed as offering an inadequate framework for a theology of ministry. In such a context, baptism may be indeed understood as merely

---

3. I am deeply indebted to Dr Ryan Lesh for his critical reading of this material and in helping me to clarify my intentions here and at several other places in this text.

4. Paul Gibson, 'A Baptismal Ecclesiology – Some Questions', p 44 below.

'the door'. Yet within the academy of liturgical scholars, any discussion of the rites of Christian Initiation always includes the eucharist as an integral part of those rites. Yet given the many centuries during which that relationship had been severed, and holy communion not administered to baptised children until they reached the 'age of reason', we should not presume that it is immediately obvious that the eucharist itself should be understood, as in the early centuries of Christianity, as integral to the sacramental action of the initiation sequence.

In the Anglican Communion, the more recent practice of communicating young children and even infants who have not yet received confirmation, has awakened a renewed awareness of this relationship between the eucharist and baptism. When I speak of a baptismal ecclesiology, the totality of Initiation is presumed to include both baptism and the eucharist. It was this presumption and others that were confronted at the IALC meeting in Oxford. When a report (issued by The Inter-Anglican Standing Commission on Ecumenical Relations – IASCER) was distributed to IALC members, several serious concerns were raised in response to the Berkeley Statement: *To Equip the Saints*. This report resulted from the previous IALC meeting of 2001, in Berkeley, California. The latter document promotes a baptismal ecclesiology as the appropriate foundation for understanding Anglican Orders, on the principle that

> ... understanding baptism as the life and ministry of the church (that is, having a baptismal ecclesiology) leads us to see ordained ministers as integral members of the body of Christ ...

This affirmation was set in opposition to periods in the church's history when 'ordination was viewed as conferring a status elevating ordained ministers above the laity'.[5]

Although the questions raised in the IASCER report surprised me, they were questions that had to be taken seriously. The report asked:

> Is it reductionist to speak of a baptismal ecclesiology? What about the other dimensions of ecclesiology? Does the notion of baptismal ecclesiology suggest a kind of egalitarianism which is sociologically impossible in any structured community?

---

5. *To Equip the Saints*, Part I, *Baptism and Ministry*.

Professor William Crockett, the IALC consultant on IASCER, addressed these questions very clearly at the Oxford meeting in a document shared with the members in attendance.

The affirmation of a baptismal ecclesiology is not intended to be reductionist or minimalist, but to be foundational for everything else that is said about the various ministries of the church. Consistent with BEM and the various bilateral dialogues, ordained ministry is discussed in the context of the ministry of the whole people of God. A baptismal ecclesiology affirms the foundation of the church's ministry in baptism. It is not intended to exclude the other dimensions of ecclesiology. It is also intended as a corrective to the tendency towards a clericalisation of the ordained ministry in the tradition, which implies a separation between clergy and laity. This does suggest an equality of status among all the baptised, but it does not imply that there is no differentiation of roles in the community. On the contrary, *Anglican Ordination Rites* states explicitly, 'In order that the whole people of God may fulfil their calling to be a holy priesthood, ... some are called to specific ministries of leadership by ordination.'[6]

Although Professor Crockett clearly states the intention of the IALC members who produced *To Equip the Saints* in 2001, even his words were considered ambivalent by some readers with regard to the distinct character of the ordained ministries and thus seemed, potentially, to imply a kind of levelling which would erode that distinction with an implicit denial of the particular *charisms* of those in Holy Order.

Such a misunderstanding of the intention of the IALC document is found in a recent book by Archbishop Peter Carnley, the then primate of Australia. In his *Reflections in Glass*, Archbishop Carnley discusses a wide array of issues facing the church today. He forcefully rebuts the proposal that is often referred to as 'lay presidency'.[7] This proposal to recognise the presidency of lay people at the eucharist is particularly associated with the diocese of Sydney in Australia, although it has found modest sup-

---

6. The IASCER report and the response by Professor Crockett were distributed as a photocopied document for discussion. For the quotation from the Berkeley Statement see p 220 below: *To Equip the Saints*, Part I, *Baptism and Ministry*. BEM indicates an extraordinary level of ecumenical agreement among the participating churches.

7. Peter Carnley, *Reflections in Glass*. (Sydney, 2004) esp ch 5, 156 ff.

port in other provinces of the Anglican Communion, particularly those areas which have a long standing Evangelical tradition with a firm Calvinist orientation. In this confrontation with the proposal of lay presidency at the eucharist, Carnley develops a convincing case for the distinctive character of the ordained ministries. Particularly, he links the ordained priesthood whose character he links to the priest's pastoral and sacramental role in the congregation, designated by the church through ordination.

Archbishop Carnley is troubled by the implications which he sees in the phrase from the Berkeley Statement quoted above: 'In order that the whole people of God may fulfil their calling to be a holy priesthood, ... some are called to specific ministries of leadership by ordination.'[8] He affirms the recovery in recent decades of a sense that all the baptised are called to ministry, and that this recovery is grounded in the New Testament teaching on the priesthood of the whole people of God (1 Peter 2:9). 'Gone are the days when the ordained priest was a one-man band who led an otherwise passive community. The whole community is now clearly seen to have a role to play.'[9] Yet he also sees a negative side to this development. He writes:

> This contemporary emphasis on the collaborative ministry of the whole people of God seems to lead to an understanding of ordained ministry in terms of the concept of enablement – the role of the ordained priest is to enable lay ministry to function as a priestly people in the world.[10]

Such an approach, Carnley suggests, envisions the ordained priest 'almost as a chairman of a group to facilitate its effective functioning'.[11]

At this point in his discussion of lay and ordained ministry, Archbishop Carnley lumps together the IALC document *To Equip the Saints* and the writings of Robin Greenwood, a leading exponent of 'collaborative ministry'.[12] The archbishop takes sharp issue with Greenwood's apparent fostering of the equality of all the baptised in the church in such a manner that the dis-

---

8. *To Equip the Saints*, Part I, *Baptism and Ministry*, p 220 below.
9. Carnley, *Reflections* 157.
10. *Reflections* 171.
11. *Reflections* 172.
12. Robin Greenwood, *Transforming Priesthood* (London, 1994); *Transforming Church, Liberating Structures for Ministry* (London, 2002).

tinctive character of the ordained priesthood is eroded. As Carnley observes, 'Greenwood ... has enormous difficulty in identifying and defining the uniquely distinguishing role of the priest.'[13] This is for Carnley the critical issue at the heart of the debate with the diocese of Sydney: the proposal that laity should be licensed to preside at the Eucharist strikes at the heart of the sacramental ministry which embodies the particular character of the ordained priesthood.

What is ordination, we may ask, if the sacramental ministry is reduced to merely a function at which anyone (presumably a Christian!) may preside? Our inherited tradition regarding ordination is grounded in the church's need to discern and select from among the laity of the church those who manifest the signs of a specific gift for pastoral oversight. This gift finds its fundamental expression in the gathering of the baptised community to celebrate the eucharist under the pastoral oversight of their ordained priest. The proponents of lay presidency need to acknowledge that if a lay person is appointed to preside at the Eucharist, through a licence or some other administrative model, this is a form of ordering, a quasi-ordination, but one which separates sacramental presidency from its integral relation to pastoral oversight and care. The result is to reduce the Eucharistic Prayer to some type of magical formula which is effective simply in its repetition in isolation from its normative context within the larger pattern of ordained ministerial care.

In support of his position, Archbishop Carnley refers to the ARCIC Agreed Statement on Ministry and Ordination, the so-called 'Canterbury Statement'. The Canterbury Statement is particularly clear on this issue:

> Not only do they [ordained priests] share through baptism in the priesthood of the people of God, but they are – particularly in presiding at the eucharist – representative of the whole church in the fulfilment of its priestly vocation of self-offering to God as a living sacrifice. Nevertheless their ministry is not an extension of the common Christian priesthood but belongs to another realm of the gifts of the Spirit.[14]

The phrase 'another realm of the gifts of the Spirit' certainly affirms a strong consensus shared by Anglicans and Roman

---

13. *Reflections* 171.
14. *Canterbury Report*, §13.

Catholics on the distinctive character of the ordained priest-hood. This distinction might be fruitfully explored with regard to the diversity of charisms which are promised to the church in the New Testament: all of the gifts of the Holy Spirit work to-gether for the building up of the Body of Christ, but the gifts are not the same to all the members. Within the mystery of our bap-tismal identity there is what we might call a radical particularity, not merely different degrees of the same gift, but different kinds, manifesting the rich diversity of the gifts of the Holy Spirit.

Unfortunately, Archbishop Carnley views both Greenwood's writings and the Berkeley Statement as proposing a view of the ordained priesthood that glosses over distinctiveness among the gifts of the Spirit. As Carnley writes, 'In advocating "total min-istry" or "collaborative ministry" we do ourselves no service by overlooking or devaluing the distinct and unique gathering role of the priest as shepherd of the flock.'[15] Whatever one may judge regarding Greenwood's writings on this subject, I can say, as a member of the IALC who contributed to the Berkeley Statement, that it was certainly not the intention of the drafters of the Statement to erode the distinctive character of the ordained priesthood. Our emphasis upon the foundational significance of baptism was intended to affirm the common ground within which all ministries, both lay and ordained, take their source, and to avoid any suggestion that ordination elevates the status of the ordained above the laity. This orientation may be seen as well in the ARCIC Statement on Ministry and Ordination that begins with an extended exposition of 'Ministry in the Life of the Church' as establishing the context for the subsequent discus-sion of ordained ministry.[16]

To discuss the theology of ministry as founded within the context of baptism moves us into a larger frame of reference; to do otherwise is to view ordained ministries in too narrow a per-spective. It suggests a change of orientation in our ecclesiology, that is, a change in how we perceive the nature of the church. For many centuries the tradition has made us familiar with a particular set of indicators as to the nature of the church. These indicators shaped our experience of the church because they are outward signs of how the life of the church as an institution in the world was expected to function. On the whole, these indic-

---

15. *Reflections*, 173.
16. *Canterbury Report*, § 3-6.

ators were grounded in clerical priorities. The recovery of a baptismal ecclesiology in no way implies that there was ever a time
in the history of the church when there were not distinctions of
role within its life. In the same context in which St Paul affirms
our unity in the one body, 'one Lord, one faith, one baptism,' he
goes on to speak of the wide diversity of gifts within that body:

> ...that some should be apostles, some prophets, some evan-
> gelists, some pastors and teachers, for the equipment of the
> saints, for the work of ministry, for the building up of the
> body of Christ, until we all attain to the unity of the faith.
> (Ephesians 4:3-13a, RSV.)

We could not ask for a clearer affirmation of the unity of all
Christians through baptism, a unity which nevertheless embraces a wide diversity of gifts.

Whereas the inherited tradition was grounded in clerical priorities, one of the extraordinary gifts which emerged from the
ordination of women, first as a disputed question, and now as a
widely-settled theological issue, was the need to reflect theologically on that inherited tradition. We came to recognise that the
ordination of women did not rupture the tradition but rather required a renewed plumbing of that tradition outside the framework of our inherited clerical model. The recovery of a baptismal ecclesiology, which is more historical, and of greater
theological integrity has played a significant role in this reclaiming of the tradition: it obliges us to seek pastoral gifts among the
whole community of baptised men and women.

This insight into the tradition on the foundation of a baptismal ecclesiology has similar implications for the current
debate about the suitability of homosexual men and women for
ordination, a question that is more closely related to the issue of
the ordination of women than many have been willing to admit.
If discernment concerning suitability for holy orders is grounded
in a baptismal ecclesiology, then the fundamental issue is not a
person's gender or sexual orientation, but rather the evidence of
the charisms that the church needs in its ordained leaders. Just
as we have come to see those charisms in women of the church,
so also, increasingly, those charged with the work of discernment are recognising these gifts in gay men and lesbian women
who present themselves to the church for the process toward
ordination.

From as early as the third century, documents speak of the

members of the church using a vocabulary which distinguishes between clergy and laity. Previous to this, the whole people of God had been spoken of using the Greek word *laos*, a term which referred to the whole community of the baptised. This term, of course, is the source for our word *laity*. Later the term came to refer to the members of the church who were not ordained. At first, the distinction of certain members of the church as clergy was linked simply to the fact that some members of the church were identified to have particular gifts, charisms, which were important for the building up of the common life of the Body of Christ. Because of these gifts, such persons were committed to particular types of service on behalf of the whole community, including but not limited to liturgical service. This service, in all its forms, was always intended to contribute to the building up of the common life of the Christian community and not to the exaltation of the minister. It was for this reason that for the first millennium of Christianity, ordination was always linked to the need of a community for a particular minister, be that bishop or priest or deacon.[17]

With the end of persecutions in the fourth century, the members of the church found themselves in a quite new situation: their worship that had been hidden from public view, could now be public. And for that worship, the Emperor Constantine erected great buildings which the rapidly-growing Christian community, now free from the danger of persecution, would use for their public liturgical rites.

The effect of this dramatic shift of status and the impact of the large buildings in which Christians now gathered for worship, known as *basilicas*, fed into the distinction between clergy and laity which had emerged in the previous century. They also contributed to the elaboration of Christian rituals by drawing upon the ceremonial practices which were attached to the emperor's public ceremonies. Ceremonial, such as the carrying of candles and incense in procession, came to be used for a bishop as he entered a basilica. This change of venue for Christian liturgical rites and the ensuing ceremonial enrichment transformed the understanding of episcopal ministry within the Christian community. Whereas this role had been that of chief pastor and

17. Cyrille Vogel, 'An Alienated Liturgy' in *Liturgy: Self-Expression of the Church*, Herman Schmidt, ed. *Consilium*, 72 (1972) 18-21.

teacher, in the new context the role of the bishop rapidly came to be seen in terms of judicial authority and power.

The bishop's normal role as pastor and presider over the Christian assembly also underwent a radical transformation in this context. In the earliest centuries, during the period when Christianity was an oppressed minority, the celebration of the eucharist was considered to be the fundamental faith-action of the entire gathered community, presided over by the chief pastor. Once the church found itself in basilicas using the great ritual ceremonies of the fourth century imperial court, the bishop's role was transformed. The loss of intimacy in their places of assembly led to a different understanding of the nature of the Eucharist. The central act of Christian worship ceased to be understood as the action of the entire gathered community, but became rather the action of the *official* members of the community, that is, the bishop and other members of the clergy, namely, the ordained. The gathering of the laity became essentially the occasion on which they might observe the performance of the sacred rituals by those specifically appointed through ordination.

Although this change in understanding unfolded only gradually, a new path had been taken which led eventually to an understanding of the church's sacramental acts as strictly limited to the authority of the ordained, with the laity functioning, at best, merely as spectators. In other words, this significant shift, which we may appropriately associate with the events of the fourth century, led in the high Middle Ages to a full-blown clericalisation in the life of the church. This became the dominant paradigm for many centuries.

The thesis of this essay, as we noted at the beginning, is that the loss of the earlier understanding of the church, grounded in what we may call a 'baptismal ecclesiology' (an interpretation of the church through the prism of baptism), gave way gradually to an 'hierarchical ecclesiology' (an understanding of the church which viewed all aspects of its life through the prism of holy orders). Through an hierarchical ecclesiology, every aspect of the church's life is perceived differently from the perception offered by a baptismal ecclesiology.

An historical evolution in the understanding of the eucharist offers us an example of how a shift in the church's self-understanding was manifested in the very practical experience of the Christian community. As was noted earlier, the eucharist had, in the earliest centuries of Christianity, been understood as the faith-action of the entire baptised community. Although the transformation was gradual, by the twelfth century the eucharistic action had come to be understood as depending entirely and uniquely upon the ministry of the ordained priest. So radical was this reversal of theology that the laity had not only ceased to be perceived as integral participants, but also their reception of sacramental communion had been reduced to merely an annual practice.

The basic question which is being posed here is as follows: what characteristics of the church define it as the Body of Christ, as the religious institution in the world which bears witness to the life, death and resurrection of Jesus Christ? We have lived with a hierarchical ecclesiology for over a thousand years. Although the leaders of the sixteenth century Reformation sought to restore balance within the church and to correct the abuses of excessive clericalism, they were greatly influenced by the clerical mentality which they sought to correct.

Among the reformers, the primary weight of leadership still remained with the clergy. For a thousand years the Christian society in general had not received a comparable formation in faith as that which the catechumenate of the early centuries had offered. 'The church' had come to refer only to the clergy, and the church today remains heir to that mindset. For some, laity as well as clergy, it is a deliberate choice, for they believe it is how the church should be constituted. But for others, even people who are committed to a recovery of the integral role of the laity in the church's life, clericalism often shapes their attitudes, at times at a deeply unconscious level.

The recovery of a baptismal ecclesiology can only be achieved as we patiently work within our inherited models of leadership to seek their transformation. That work will require us to define issues in the context of the new realities of the church's life in the twenty-first century. Our world is utterly different from that of the early centuries of Christianity. We may gain insight through a knowledge of history, but we will certainly not find there a blueprint for the church today.

As noted earlier, for about a millennium the interpretation of the church's life has been through the prism of a clerical or hierarchical self-understanding. A baptismal ecclesiology is not reductionist in that it seeks to deny or eliminate the legitimate role of ordained leadership in the church, but rather affirms that the church is founded upon the sacrament of baptism; the fundamental sacraments of Christian identity (baptism and eucharist), are the visible signs shared by all members of the church, whether ordained or lay. While affirming a baptismal ecclesiology, how do we avoid any hint of an erosion of the integral and distinct role which the ordained priesthood fulfils in the sacramental life of the church? Archbishop Carnley responds to this concern by focusing on the ministry of the priest-presider at the eucharist. The Great Thanksgiving over the bread and wine is, he writes,

> ... the 'verbal centre' of the Eucharistic event. Indeed, the *anaphora* is the quintessential prayer in which the church prays what it believes. It is no coincidence that it has the same Trinitarian structure as the Creed: thanksgiving is made for Creation by God the Father, thanksgiving for redemption through Christ the Son, and thanksgiving for our continuing human transformation and renewal through the gift of the Spirit. It is a prayer that moves from *berakah* (blessing) to *haggadah* (narrative) to *shikhinah* (presence).

He continues,

> ... it is in this prayer *par excellence* in which we see the ordained person actually doing exactly what he or she is authorised and commissioned by ordination to do as shepherd of the community – interpreting the church to itself and forming it as the Body of Christ. ... It is the central prayer in which, culminating in communion, the community is formed as the Body of Christ. And given the seamlessness and unitary nature of the ministry of liturgical oversight and pastoral oversight, this is why it is appropriate for those authorised by ordination for this distinct ministry to lead the reciting of it. To do otherwise would be to perpetrate the symbolic confusion of saying one thing and doing another. At this point the pastoral and the liturgical oversight of those ordained priest coincide: their pastoral work becomes a liturgical work and the liturgical becomes the pastoral. This is why it is appropriate that those ordained to ministerial priesthood should preside immediately and directly at the eucharist, and why it is inappropriate for lay people to do so. To fracture this seamless pastoral and liturgical ministry at this point would result in symbolic nonsense.[18]

---

18. *Reflections*, 177-9.

I have quoted Archbishop Carnley at length because it strikes me that he has presented a critical insight into this other dimension of a baptismal ecclesiology, and that it clarifies the distinction and complementarity of roles within the Body of Christ. A comprehensive baptismal ecclesiology does not seek to reduce the understanding of holy orders to one that views the church's ordained ministers merely as enablers of the laity.

The adoption of a baptismal ecclesiology requires a rich sacramental theology if the ordained ministry is not to be reduced to merely a set of liturgical functions. Ordained priests have a very specific role in the life of the church – to be sign bearers for the building up of the entire community of the faithful and to provide pastoral oversight, that is, to preside in the fullest sense over the fundamental faith-actions of Christian identity as the crucial embodiment of their ministry of pastoral care.[19]

In an essay on the theology of Michael Ramsey, Archbishop Rowan Williams writes that:

> The presence of the ordained is not dictated by juridical requirements or by some theory of occult powers given only to the clergy. They are there presiding in the assembly in order to show something – the unity of the church in the cross and resurrection of Jesus. Without the apostolic ministry, the problem is not a defect of 'validity' in the usual Catholic sense but a defect of clarity and intelligibility in the symbolic communication of the gospel of God.[20]

In his dissertation, Peter Waddell notes that in this teaching, Ramsey is following the characteristic Anglican approach to the role of the ordained priest in the celebration of the eucharist.

It is important to notice that there is also an emerging ecumenical consensus on this question. The distinguished Roman Catholic sacramental theologian David N. Power writes of the need to search for a

> church structure and a practice of ordination that is appropriate to an awareness that the community of faith is the

19. I am indebted to Peter M. Waddell for sharing with me his as yet unpublished doctoral dissertation submitted to the University of Cambridge in 2001: *The Eucharistic Priesthood of the Ordained Ministry: A Contemporary Anglican Proposal*.

20. Rowan Williams, 'Theology and the Churches,' in *Michael Ramsey as Theologian*, Robin Gill and Lorna Kendall, eds. (London, 1995) 16.

ecclesial subject of celebration, so that the act of the ordained minister is understood in this context.

… It is the intersection between the role ascribed to the ordained priest and the doctrine of the sacrifice of the Mass in Catholic doctrine that still creates severe difficulties for other western churches. … Nonetheless, one aspect of Trent's accent on the role of the priest remains important, and that is the issue of the sacramental nature of ministry and the pertinency of this to the life of the church, inclusive of its worship. Current ecumenical dialogue shows a common concern for this sacramentality, even if it is difficult to come to an agreed proposition on it.

However, both Catholics and others may see a possibility of retrieving Trent's concern when the ordained ministry is spoken of less in terms of the power that it possesses and more in terms of what it signifies and thus contributes to the life of the church and to its sacramental acts.[21]

This reciprocity between the community of faith and the ordained priest is echoed by Archbishop Carnley in his concluding comments on this question:

The priest actively presides, not just by giving the blessing and pronouncing the absolution, but also and quite specifically in the rehearsal of the *anaphora* in the presence of, and in dialogue with, the people of God.[22]

Seen in this perspective, the baptismal vocation of the ordained manifests in the celebration of the eucharist its profound complementarity with the vocations of the gathered members of the community of faith in a shared acknowledgement of the diverse gifts of the Spirit which together contribute to the building up of the common life of the Body of Christ.

British theologian Paul Avis brings marvellous insight to these questions in the concluding essay of his revised edition of *Anglicanism and the Christian Church*. Writing about the divisions among the various Christian traditions, Avis observes that:

There are many thousands of Christian communions, large and small, in the world. Doubtless each has its own integrity after a fashion and each can appeal to the dominical promise: 'Where two or three are gathered together in my name, there

---

21. David Power, *The Sacrifice We Offer* (New York, 1987) 160-1.
22. *Reflections*, 179.

I am in the midst.' Each must learn to regard the others as genuine expressions, albeit with limitations due to history, theology and other factors, of the mystical Body of Christ. We need to work for greater mutual understanding in the context of total mutual acceptance on the basis of our baptism into Christ and the fundamental trinitarian baptismal faith of the church. This can be done, I believe, without sacrificing or compromising what is distinctive and precious in our own tradition. This is the key to finding a new paradigm for Anglicanism, and indeed for ecumenical Christianity.[23]

What we have referred to as a hierarchical ecclesiology, Avis calls 'the apostolic paradigm,' and he sees its problems as being, as we noted earlier, ecumenically divisive. 'The apostolic paradigm,' he writes, 'presupposes that there is one true church. It sits uncomfortably with ecumenical theology.'[24] In its place, Avis proposes a baptismal paradigm, and goes on to say that Anglicanism has never lost it: 'Its official formularies and its classical divines have upheld it,' and it was later affirmed in the Chicago-Lambeth Quadrilateral. The Lambeth Conferences 'have succeeded in transcending the limitations of the "apostolic paradigm", and have grounded their messages to the Anglican Communion and to the wider ecumenical community "on the reality of the christological foundation of the church in holy baptism and the baptismal faith".'[25]

To the idea that a baptismal ecclesiology is reductionist, Avis responds that

... baptism is the foundational sacrament of Christian initiation and, as a sacrament, it includes the Word of God. The baptismal model of ecclesiology means digging down to the foundations, to the bedrock of ecclesial reality.[26]

In his final paragraph, Avis writes 'The baptismal paradigm, as I understand it, involves an almost mystical, certainly intuitive, perception of that fundamental ecclesial reality.'[27] Given such an understanding of the baptismal paradigm, it seems reasonable to suggest that a baptismal ecclesiology offers us the

---

23. Paul Avis, *Anglicanism and the Christian Church* (London, 2002) 346.
24. Avis, *Anglicanism* ,347-8.
25. *Anglicanism*, 352.
26. *Anglicanism*, 354.
27. *Anglicanism*, 354.

most adequate theological context for an affirmation of the 'one Lord, one faith' which all Christians share through the one baptism.

A Baptismal Ecclesiology – Some Questions

Paul Gibson

The 2001 Berkeley Statement of the International Anglican Liturgical Consultation placed a theology of ministry firmly within a baptismal ecclesiology. The statement puts it, 'Through the Holy Spirit God baptises us into the life and ministry of Christ and forms us into the *laos*, the people of God.'[1] The statement notes various interpretations of the relationship between the people of God and the ordained ministry in the course of Christian history, but now understands, 'baptism as the foundation of the life and ministry of the church (that is, having a baptismal ecclesiology) [which] leads us to see ordained ministers as integral members of the body of Christ, called by God and discerned by the body to be signs and animators of Christ's self-giving life and ministry to which all people are called by God and for which we are empowered by the Spirit.'[2]

I have no quarrel with the theological democracy on which this ecclesiology is based – with the principle that all members of the church are equally 'living stones' in the temple of Christ's spiritual house.[3] Nor have I a quarrel with the principle that all are equally called to a gospel-filled life of service no matter what their role and function in the Christian community may be. The church's ministers are in the church, not over the church. However, I do find myself asking if the equality established by baptism can carry the full freight of a theology of ministry and order. It is not that it is wrong, but whether it is partial, and if some review of our understanding of baptism in the Christian life is now overdue.[4]

---

1. *To Equip the Saints*, p 219 below.
2. Ibid., p 220 below.
3. 1 Peter 2:4f.
4. If the IALC had defined baptism as the water rite and the eucharist combined – which I believe is the proper definition of Christian Initiation – there would be no need for the rest of this paper. However, it is my sense that most readers understand baptism to mean the water rite alone. I believe an ecclesiology must have a broader and deeper base. [The Toronto Statement on Christian Initiation 'Walk in Newness of Life' (IALC IV) and the Boston Statement on Children and the Eucharist (IALC I) both state that baptism admits to the eucharist regardless of age. *Eds*].

The Jewish Encyclopedia defines baptism as, 'a religious ablution signifying purification or consecration.' For instance, God told Moses to make the people wash their clothes before the revelation at Sinai, an act which the rabbis interpret as complete immersion.[5] (Exodus 19:10) Moses washes Aaron and his sons before they offer sacrifice. (Exodus 29:4) A person healed of leprosy is commanded to wash his clothes, cut off his hair, and bathe himself in water. (Leviticus 14:8) A man who has a nocturnal emission must bathe his whole body in water and be unclean until the evening. (Leviticus 15:16) A couple who have sexual intercourse in which semen is discharged by the man must both wash. (Leviticus 15:18) And when a woman menstruates anyone who touches her bed must wash their clothes and bathe in water. (Leviticus 26:7f) And so on. These are only a few examples.

With the prophets the emphasis on washing shifts from the concerns of cult and taboo to morality and *inner* purity. 'Wash yourselves, makes yourselves clean,' says Isaiah, 'remove the evil of your doings from before my eyes: cease to do evil. Learn to do good, seek justice, rescue the oppressed, defend the orphan, plead for the widow.' (1:16f) Life-giving water is now associated with the Spirit of God: 'I will pour water on the thirsty land, and streams on the dry ground; I will pour my Spirit on your descendants, and my blessing on your offspring.' (44:3) Ezekiel pictures Jerusalem as a naked and abandoned woman covered with blood when God comes to her rescue, covering her with a cloak, bathing her with water and anointing her with oil. (16:3-9) Ezekiel also speaks of God sprinkling cleansing water on the nation, and giving the people a new heart and a new spirit. (36:25f) And he offers the image of a great and nourishing river flowing out of the temple, with healing power that can make fresh even the stagnant seas. (47:1-12)

We can see from this brief review that the water rituals of the religion of the Hebrews had three facets. There was cleansing of people who had suffered a disease or broken a taboo or were simply alienated from God. There was their restoration to full status in the community. And there was cleansing and restoration of the nation, conceived at least in the terms of a baptismal metaphor. There is always a tension between the personal/individual, and the corporate. The corporate dimension lays the

---

2. *Jewish Encyclopedia*, website version.

foundation of a baptismal ecclesiology, but the individual dimension secures the personal element, which remains intact even within a Christian understanding of baptism (as we shall see).

John the Baptist stood somewhere in this tradition, offering his listeners cleansing and consecration to God's future. The essence of his teaching was that God was coming to put the world's house in order – violently and definitively. Those who wish to find themselves in the safety of the right side must prepare for the cataclysmic event with repentance and with baptism which seals it. We do not know if John's penitents were baptised only once or repeatedly. Obviously, Jewish practice took for granted that repeated washing and bathing would be part of the life of every observant Jew.[6] However, repeated baptism may not have been unknown among the earliest Christians as is evidenced by 'Otherwise, what will those people do who receive baptism on behalf of the dead? If the dead are not raised at all, why are people baptised on their behalf?' (1 Corinthians 15:29) Did this involve a baptism sequential to their own?

We do not know if John actively baptised people himself, plunging them under the water of the river, or if they immersed themselves in response to his admonition. There is no evidence that John created a baptised community, an *ecclesia*, although one commentator[7] at least has suggested that John's choice of the Jordan as the location of his baptisms had political and national significance: the Jordan was the last barrier crossed by the people when they entered the promised land. They came from the wilderness, through the Jordan, and into the land. To practise baptism at that particular place was a recapitulation of the final event of the exodus: out of the wilderness, through the Jordan, into the land.

John, it is suggested, was not trying to found a church. John was trying to refound the nation, this time on the basis of repentance and apocalyptic hope. His baptism was as much political

---

6. Hebrews 6:2 and 9:10 refer to 'baptisms'.

7. See John Dominic Crossan, *Jesus: A Revolutionary Biography* (San Francisco, 1994) 43f. Crossan writes, 'What [John] was forming ... was a giant system of sanctified individuals, a huge web of apocalyptic expectations, a network of ticking time bombs all over the Jewish homeland. Its magnitude insured a lasting memory, but its diffusion made it both possible and necessary for Antipas to strike precisely at John himself and at John alone.'

as religious. There is little doubt that Jesus was for a time a member of John's movement, that he submitted to John's call for repentance and the cultic act which sealed it. According to Matthew, when John (who was obviously familiar with Jesus' reputation) questioned his need for repentance, Jesus replied, 'It is proper in this way to fulfil all righteousness.' (3:15) *The Interpreter's Dictionary of the Bible* suggests that the first meaning of righteousness is not goodness or holiness or personal blamelessness but behaviour which is appropriate to a relationship. It is appropriate for kings to care for their people, for parents to feed and educate their children, for employers to pay their workers adequate wages. Such behaviour is righteous. Jesus, whose relationship is increasingly with the common people and with marginalised members of society, identifies with them unconditionally in the rite of John's baptism. He fulfills righteousness by conforming to the behaviour appropriate to his emerging relationship with humble followers. (Matthew 3:15) It is appropriate for him to bring good news to the poor, release to captives, sight to the blind, freedom to the oppressed, and to proclaim 'the year of the Lord's favour'. (Luke 4:18f)

There is also little doubt that Jesus eventually broke with John's movement. According to Matthew's account of the tradition, John sent messengers to him to ask who and what he was. Jesus replied that the signs of God's reign were being realised in his ministry. He recognised and praised John's prophetic role but said that God's empire was being discovered in ways that were less fiercely ascetic and more overtly compassionate. John had demanded repentance as a condition of baptism. It would seem that Jesus treated people as members of God's empire in the hope that they would repent and change their lives. The stages are reversed. The story of Zacchaeus is paradigmatic. Jesus looked up into the tree where Zacchaeus had climbed and said, 'Hurry on down; for I must stay at your house today.' (Matthew 9:15) Zacchaeus then promised to undo the damage of his corrupt and exploitative career.

The synoptic gospels give us little if any evidence that Jesus baptised. Jesus does appear to advocate baptism in two passages: in Mark 16:16 he is quoted, 'The one who believes and is baptised will be saved,' and in Matthew 28:19 (a much questioned passage) Jesus tells the eleven 'to make disciples of all nations, baptising them.' Jesus makes other references to baptism

(Mark 10:40, Luke 12:50) but using the word as a metaphor for martyrdom.

On the other hand, John's gospel does say that Jesus baptised in the Judean countryside. (3:22) John the Baptist's disciples seem to complain about this. (3:26) The Pharisees also hear that Jesus is baptising more disciples than John. (4:1) And then John the evangelist seems to remember that this is inaccurate. 'Oops!' he seems to say, actually 'it was not Jesus himself but his disciples who baptised.' (4:2) In spite of this, John's gospel abounds in baptismal symbolism – the changing of the water of purification into wedding wine, the encounter with the Samaritan woman at the well (which immediately follows John's admission that Jesus himself was not baptising), the healing of the paralytic by the pool of Beth-zatha, the water and blood which flowed from Jesus' side on the cross – but no other evidence that Jesus may actually have performed baptismal rites. Indeed, the gospels as a whole provide us with little of such evidence, let alone a baptismal ecclesiology.

The Acts of the Apostles and the epistles are much more open to an ecclesial view of baptism. A notable example is the mass conversion on the day of Pentecost. At the conclusion of Peter's sermon 3,000 people are baptised. (Acts 2:41) This is followed by a beautiful verse in which the ideals of ecclesial life are wonderfully expressed: 'They devoted themselves to the apostles' teaching and fellowship, to the breaking of bread and the prayers.' (2:42) However, as the description of the young church's activity goes on it becomes difficult to believe that the account is literally historic. Were 3,000 people all together with their property in common? (2:44) Did 3,000 people day by day spend much time together in the temple? Admittedly, the text suggests that they broke bread from house to house and not all in one place, but the organisation required for such arrangements for so many people and celebrations raises serious practical questions. I suggest that we are indeed in the presence of the beginnings of a baptismal ecclesiology in which a theological ideal is expressed as history, but it is not the only baptismal model to be examined.

Before we jump into a baptismal ecclesiology we should notice how personal and individual some New Testament baptisms are. Perhaps the most extreme example is the baptism of the Ethiopian eunuch by Philip. (Acts 8) He hears a christological interpretation of Isaiah 53 and noticing some water says, 'What prevents me from being baptised?' The chariot stops and Philip baptises him. The text says that the Spirit of the Lord snatched Philip away and that the eunuch went on his way rejoicing. He was part of no visible *ecclesia*. In fact, there is no reason to believe he would ever see a Christian community or even another Christian, unless he himself were responsible for their conversion.

Paul was baptised three days after his conversion experience on the road to Damascus. The Philippian jailer and his family were baptised 'without delay'. There is little evidence in these accounts that baptism was overtly communal and ecclesial, although it is assumed elsewhere that those who were baptised were intimately related to a Christian community.[8] On the contrary, baptism has more in common with many of the personal purification rites of ancient Judaism through which an individual achieves recovery of purity in the sight of God and consequently recovers a place among the holy people. Even Paul's theology of baptism in Romans 6, which may have been written with one eye on potential Hellenistic converts whose religious background often took for granted that salvation involved identification with the myth of a dying and rising god, says nothing to assume an immediately ecclesial context. It may be assumed that those who are baptised will find their place in the baptised community but the baptism itself may be as personal as a healed leper washing after he is judged free of the disease. Paul seems to be primarily concerned with personal freedom from slavery to sin and new life as the free gift of God.

It is true that there are a number of texts in which baptism is linked to the corporate body. In 1 Corinthians 12 Paul speaks of the community as a body composed of many members, each with its own function. In Galatians 3 he speaks of the baptised as 'clothed with Christ,' in a community in which there is no longer Jew nor Greek, male and female, slave and free.[9] The Pauline

---

8. See 1 Corinthians 12:13.
9. It should be noted that these categories are not entirely equal in Paul's thinking. His teaching on circumcision probably negates any difference between Jew and Greek – neither circumcision nor its absence makes any difference. However, the differences he elsewhere raises between men and women (see 1 Corinthians 14:34) and his willingness to leave the institution of slavery unchallenged, indeed his return of the

author of Ephesians emphasises an analogy between the relationship of husband and wife and Christ and the church which is the basis of a certain dimension of ecclesial theology. However, each of these examples of an ecclesial theology would be as applicable to a lay community – for instance, monks or nuns – as to the ordered church as we begin to find it in the pastoral epistles. They are about gifts and charisms and dispositions of relationship. But if the Berkeley Statement is about the ordered church, the institutional church (to use a suspect but accurate term), then it is questionable that the New Testament provides us with a theological basis for the discussion.

I suggest that baptism in the apostolic church may have been primarily a matter of personal crisis, i.e. a moment of decision or judgement. You came to the point of belief and this is what you did. Certainly it opened the door to the community because that is what it is: an open door. It was an act of commitment and conversion. The nature of the community was based on what happened after commitment, not on the moment of arrival. Even the first letter of Peter, whose early chapters are regarded by some scholars as possibly a baptismal liturgy, talks about what is going to happen to the neophytes who must now 'grow into salvation'. (2:2) They are invited to something beyond the door: 'Like living stones, let yourselves be built into a spiritual house, to be a holy priesthood, to offer spiritual sacrifices acceptable to God through Jesus Christ.' (2:5)

I suggest that a theology of ministry and order (specifically, but not exclusively, ordained ministry and order) should be built on a eucharistic ecclesiology. As we have seen, there is scanty evidence that baptism (especially as practised by John) was central to Jesus' method. However, the table of mutual acceptance and service was central, indeed indispensable. Jesus' distance from John can be explained by his willingness to eat and drink (frowned on by John) with sinners who may not yet have formally repented. He was even willing to eat and drink with those with whom he disagreed profoundly, using the table as an opportunity to challenge rather than isolate himself from their prejudices. (see Luke 7:36-50) According to Luke, when a dispute broke out among the disciples at the last supper as to which of them was greatest, Jesus replied, 'The leader [must be]

---

escaped slave Onesimus to his master (Philemon 12), throw a shadow over his doctrine of equality.

like the one who serves. For who is greater, the one who is at the table or the one who serves? Is it not the one at the table? But I am among you as one who serves.' In John's version of the last supper Jesus acts out this theology by insisting on washing the feet of the others. Even more he illustrates the double movement of service when he tells Peter that he will have no part in him if he does not accept the washing of his feet. (13:8) An ecclesiology built on the table demands not only that there are servants (ministers) but also that others accept their service.

What happened between the last supper and the development of an ecclesial understanding of baptism as we begin to find it in Justin and discover it fully grown in *Apostolic Tradition*? There are two areas for exploration. Did a conservative leadership in the more Jewish Jerusalem church seek to return to the more rigid standards of John the Baptist when Jesus' more flexible and tolerant approach was no longer in daily view? This would be consistent with their attempts to insist that Christians must first be Jews, i.e. circumcised. And second, were Christian communities seduced into a 'high' view of initiation by the mystery cults of their cultural context, from whose ranks many converts may have been drawn? A third factor may have been the need to run a tight ship in an ocean of persecution. Where it was at best illegal and at worst very dangerous to be a Christian at all, the gateway of baptism could function as an important screen to ensure the probable fidelity of the faithful.

As Jesus' tolerant approach to sinners in the hope that they would turn towards the reign of God was replaced by higher and higher moral standards developed and expanded from the list of required abstentions adopted at the so-called Council of Jerusalem (Acts 15:20), baptism became a barrier rather than a door. Growing numbers of would-be Christians hesitated before entering a community which would submit them to humiliating discipline and to second-class status if they should slip in their moral behaviour after baptism.[10] The emperor Constantine is said to have delayed his baptism until his deathbed in case he should not be able to meet the high standards of the Christian

10. Edward Yarnold, *The Awe-Inspiring Rites of Initiation* (Slough, 1971) 7. Yarnold says, 'many who were convinced of the truth of Christianity preferred to postpone baptism at least until the passionate time of youth was over. Baptism involved such a radical change in life that one would not receive it until one felt completely ready.'

community. Thus a two-tiered Christianity was invented composed of the very good (eventually often monks and nuns) and the ordinary (often catechumens). Baptism was in danger of becoming admission to the élite rather than to the *plebs sancta Dei*. The shift from the simplicity of the baptism of the Ethiopian and of Paul to rituals that are almost Masonic in tone and structure is remarkable. Edward Yarnold says, 'The ceremonies took place at night, some of them in the dark, after weeks of intense preparation; they were wrapped in secrecy, and the candidate knew little about them until just before or even after he had received them.' Yarnold says he might have called his own book on the subject, 'The Spine-chilling Rites of Initiation.'[11] Lent, which was originally a period of more intense catechesis before the baptisms at Easter, became a season of penitence characterised in many parts of the west by the imposition of ashes on its opening day.

Years ago I undertook an amateur study of Indonesia. One of the books I read suggested that the Islamic penetration of Indonesia had been remarkably easy. The old religion of the archipelago, and especially of Bali, had been Hindu/Buddhist but it was a religion very much in the hands of an economic, social, and perhaps intellectual élite. Islam arrived on the boats of Arab traders with a simple religion that anyone could grasp. Pray briefly five times a day, be socially responsible (give alms), recognise every other Muslim as part of a universal brotherhood, go on a pilgrimage if you can afford it. And the middle class of shopkeepers and *petit bourgeoisie* embraced it. Today Indonesia has the largest Muslim population in the world. I have to ask if Islam's rapid conquest of the Christian Middle East and north Africa in the seventh century was as much the consequence of élitism as of military subjugation.

Eventually the whole complex process of preparing for admission by baptism to the *ecclesia* imploded, especially when Christianity was the official religion and the majority of candidates were children. Some fossils of the old élitist tradition remained. However, during the last fifty years of our era there have been serious attempts to revive the practice of the fourth century, to tie baptism to Easter and prepare candidates not only by catechesis but also by scheduled ritual events at fixed intervals before their initiation. I have no problem with the instruc-

---

11. Ibid. ix.

tion of candidates for baptism, or with giving them opportunity
to express the doubts, anxieties, and personal insights that they
will bring to their lives as Christians. But I seriously question the
notion that baptism defines the church except as the sign of the
crisis that everyone brings to the experience of faith and of consecration to its vision.

I do not believe we may ground a theology of ministry on a
baptismal ecclesiology because I do not believe baptism is about
the structure of the church. Baptism is the door; the table is
where structure and order are defined. All are there as guests;
each one has a role to play, some more fixed than others. When
we have a festal family dinner we need someone to prepare the
food for the table. We need someone to furnish it with plates and
cutlery. We need the host. We need people who will share the
food, passing it to one another, making sure everyone is included,
serving one another. We need conversation, the telling of our
story, not only in its historic terms but also in its current terms.
The principles of this homely scene belong equally to the eucharist and our theology of ministry must be drawn from the
mutuality, interaction, humble service, and organisation they
secure. The table demands ordered relationships and may therefore be the model of the church's order. Insofar as baptism is
considered apart from the eucharist, its emphasis is on response
and acceptance.

The Theology of Ordained Ministry in the Berkeley Statement

William R. Crockett

This article is offered as a commentary on Part 1 of *To Equip the Saints* (The Berkeley Statement), 'The Ordered Nature of the Church,' which deals with the theology of ordination. Part 2 deals with the liturgy of ordination. In this article we shall take note of issues that are the subject of ongoing debate in the Anglican Communion and raise questions where further theological reflection is needed. The Berkeley Statement needs to be read in the context of (a) the earlier statements of the International Anglican Liturgical Consultation, (b) the multilateral and bilateral ecumenical dialogues in which the Anglican Communion is engaged, and (c) the liturgical scholarship, ministry studies, and sacramental theology of the last several decades.

The liturgy and theology of ordination have been the subject of three successive sessions of the IALC. A preliminary conference was held in Järvenpää, Finland in 1997. Further work was done at a meeting in Kottayam, India in 1999. This preparatory work came to fruition in the full consultation held in Berkeley, California in August, 2001. At Järvenpää it was recognised that the variety of bilateral agreements and the reality of full communion with some churches and united churches in some provinces form part of the present ecumenical context in which Anglicans reflect on the meaning of ordination.

Järvenpää notes that there has been significant ecumenical convergence on a variety of issues concerning ordination in both multilateral and bilateral agreements. These include (1) 'Baptism as the foundation in which a theology of the ministry of the whole people of God is rooted;' (2) Apostolic succession is understood primarily as a characteristic of the church as a whole in its varied witness and cannot be limited to ministerial succession; (3) 'Different forms of ministry are based on different gifts (*charismata*) given by God for the mission of the church;' (4) Recognition that 'the church needs persons who are publicly and continually responsible for pointing to its fundamental dependence on Jesus Christ . . . [and that] the ministry of such persons, who since very early times have been ordained, is constitutive for the life and witness of the church;'[1] (5) 'Ordination is always presided over by persons in whom the church recognises the authority to transmit the ministerial commission by imposition of hands and prayer;' (6) 'Ordination is accepted in most denominations to be for life;' (7) 'Recognition of the true ecclesial status of other communions precedes the mutual recognition of ministries.'[2]

In his keynote address at the Järvenpää conference, 'Ordination as God's Action through the Church,'[3] Paul Bradshaw helped to establish the foundations for the theology of ordination found in the Berkeley Statement. In the Pauline communities in the New Testament, there were a variety of complementary ministries based on the variety of gifts (*charismata*) given by the Spirit. While these gifts of ministry included a variety of leadership roles, there was no difference in status between those exercising leadership roles and the other members of the community. Ordination did not imply clericalism, which implies a separation between clergy and laity. The distinction between 'clergy' and 'laity' emerged only slowly in the life of the early church. By the third century the leadership roles in the church were structured in the three offices of bishops, presbyters, and deacons. Edward Schillebeeckx interprets this change not as a shift from charismatic to institutional ministries, but as an institutionalisation of the charisms of the Spirit. 'The development of ministry in the early Christian churches was not so much, as is sometimes claimed, a historical shift from *charisma* to institution but a shift from the *charisma* of many to a specialised *charisma* of just a few.'[4] While this represents a fundamental sociological shift, there is continuity in the theological understanding of ministry as a charism of the Spirit.[5] Bradshaw and Schillebeeckx both note, however, that gradually a hierarchy of ministries became established, largely influenced by the social structures of the ancient world.

Bradshaw observes that in the liturgical traditions of the

---

1. BEM, Baptism 8.
2. Järvenpää 62.
3. Järvenpää 8–15.
4. Edward Schillebeeckx, *The Church with a Human Face: A New and Expanded Theology of Ministry* (New York, 1985) 121.
5. Schillebeeckx, *The Church with a Human Face*, 125–33.

early church,[6] ordination is understood as an act of God working through the whole church. He points out that one of the
major distortions in our traditional theology of ordained ministry is that it has been divorced from ecclesiology. Ordination is
a process which begins with the community's recognition of
God's call. In the ordination rite this finds liturgical expression
in the community's prayer for the bestowal of the gifts and
graces necessary for the effective exercise of the particular office
to which the person is being ordained, culminating in the community's acceptance of the new role of the minister among
them.[7] In the patristic period ordination always meant appointment to a particular community. The Council of Chalcedon regarded absolute ordinations as invalid.[8]

To Equip the Saints begins its reflection on the theology of ordained ministry by placing it in the context of a theology of mission. This missiological starting point reflects both the IALC's
earlier statement on baptism and a growing ecumenical consensus that a theology of mission ought to provide the starting
point for reflection on a theology of ministry and ordination. In
Walk in Newness of Life, its Toronto Statement on Christian
Initiation, the IALC affirmed that 'Mission is first and foremost
God's mission to God's World ... The primary agent of mission
is God the Holy Spirit, who brings into existence a community of
faith to embody this mission and to make God's new order manifest in a broken world.'[9] In the ecumenical context, a prime example of this approach is found in the Niagara Report of the
Anglican-Lutheran Consultation on Episcopé, which begins its
reflection on ministry in the context of the nature of the church
and its mission. This mission is the mission of the Triune God towards the world in which the church participates. Mission is
God's gift and all ministry is to serve that mission.[10] The understanding of mission in all these documents is that mission is
'God's mission' in which the church participates.[11]

Since it is the church which is the primary agent of God's

6. For the early ordination rites see Bradshaw 1990.
7. Järvenpää, 9–11.
8. Schillebeeckx, *The Church with a Human Face*, 154–56.
9. *Walk in Newness of Life*, Section 2: God's Mission 1.
10. *Niagara Report*, Sections 11–24.
11. For the history of the concept of 'God's mission' see David J. Bosch,
Transforming Mission: Paradigm Shifts in Theology of Mission (Maryknoll,
NY, 1991) 389–93.

mission, reflection on mission leads directly to ecclesiology, reflection on the nature of the church. The Berkeley Statement affirms that all ministry in the church is grounded in a baptismal ecclesiology. The new community, the church, is called into being by God, who

> through the Holy Spirit baptises us into the life and ministry of Christ and forms us into the *laos*, the people of God, who as signs and agents of God's reign participate in God's mission of reconciling humanity and all creation to God ... The foundation of the life and ministry of the church is therefore baptism.[12]

The affirmation of a baptismal ecclesiology as foundational for a theology of ministry is sometimes misunderstood as a reductionist or minimalist understanding of the nature of the church, which does not take sufficiently into account the perspectives offered by the eucharistic and communion ecclesiologies which are also prominent themes in ecumenical dialogues. The affirmation of a baptismal ecclesiology is not intended to be reductionist or minimalist, but to be foundational for everything else that is said about the various ministries of the church. Consistent with BEM and the various bilateral dialogues, ordained ministry is discussed in the context of the ministry of the whole people of God. A baptismal ecclesiology affirms the foundation of the church's ministry in baptism. The other dimensions of ecclesiology build on this foundation.

A baptismal ecclesiology is also intended as a corrective to clericalism. A baptismal ecclesiology affirms an equality of status among all the baptised. It 'leads us to see ordained ministers as integral members of the body of Christ, called by God and discerned by the body to be signs and animators of Christ's self-giving life and ministry to which all people are called by God and ... empowered by the Spirit.'[13] This does not imply that there is no differentiation of roles in the community. On the contrary, the Berkeley Statement states clearly that 'in order that the whole people of God may fulfil their calling to be a holy priesthood . . . some are called to specific ministries of leadership by ordination.'[14] This differentiation of roles is not to be understood in a purely functional sense, however, but in the Pauline

---

12. *To Equip the Saints*, Part I: *The Calling of the People of God*, p 219 below.
13. *To Equip the Saints*, Part I: *The Calling of the People of God*, p220 below.
14. *To Equip the Saints*, Part I: *Baptism and Ministry*, p 220 below.

sense of complementary gifts of ministry which build up the Body of Christ and enable it to participate in God's mission in the world.

In common with the various ecumenical dialogues on ministry, the Berkeley Statement recognises that the structure of ordained ministries has evolved both historically and culturally. Recent scholarship has emphasised the variety of forms which ordained leadership took in the earliest period of the church, reflecting the social setting of the early communities and the models of leadership to be found both in Jewish and Greco-Roman culture.[15] By the end of the second century, the variety of ministries of leadership that was evident in the New Testament period became ordered in the threefold pattern of bishops, presbyters, and deacons. This threefold pattern of ministry continues to interact with various aspects of culture.

The recognition in the Berkeley Statement of the variety of ways in which the ordained ministry has been shaped by different cultures reflects a heightened awareness of the pluralism of cultures within the worldwide Anglican Communion. The importance of the inculturation of liturgy was affirmed in the York Statement of the IALC.[16] The Berkeley Statement recognises that this cultural shaping of the forms of ordained ministry is of theological as well as sociological significance. 'The gospel both affirms and challenges these cultural expressions of relationships and leadership.'[17] The people of every culture are called to discern theologically the ways in which the patterns of ordained leadership that prevail in their cultures serve or fail to serve the ministry of the whole people of God. Having reflected on the missionary and ecclesiological context for the ministry of all the baptised, having located the ministry of the ordained in the context of the baptised community, and having reflected on the historical and cultural shaping of ordained leadership, the Berkeley Statement goes on to reflect theologically on the particular roles of bishops, presbyters, and deacons.

The ministry of bishops is understood as a 'ministry of oversight (*episcopé*) which historically found its focus in the office of the bishop.'[18] This approach to the ministry of bishops reflects

---

15. See Bradshaw 2002, 193–201.
16. *Down to Earth Worship*.
17. *To Equip the Saints*, Part I: *Cultural Shaping of Ministry*, p 220 below.
18. *To Equip the Saints*, Part I: *Bishops*, p 221 below.

recent bilateral and multilateral ecumenical work.[19] In ecumenical studies it is recognised that it is the ministry of oversight (*episcopé*) 'which constitutes the heart of the episcopal office'.[20] In the earliest communities the ministry of *episcopé* was variously structured, but by the third century this ministry 'found its focus in the office of the bishop'. Among the various gifts of ministry, the ministry of *episcope* (oversight) is a ministry of leadership in mission, teaching and common life which serves to express and promote the visible unity of the church. It is recognised ecumenically that every church needs this ministry of unity in some form.[21] The Anglican tradition, having retained the episcopal office, understands the ministry of the bishop as a ministry of personal *episcopé*: 'the bishop is the sign of unity and of continuity with the apostolic tradition of faith and life.'[22] Theologically, the Berkeley Statement sees the bishop's role summed up in the Virginia Report of the Inter-Anglican Theological and Doctrinal Commission: 'The calling of a bishop is to represent Christ and his church, particularly as apostle, chief priest, teacher and pastor of a diocese; to guard the faith, unity and discipline of the whole church; to proclaim the word of God; to act in Christ's name for the reconciliation of the world and the building up of the church; and to ordain others to continue Christ's ministry'[23]

Consistent with its emphasis on the historical and cultural shaping of ministry, the Berkeley Statement pays particular attention to the way in which the bishop's role has been shaped by the historical, cultural, and social contexts in which the episcopal office has developed:

> In the pre-Nicene period ... the bishop was teacher and pastor and the bond of communion both within the local church and between the various local and regional churches. Bishops also exercised a ministry of prophetic witness. In the period after Constantine ... the bishop became part of the

---

19. See *Niagara Report*, Sections 40–59 and Peter Bouteneff, ed., *Episkopé and Episcopacy and the Quest for Visible Unity* [Faith and Order Paper no 183] (Geneva, 1999).

20. *Niagara Report*, Section 54.

21. See *The Nature and Purpose of the Church: A Stage on the Way to a Common Statement* [Faith and Order Paper no 181] (Geneva, 1998) Section E, 89 - 97.

22. *To Equip the Saints*, Part I: Bishops.

23. *Virginia Report*, 3.17.

hierarchical administrative structure of the empire on the model of the imperial civil service. In the feudal period in the West the bishop was both spiritual and temporal lord. After the Reformation [and during the period of colonialism] ... the imperial and feudal models of episcopacy continued to predominate ... [but were later] modified by an increased sense of the role played by the bishop in leading the mission of the church and by a heightened emphasis on the apostolic nature of the episcopate. In the Anglican Communion today a renewed model of episcopal leadership is emerging, one that more fully reflects the servant ministry of Jesus and the baptismal calling of the whole people of God. In this style of episcopal leadership, the ministries of all the baptised are nurtured in ways which are personal, collegial, and communal.[24]

According to the Berkeley Statement, 'the calling of presbyters is 'to share with the bishops in the overseeing of the church.'[25] The Berkeley Statement affirms the description of the presbyter's role found in *BEM*: 'Presbyters serve as pastoral ministers of word and sacraments in a local eucharistic community. They are preachers and teachers of the faith, exercise pastoral care, and bear responsibility for the discipline of the congregation ...[26] The Berkeley Statement notes that:

The New Testament uses the term *presbyteros* in reference to the 'elders' of Christian communities (Acts 15:4-6; 20:17), and the language of priesthood to speak of Christ (Hebrews 4:14-5:10) and of the whole community of the baptised (1 Peter 2:4-5; Revelation 1:6). When applied to Christ, priestly language refers to the sacrificial nature of his death (Hebrews 7:26-28) and to Christ's intercession before God on behalf of all creation (Hebrews 7:23-25; Romans 8:34). When applied to all the baptised, priestly language refers to the 'living sacrifice, holy and acceptable to God' (Romans 12:1) which they offer. As the ordained ministry developed, language of priesthood became increasingly applied first to the office of bishop and then derivatively to the presbyterate, and sacrifi-

---

24. *To Equip the Saints*, Part I: Bishops. Cf *BEM*, Ministry 26; *Virginia Report*, 3.22.
25. *To Equip the Saints*, Part I: Presbyters / Priests quoting *Virginia Report*, 3.22.
26. *BEM*, Ministry, 30.

cial and vicarial interpretations of this ministry were overlaid upon the earlier presbyteral understanding.[27] At the
time of the Reformation, the Anglican ordinal retained the
term 'priest,' but interpreted this office as one in which the
minister unites the proclamation of the word, the administration of the sacraments, and the pastoral care of the community.[28]

The linguistic and cultural shaping of the role of the presbyter is highlighted in the Berkeley Statement: 'In the various
languages used in the Anglican Communion today, different
terms are used for the office [of presbyter/priest], with different
connotations arising from historical, cultural, and linguistic factors.'[29] It is recognised that some provinces use the term 'presbyter' in their ordination rites, while others use the term 'priest'.
It is also recognised that neither term exhausts the meaning of
the office and that 'ordination rites should make use of a wide
range of imagery in order to bring out the multi-faceted meaning of this office.'[30] This recognises the metaphorical and symbolic character of all religious language, and the multivalent
character of religious symbols.

This recognition of the nature of religious language and symbols is of vital importance. When priestly language is used either
of Christ, the baptised community, or the ordained, it is not used
in a literal sense, but in a metaphorical or symbolic sense, which
allows for a wide range of meaning reflecting different historical, cultural, and linguistic contexts. The use of priestly language for the presbyterate in the Anglican tradition provides a
good example. While Thomas Cranmer retained the term
'priest' for this office at the time of the Reformation, the language of the Ordinal transformed the meaning of the term. In the
medieval context, the term 'priest' had as its primary connotation the offering of sacrifice. In the Anglican Ordinal the term

---

27. See Bradshaw 2002, 201–06; Schillebeeckx, *Church with a Human Face*,
144–47.
28. *To Equip the Saints*, Part I: *Presbyters/Priests*, p 224. For the interpretation of ministry and priesthood in the Anglican tradition see Stephen
Sykes, John Booty, and Jonathan Knight, eds., *The Study of Anglicanism*,
rev. ed. (London, 1998) 321–33. For the history of the Anglican Ordinal
see Bradshaw 1971.
29. *To Equip the Saints*, Part I: *Presbyters/Priests*, p 224.
30. *To Equip the Saints*, Part I: *Presbyters/Priests*, p 224.

'priest' had a primarily pastoral connotation, which included the ministry of word, sacrament, and pastoral care. The Berkeley Statement recommends that:

> provinces that use the term 'priest' (or a translation thereof) may be guided by the interpretation of the term in *Baptism, Eucharist and Ministry*: 'Ordained ministers are related, as are all Christians, both to the priesthood of Christ, and to the priesthood of the church. But they may appropriately be called priests because they fulfil a particular priestly service by strengthening and building up the royal and prophetic priesthood of the faithful through word and sacraments, through their prayers of intercession, and through their pastoral guidance of the community.[31]

How is the ministerial priesthood of the presbyterate related to the priesthood of all the baptised? Neither the various ecumenical agreements nor the Berkeley Statement go very far in addressing this question. ARCIC declares that the ministerial priesthood 'is not an extension of the common Christian priesthood but belongs to another realm of the gifts of the Spirit,' but does not develop what this means.[32] This is an issue, therefore, which needs further theological reflection. What the Berkeley Statement does make clear is that the priestly ministry of the presbyter is a 'sacramental, pastoral, and teaching' ministry which, like all ministries of leadership in the church, must be in the service of the priesthood of the baptised community if it is to be consistent with a baptismal ecclesiology.

In a recent book,[33] Paul Avis points a way forward in the interpretation of the priesthood of the ordained ministry by exploring the concept of representation, taking his cue from F. D. Maurice.[34] F. D. Maurice distinguished between a representative

---

31. *To Equip the Saints*, Part I: *Presbyters/Priests*, p 224; *BEM*, Ministry, 17.
32. *Final Report*, 13. Probably the best exegesis of this text can be found in J. M. R. Tillard, *What Priesthood Has the Ministry?* [Grove Booklet on Ministry and Worship no 13] (Bramcote, Notts, 1973). Tillard relates the language of priesthood as applied to all the baptised people of God in 1 Peter 2:9 to its background in Exodus 19:6. This is a priesthood of holiness of life. On the other hand, he relates the language of priesthood as applied to the ordained in a highly analogous way to the Levitical priesthood.
33. Paul Avis, *A Ministry Shaped by Mission* (Edinburgh, 2005).
34. Frederick Denison Maurice, *The Kingdom of Christ*, A. R. Vidler ed. (London, 1958) 2: 145–46.

and a vicarial priesthood. He argued that ministerial priesthood
has to do with representation, not mediation. The ordained ministry does not mediate between God and the community, but
represents God to the community and the community to God.
The priest represents Christ to a community which is already
united to Christ in baptism. Similarly, R. C. Moberly argued in
his classic work *Ministerial Priesthood* [35] that the ministerial
priesthood is not a mediatorial priesthood, but a representative
priesthood, which acts as the representative and organ of the
whole body in the exercise of responsibilities which belong to
the body as a whole. Does the ordained ministry represent
Christ or the church? Avis argues that this is a false dichotomy.
If the ordained ministry is a representative rather than a mediatorial priesthood, the church's ministers can be seen to represent
both Christ and the church, because Christ cannot be separated
from his body. Within the baptised community the ordained
ministry exercises a public, representative ministry. Does this
inevitably lead to hierarchy, social stratification, and clericalism? Avis argues that clericalism is not intrinsic to ordained
ministry, and that an egalitarian, socially holistic, and interde-
pendent interpretation of the relationship between the ordained
and the baptised community is equally possible. From the perspective of the Berkeley Statement this would be consistent with
a baptismal ecclesiology.

The Berkeley Statement acknowledges the diversity of understanding and practice in the Anglican Communion today
with regard to the diaconate. During the medieval period and in
the post-Reformation period in the Church of England the diaconate became a transitional order, commonly leading to the
priesthood. Today, in some provinces of the Anglican Communion, the diaconate is being renewed as a distinct office, but
different models are being proposed, so that the shape of a
renewed diaconate is a matter of ongoing debate in the communion. In some parts of the Communion, particularly in North
America, a renewed diaconate is understood to be directed towards the servant mission of the church in the world. In this
model, the liturgical role of the deacon expresses the interface
between the world and the baptised community. The distinctive
nature of the diaconate, however, is not servant ministry in itself, which belongs to all the baptised, but the calling of the dea-

---

35. R. C. Moberly, *Ministerial Priesthood* (London, 1969) 242.

con is to embody and activate the Christ-like service of the whole people of God in the world. It is this model which is primarily reflected in the Berkeley Statement. The Berkeley Statement challenges the prevailing view within Anglicanism that the diaconate is the basis for the servant character of all three orders of ministry and affirms that baptism is the basis for the servant character of all the church's ministries.

On the other hand, particularly in the Church of England and in parts of Australia, another model for a renewed diaconate has emerged which draws on the work of John N. Collins, who calls in question the prevailing interpretation of *diakonia* as 'service.' In his classic work *Diakonia: Reinterpreting the Ancient Sources* [36] and his newer book *Deacons and the Church: Making Connections between Old and New* [37] Collins argues that in classical Greek usage the word group *diakonia/diakonos* is not primarily related to 'service' but to 'commissioned agency,' especially for a 'sacred mission.' The *diakonos* is more like an 'ambassador' than a 'servant.' According to Collins, 'service' is the duty of every Christian rather than the essence of a particular ministry. The Church of England report *For such a time as this: A renewed diaconate in the Church of England* [38] took up Collins' work and concludes that deacons are ambassadors whose mission is to make connections and build bridges between the church and the world. While this affirms the ministry of the deacon as a 'go-between' between church and world, it does not limit the distinctive office of the deacon to the service role, but includes the proclamatory, liturgical, and pastoral dimensions as integral to the deacon's ministry. The fundamental understanding of the diaconate and the shape of a renewed diaconate, therefore, remain matters of ongoing debate.

What is the relationship between the three orders of ministry? In his keynote address at the Järvenpää conference Paul Bradshaw argued that the episcopate, presbyterate, and diaconate are 'three separate orders of ordained ministry, rather

---

36. John N. Collins, *Diakonia: Re-Interpreting the Ancient Resources* (New York, 1990).

37. John N. Collins, *Deacons and the Church: Making Connections Between Old and New* (Harrisburg, PA, 2003).

38. Working Party of the House of Bishops, Church of England, *For Such a Time as This: A Renewed Diaconate in the Church of England* (London, 2001).

than three different degrees within one ministry, [therefore] . . .
we must not rule out the possibility of direct ordination to any of
the orders.'[39] The Berkeley Statement continues this line of
thinking:

> Because the three orders are viewed as distinct ministries, di-
> rect ordination to the presbyterate, and even the possibility
> of direct ordination to the episcopate, are being advocated by
> some in the Anglican Communion. There is historical prece-
> dent for both sequential and direct ordination. In the pre-
> Nicene church, direct ordination was commonly practised,
> and sequential ordination did not become universal until the
> eleventh century. Provinces may therefore wish to consider
> the possibility of direct ordination to the episcopate and to
> the presbyterate.[40]

I will not take up the matter of direct ordination here, since
John Gibaut has contributed an article on this subject in the present volume, but will simply note that the question of the relationship between the three orders remains a matter of ongoing
debate within the communion. The interest in direct ordination
has arisen primarily in some areas within the communion where
there has been a renewed understanding of the diaconate as a
distinct order of ministry rather than a transitional order, thus
raising the question of direct ordination to the presbyterate. In
other parts of the communion, however, the diaconate is regarded
as foundational for all three orders and sequential ordination is
defended. This is the position taken in the Church of England's
report on a renewed diaconate.[41]

The final section of Part 1 of the Berkeley Statement takes up
the question of the meaning of the act of ordination itself. *BEM*
has a whole section on the meaning of ordination, which The
Berkeley Statement quotes with approval as consistent with an
Anglican understanding:

> Ordination denotes an action by God and the community. . . .
> The act of ordination by the laying on of hands of those ap-
> pointed to do so is at one and the same time invocation of the

---

39. *Järvenpää*, 12.
40. *To Equip the Saints*, Part I: *Direct Ordination*, p 225.
41. Working Party of the House of Bishops, Church of England, *For
Such a Time as This*, 37–38.

Holy Spirit (epiklesis); sacramental sign; acknowledgment of gifts and commitment.

This reflects a sacramental understanding of ordination, acknowledging the act of ordination as an effectual sign of the bestowal of grace. The context for this interpretation is the contemporary renewal of sacramental theology, which understands sacraments as symbolic actions expressive of God's self-giving in the context of the liturgical community.[42] Since grace is God's self-gift towards us and in us, personal and relational language is particularly appropriate to express the nature of sacramental action. Sacraments are prayer-actions that express God's gracious encounter with us through the instrumentality of sacramental signs:

Ordination is a sign of the granting of this prayer by the Lord who gives the gift of the ordained ministry. ... Ordination is a sign performed in faith that the spiritual relationship signified is present in, with and through the words spoken, the gestures made and the forms employed.[43]

This interpretation of sacramental activity is consistent with the classical Anglican understanding of sacraments as 'moral instruments' of grace, which was first developed by Richard Hooker in the sixteenth century.[44] In this view, sacramental activity is seen as analogous to the offer and acceptance of a gift between free moral agents.

The importance of a baptismal ecclesiology emerges again at this point. The Berkeley Statement concludes its interpretation of the meaning of ordination by pointing out that the act of ordination is an action of the whole community:

It is the community as a whole, with the bishop presiding, which recognises the divine call and the gifts of ministry of those who are to be ordained. It is the community as a whole which, through prayer with the laying on of hands by the bishop as the focus of the church's unity, seeks from God the necessary increase of those gifts and graces for the effective exercise of the ministry. It is the community as a whole which authorises and sends forth the ordained in God's name to lead the baptised in Christ's mission and ministry.[45]

---

42. See James F. White, *Sacraments as God's Self Giving* (Nashville, 1983).
43. *BEM*, Ministry 43.
44. Richard Hooker, *Laws of Ecclesiastical Polity*, 5.57.4,5.
45. *To Equip the Saints*, Part I: *The Act of Ordination*, p 227.

The Berkeley Statement does not take up the question whether ordained ministry is to be understood functionally or ontologically, and the question of the indelibility of orders. These are questions that require ongoing theological reflection. The notion of the 'sacramental character' which Augustine distinguished from the grace of baptism was applied by the medieval theologians to the sacrament of ordination. In the patristic period there was no explicit notion of indelible character. As we have already seen, ordination was not regarded as absolute, but was related to appointment to a particular community. Both multilateral and bilateral ecumenical dialogues speak of ordination as a lifelong commitment. The difficulty with the notion of 'indelible character' is that it suggests a difference in ontological status between the ordained and the laity, which can undermine the complementarity of ministries within the baptised community. On the other hand, a purely functional understanding of ordained ministry reduces ordained ministry to the particular roles exercised by the ordained, leaving out of account the personal dimension of ministry.

A relational or covenantal model offers alternatives to functional or ontological views. Ordained ministry is neither a status nor a set of functions, but a charism of the Spirit. It is a gift, not an individual possession. It is a relational reality, a service to the community. In the language of *BEM*, ordination establishes a 'new relation' between the 'minister and the local Christian community and, by intention, the church universal.'[46] It is 'in recognition of [this] God-given charism of ministry, [that] ordination to any one of the particular ordained ministries is never repeated.'[47] ARCIC adopts what could be called a covenantal model, affirming that 'just as Jesus Christ has united the church inseparably with himself, and as God calls all the faithful to life-long discipleship, so the gifts and calling of God to the ministers are irrevocable. For this reason, ordination is unrepeatable in both our churches.'[48]

---

46. *BEM*, Ministry 42.
47. *BEM*, Ministry 48.
48. *Final Report*, Ministry and Ordination 15.

What History can tell us about Ordination

Paul F. Bradshaw

In the post-modern ethos of our present age, there are many who share Henry Ford's view that 'history is bunk'; and that includes a good number of Christian clergy. Why should we bother to study the history of ordination practice? Why can't we simply create what we think are appropriate ordination rites for our needs, guided by what we read in the New Testament? Well, of course we could attempt do so, and there are a number of Christian denominations that have tried to do just that. But the New Testament on its own does not give us a complete picture of early Christian thought and practice in this area, and there is much that we would not know were it not for the remains left by later generations. If we believe that Christian doctrine and liturgy need to be true to their roots in the apostolic age, we need to discover, as far as we can, what it was that the first generations of Christians did and thought, and how and why in later centuries things changed to produce ideas and practices that in some cases have remained with us down to the present day.

There are, for instance, a few signs in the New Testament that at least some early Christian appointments to office or commissioning for a particular ministry involved both prayer and laying on of hands (Acts 6:6, 13:3; the laying on of hands is not explicitly mentioned in the appointment of elders in Acts 14:23, prayer is not explicitly mentioned in 1 Timothy 4:14 and 2 Timothy 1:6, and neither are mentioned in Titus 1:5). But what was the connection between these two actions? And what sort of prayer was used? And was there anything else involved in the process? Were it not for later evidence, we would have no hope of trying to answer these and similar questions, and in our attempts to be true to the scriptures in our own practice might well come up with ways of doing things that seem to be quite different from what actually was once the case.

For example, in composing the first Anglican Ordinal in 1550, Thomas Cranmer tried to produce something that was true to the New Testament, but he thought that prayer and the imposition of hands were two separate and successive actions in the apostolic age, that the local Christian community first engaged in an act of prayer and then subsequently hands were laid on the candidate to commission him for ministry. Thus the bidding before the litany in the rite for consecrating a bishop states:

> Brethren, it is written in the gospel of St Luke, that our saviour Christ continued the whole night in prayer, or ever that he did choose and send forth his twelve Apostles. It is written also in the Acts of the Apostles that the disciples which were at Antioch did fast and pray, or ever they laid hands upon or sent forth Paul and Barnabas. Let us therefore, following the example of our saviour Christ and his Apostles, first fall to prayer, or that we admit and send forth this person presented unto us to the work whereunto we trust the Holy Ghost hath called him.

Cranmer also appears to have thought that the act of prayer was general intercession for all sorts of needs, including a brief petition for the candidates, since that is all that he provided in the rite for deacons.[1]

Election

If we were to judge on the basis of the New Testament alone, we might possibly think that candidates were regularly chosen by casting lots (see Acts 1:26), though few churches, even those that think of themselves as conforming closely to scripture, have adopted this as their normal way of choosing ministers. When we turn to other evidence for early Christian history, however, a somewhat different picture emerges.[2] It appears from this testimony that the election of candidates for office, or at least the opportunity to raise objections to any who had been nominated, was the normal practice in Christian churches both Eastern and Western. This was not understood as a mere incidental preliminary to the ordination, but as an integral part of it, just as the catechumenate was of Christian initiation. Nor was it (at least in theory) seen as expressing the right of Christian communities to choose the people that they wanted as their leaders, even if in practice that was often what happened. On the contrary, it was understood as the means by which God's choice of a person for office was discerned and made manifest: it was God who chose

---

1. For further details of the first Anglican Ordinal, see Bradshaw 1971, chapters 1-2.
2. Further details of the ancient ordination practices mentioned in this essay, together with English translations of the relevant texts, can be found in Bradshaw 1990.

and called, and that call was revealed through the vote of the community. That ordination was God's action rather than the result of human choice alone is made clear in many ancient ordination texts, e.g. 'you who from generation to generation ordain holy bishops: make, God of truth, this man also a living bishop ...' (fourth-century *Sacramentary of Sarapion*); 'Lord, fill this man, whom you have willed to undertake the rank of the presbyterate ...' (one of the prayers of the Byzantine rite); 'we beseech you that you would grant that these your servants, whom you deem worthy to call to the office of Levites ...' (collect for deacons in the *Leonine Sacramentary*).

In the case of a bishop, a candidate was not only selected by the local church but eventually also required to have the approval of the other bishops, and it was this requirement, rather than any theory of sacramental transmission, which led to the presence and involvement of the latter in the rite of episcopal ordination. Thus, Canon 4 of the Council of Nicea in AD 325 ruled that all the bishops of the province ought to attend the ordination, but if that were not possible, then a minimum of three was required, with the rest sending their approval in writing. Canon 6 permitted a majority verdict to suffice where unanimity could not be reached, and similar legislation was repeated in later councils. In the case of the presbyterate and diaconate, while the right of nomination seems generally to have rested with the bishop, he did not normally act without the consent of the clergy and people. Vestiges of this can still be seen in the later rites of East and West, where the congregation are invited to acclaim the ordinands as worthy, or (in the Roman tradition) are given opportunity to express any objections to them.

The importance originally accorded to the election can be seen in the Greek word that came to be used by Christians as the technical term for ordination *cheirotonia*, and its associated verb, *cheirotoneo*. The root meaning of the noun was 'the lifting up of the hand', and it was used in classical Greek to signify an election. Early Christianity, on the other hand, extended it to designate not just the first half of the process of ministerial appointment but the whole action – both the election and the prayer with the laying on of the hand. The ambiguity of the word, however, led to its being understood by the late fourth century as referring primarily to the lifting up/laying on of the hand in prayer rather than to the raising of the hand in voting. This then resulted in that second gesture being accorded greater sacramental significance and the act of election given reduced importance in the process, leading to its eventual decline and virtual disappearance in many places. A somewhat parallel development can be seen with regard to baptismal practice. Whereas the church in the first three centuries seems to have attached great importance to the reformation of the candidate's way of life as part of the process of becoming a Christian, and regarded the baptism as ineffective if he or she were still sinning, by the late fourth century the emphasis appears to have shifted to the ritual action in isolation from these preliminaries, and to stress being laid not on outward and visible signs of conversion as a necessary part of baptism, but on the invisible inner effects on the soul brought about by the ritual itself.

Furthermore, the requirement for other bishops to be present at an episcopal ordination also in time brought about a major shift in the theology of that rite. It eventually became expected that the ordinand himself would travel to where the archbishop or patriarch was, rather than have his superior travel to the particular diocese. So, for example, someone elected by an Italian diocese would go to Rome for the confirmation of his election by the pope and for his ordination there. Hence candidates for the episcopate were no longer ordained in their own cathedral nor in the presence of their own ecclesial community. This in the end almost completely severed the connection between the clergy and people of the diocese and the process of the ordination of their bishop. Not only was their act of election reduced in significance but also they had no part to play in the liturgical and sacramental action, which was now seen as concentrated in the hands of the episcopal authorities alone. It also severed the solemn seating of the bishop in his own episcopal chair, *cathedra*, from the act of ordination to create a distinct rite of enthronement at a later date, and so encouraged the idea that ordination and jurisdiction might be distinguished from one another.

While some of the sixteenth-century Reformers did try to restore election to its ancient place in the process of ordination, that was not the case in England. Its absence formed one of the Puritan objections to the Anglican Ordinal in the reign of Elizabeth I, but although John Whitgift in his controversy with Thomas Cartwright was willing to admit that in some places in the apostles' time and even up to Cyprian's era the people did elect their ministers (while denying that the verb *cheirotoneo* meant 'elect'), yet he refused to accept that this was always necessary and claimed that 'now in this state of the church it were most pernicious and hurtful'.[3]

Prayer

Disputes between Anglicans and Roman Catholics as to the validity of Anglican ordinations have over the centuries tended to narrow the understanding of 'prayer' in these traditions down to the ordination prayer itself, or even to a particular formula of words. However, sources from the early centuries of Christianity reveal a much broader concept, which included the prayer of the whole assembled congregation as well as an ordination prayer proper. There is no rite known to us from that period that lacks both of these elements, and like the act of election, it reveals that the action of ordination was not seen as something done by the bishop or other ordained ministers alone but as an act of the whole body of the church – or rather as the act of God working in and through the church.

The prayer of the people was usually introduced by a bidding and might then take the form of silent intercession or a litany in which there were particular petitions for the candidate. In later rites in East and West this element tended either to be reduced in extent or even moved to a different location altogether in the service, away from the ordination prayer, as its original central importance was forgotten.

The ordination prayer proper in the older sources, after first giving thanks and praise for God's gifts of ministry to the church, tends to focus on asking God to bestow on the ordinand the appropriate personal qualities needed for the effective exercise of the ministry to which he has been appointed. So, for example, in what seems to be the primitive core underlying one of the ordination prayers for a bishop in most of the Eastern traditions God is asked to make him a true shepherd, giving his life for the sheep, and (using a quotation from Romans 2:19-20) a guide of the blind, a light of those in darkness, a teacher of the ignorant, and a lamp in the world. It tends to be later strata of the prayers that seek the bestowal of the gift of the office itself and of its powers, as the emphasis shifted from seeing the elec-

---

3. *The Works of John Whitgift*, John Ayre ed. (Cambridge 1851-53) I: 339-425.

tion as that which appointed someone to office, and the prayer
with laying on of hands as then requesting appropriate gifts for
its exercise, to seeing the prayer itself as the act of ordaining. It is
in these later strata that we often find an explicit invocation of
the Holy Spirit on the candidate, as well as christological and ecclesiological references that are frequently lacking in the older
prayers, as doctrinal precision and theological reflection on the
nature of the ordained ministry developed. The agency of the
bishop in bestowing the office is also sometimes mentioned,
another sign of the way in which ordination was ceasing to be
understood as the act of the community. So, for example, one of
the prayers for a bishop in the eighth-century Byzantine rite
asks: 'O Lord of all, strengthen by the advent, power, and grace
of your Holy Spirit him who has been elected to undertake the
gospel and the high-priestly dignity, by the hand of me, a sinner,
and by that of the bishops who minister with me ...'

Another marked feature of the oldest strata is the almost total
absence of sacerdotal language to define the particular order,
which was only gradually added in later centuries, as in the case
of the eight-century Byzantine text just quoted. Even the ancient
Roman prayer texts, which are unusual in making extensive use
of Old Testament cultic imagery, are insistent that what they
seek is actually the spiritual counterpart of those former physical realities, rather than portraying the Christian ministries as
their direct descendants. Thus while the prayer for a bishop in
this tradition does centre around the images of the vesting and
anointing of the high-priest, the priestly robe is understood as
being symbolic of the adornment of mind and spirit required of
a Christian bishop, and God is asked to bestow on the ordinand
the personal qualities which correspond to the richness of that
outward dress, and also to sanctify him with a spiritual unction
corresponding to the oil which was poured on the head of Aaron
and flowed over his body.

The Imposition of the Hand

As we saw at the beginning of this essay, the relationship between prayer and the laying on of the hand is ambiguous in the
New Testament, and it is only later evidence that makes it clear
that the early Christians employed the manual gesture in association with the ordination prayer. Indeed, it would seem that
originally it functioned simply to indicate the person for whom

prayer was being made, and thus was ritually subordinate to the act of prayer. It appears to have achieved greater prominence when the verb *cheirotoneo* came to be understood as denoting the imposition of the hand rather than the election, as indicated above. And it was later still that the notion emerged in some quarters of grace being transmitted from ordainer to ordinand by this physical gesture.

The presence of other bishops at the ordination of a bishop in order to testify to episcopal approval and acceptance of the person elected by his diocese inevitably led to their being more actively involved in the rite itself. From early times one of the bishops (eventually the archbishop of the province) came to preside over the rite, and others assumed certain liturgical roles within it. However, it was only in the West that the involvement of the other bishops in laying hands on the head of the candidate came to be normative practice. In Eastern rites this custom does not feature at all, as it once did not in the Roman rite, where the pope alone performed the imposition of the hand. The corporate laying on of hands appears to have entered Western practice through the influence of a Gallican document known as the *Statuta Ecclesiae Antiqua*, perhaps composed by Gennadius of Marseilles at the end of the fifth century. This collection of brief directions about what to do at ordinations seems to have been assembled from the anonymous church order known as the *Apostolic Tradition*, formerly attributed to Hippolytus of Rome, and from other sources rather than on the basis of what was already current practice in the region. Nevertheless, in the course of time it came to be regarded as authoritative and its directions incorporated into the liturgical books containing the ordination prayers. In this way from the eighth century onwards the laying on hands by all bishops present became established practice not only in the Gallican region but also throughout the West, including Rome itself. Nevertheless, why at least three bishops should be required for this action and not just one remained a matter of discussion among scholars. It was widely believed from the Middle Ages onwards that the other two were there for safety reasons, in case the presiding bishop should be sacramentally defective in some way or lack the requisite intention and thus unable to transmit the grace of orders, 'a threefold chain is not easily broken' being a common aphorism. The debate was only brought to an end in the Roman Catholic Church in 1944 when

Pius XII declared in his Apostolic Constitution *Episcopalis conse-crationis* that the other two bishops were co-consecrators and not simply assistants to the presiding bishop, as many had thought.

The *Statuta Ecclesiae Antiqua* also affected the rite for pres-byters in a similar way. Its directions followed those of the *Apostolic Tradition* in providing that other presbyters present should join the bishop in laying hands on the candidate. Although such an action is unique among the extant sources of ancient ordination practice Eastern and Western, yet as a result of the influence that the *Statuta Ecclesiae Antiqua* came to have, the gesture later became normative practice in Western rites, though again not in the East.

The insertion of the directions from the *Statuta Ecclesiae Antiqua* into Western ordination texts seems to have been re-sponsible for another significant change in practice: the separa-tion of the laying on of hands from the ordination prayer itself. Because the direction concerning the imposition of hands for each order of ministry was placed before the prayers relating to that order in the text, this could easily be understood to imply that the action itself was to be performed prior to the prayer being said and not during it; and when the custom grew of or-daining more than one person at a time, this provided a very convenient arrangement: hands were laid on each candidate in turn in silence and then the prayer was said once for all of them, which continues to be the Roman Catholic practice to the pre-sent day, even when there is only one person to be ordained. This was something that did not happen in Eastern traditions, where no more than one person is ever ordained to a particular office on the same occasion, and the presiding bishop's hand is often laid on the candidate throughout several prayers and other formularies.

There is another particularly interesting development in rela-tion to the imposition of hands in the rite for bishops. As early as the fourth-century *Apostolic Constitutions* deacons are directed to hold the book of the gospels open over the head of the ordinand at the point in the service at which one would have expected the imposition of the hand. The latter is not explicitly mentioned, which raises the possibility that the imposition of the gospel book may here have been intended to replace rather than merely supplement the imposition of the hand. This ceremony was not something invented by the author of this particular church order, since there is other evidence that it was practised at Antioch before the end of the fourth century. Later commentators offer a variety of explanations as to its meaning – such as that it symbolised the descent of the Holy Spirit, submission to the law of God, or the sacred word given to the bishop to transmit to others – and the later evidence makes clear that it was now, if not earlier, ancillary to the imposition of hands and at this time was in most ecclesiastical traditions performed by bishops rather than deacons. It seems likely, however, that its original purpose was to represent Christ himself ordaining the bishop. The later Jacobite and Maronite traditions express this idea in a somewhat different way, by deferring the ordination not only of bishops but also of presbyters and deacons until after the eucharistic consecration has taken place, when the presiding bishop then extends his hands over the consecrated bread and wine three times before proceeding to lay his right hand on the ordinand.

The kiss

Little attention has been paid to this universal feature of all ancient ordination rites, Eastern and Western. It is not, as might be thought at first sight, merely the kiss of peace that normally occurs within eucharistic rite, as it follows immediately after the ordination no matter when that takes place in relation to the rest of the eucharistic celebration. In spite of it not being referred to in the New Testament, its ubiquity suggests that it was regarded as of some considerable significance within early Christianity. Although oldest sources explicitly mention it only in relation to the ordination of a bishop, all later rites include the practice in the rites for presbyters and deacons as well, and this was probably true of earlier times. The oldest custom seems to have been for the exchange to take place between the newly ordained and the whole congregation, and thus appears to have been intended to express their acceptance of their new relationship with the person. However, in later rites the action became clericalised and the laity were excluded from involvement in it, thus changing its significance and implying that it was now seen as symbolising acceptance into the particular order. Precise practice varied. In the Byzantine tradition, for example, it became an exclusively episcopal action: only the bishop (or in the case of the episcopate, all the bishops) kissed the newly ordained; while in other traditions (e.g. Coptic and Roman) the kiss is described as being given by the newly ordained to the other ministers present.

Later Elaboration

The centrality of the elements described above to the traditional process of ordination became obscured in the course of history as secondary accretions were added to the rites. In most cases the number of prayers multiplied, so that it became less clear which was the core ordination prayer and how it related to the prayer of the people. More powerful still, however, was the addition of a variety of symbolic ceremonies, chief among them being the vesting of the newly ordained with the robes and insignia of their office at the end of the rite and the bestowal on them of various instruments associated with that office and / or the performance by them of liturgical actions that were distinctive of the office. At first the ancient Roman tradition resisted this development, requiring the ordinand to be vested in accordance with the order to which he was to be ordained before and not after the ordination prayers were said and including no further post-ordination ceremonies at all in the case bishops, presbyters and deacons; but in the end it followed the general trend.

The idea of handing over instruments of office, the *porrectio instrumentorum* or *traditio instrumentorum* as it came to be called in the West, appears to have been introduced in imitation of the practice of similar actions as the core of admission to civil office. It had earlier been the central ceremony of admission to what became known as the minor orders – such as sub-deacons and readers – rather than laying hands on them, which only tended to develop in relation to these orders in Eastern rites, as the ritual of their appointment gradually became assimilated to those of the major orders to varying degrees in the different traditions. Thus, for example, a reader was appointed by handing to him the book from which he would read. In the course of time, particularly in the West, similar ceremonies were adopted for both presbyters and deacons, while in the case of bishops the bestowal of episcopal insignia of every kind became increasingly elaborate. Presbyters in the West eventually received the paten and chalice, deacons the book of the gospels.

In the West a further practice was also introduced in relation to bishops and presbyters, an anointing. The anointing of the hands of newly ordained presbyters is first found in eighth-century Gallican texts, while the same ceremony occurs in slightly later texts in relation to bishops. By the ninth century, a further anointing, this time of the bishop's head, was added to the rite. Apparently the petition in the ordination prayer for the bestowal of 'the dew of heavenly unction' was interpreted literally and thought to refer to a physical anointing, and since Frankish kings were already anointed on the head at their coronations, in imitation of Old Testament practice, the same was now done to bishops, the action being inserted into the very middle of the ordination prayer itself, thus dividing it in two, and eventually accompanied by the hymn, *Veni, Sancte Spiritus*.

The multiplication of ceremonies not only obscured what had been the central elements of the rite but also confused Western medieval theologians in their attempts to define what were the essentials of what was now understood to be the sacrament of ordination. Since they did not know the history of the rites, they had to base their judgements solely on what they observed in current practice. Some believed that the essential ritual action and the words which effected the ordination – its 'matter' and 'form' in scholastic terminology – had been instituted by Christ himself, while others thought that the church had been left to determine what they should be. Thus, Pope Innocent IV (1243-1254) claimed that, if the church had not established the various rites, it would have been quite sufficient for an ordaining bishop merely to have said 'May you be a priest' or 'May you be a bishop'. While some argued that the imposition of hands must be essential, because it went back to apostolic times, others, including Thomas Aquinas, inclined to the view that the *traditio instrumentorum* and its accompanying formula were the indispensable elements, because they more clearly signified the transmission of power, while still others thought that the priestly anointing must constitute at least part of what was vital.

The sixteenth-century Reformers, by insisting that only what was found in the New Testament could be regarded as essential and by reshaping ordination rites accordingly, did manage to come nearer to the theory and practice of primitive Christianity, even if they did not always get it completely right. Yet even they introduced some new elements of their own, the most common of which were a sermon on the nature of the office to be conferred and a public examination of all the candidates within the ordination rite itself, in which they were required to respond to a series of questions about their beliefs and intentions. This latter was doubtless inspired by the Reformers' desire to ensure that only those truly called by God, espousing sound doctrine and following an appropriate way of life should be admitted to the ordained ministry, and even though not explicitly mentioned in the New Testament, it did have some precedent in the medieval rite for bishops.

Conclusion

Such historical knowledge does not provide us with a blueprint that we must necessarily follow in our practice today. But it does at least enable us to distinguish older from newer elements in the tradition, and to discern how and why things have changed over time. Whether such changes are then to be regarded as positive developments to be welcomed and perpetuated, or as losses to be rectified in future revisions of rites is, however, something that churches today need to ponder for themselves.

By Public Prayer and the Imposition of Hands: The Prayer of the People and the Ordination Prayer

Richard Geoffrey Leggett

Introduction

Within the last century Christians of many traditions have redis-covered ordination as an act of the entire assembly, gathered in its various orders, each with its part to play. This rediscovery has necessitated a re-evaluation of our ordination rites to deter-mine how well the various liturgical elements express this re-newed understanding. We have come to realise that it is not just the content of a text or an action that is important, but also its place within the liturgical context, the gestures and postures that accompany it and the identity of those who recite or enact it.

For Anglicans, the Preface to the Ordinal of 1550 describes our fundamental understanding of the content of the ordination process and rite:

> ... no man by his own priuate aucthoritie, might presume to execute any of [these offices], except he were first called, tried, examined, and knowen, to haue such equalities, as were requisite for the same. And also by publique prayer, with imposicion of handes, approued, and admitted thereun-to.[1]

In our tradition, 'publique prayer, with imposicion of handes' has included of first importance (1) a general litany with special suffrages, (2) proper collects to conclude the litany and (3) the laying on of hands with imperative formula and of second im-portance (4) silent prayer, (5) the singing of the *Veni Creator Spiritus* or *Veni Sancte Spiritus* and (6) an ordination prayer for presbyters and bishops. If we consider the eucharistic structure to consist of (a) the gathering of the community, (b) the proclam-ation of the word of God, (c) the prayer of the faithful, (d) the holy communion and (e) the commissioning of the community, then the elements of public prayer and laying on of hands men-tioned above have usually been interpolated into the eucharistic structures of the gathering and the prayer of the faithful.

---

1. First ... *BCP*, 292.

This distributed character of the classic Anglican ordinal is the result of a lengthy historical development. We shall trace that development by looking first at liturgical structure, i.e. how the elements have been interpolated into the rite, and then content, i.e. the elements of the 'publique prayer'. We shall conclude with the recommendations of the Berkeley Statement and some suggestions towards an agenda for future revision.

STRUCTURE

The New Testament and Patristic Period
When we consider the accounts of the commissioning of individuals for office or special ministry in the Acts of the Apostles, there is a close association between the prayer of the community and the setting apart of the individual(s) for this office or ministry. In Acts 1:15-26 the community's prayer for discernment directly preceded the casting of lots and the subsequent enrolment of Matthias as an apostle. The account in Acts 6:1-6 of the appointment of the seven tells us that the community chose the candidates who then stood before the apostles 'who prayed and laid hands on them'.[2] Similarly the commissioning of Paul and Barnabas by the prophets and teachers in Antioch reveals a close association between corporate prayer and commissioning: 'Then after fasting and praying [the prophets and teachers] laid their hands on [Paul and Barnabas] and sent them off.'[3]

One of the earliest witnesses to the relationship between the prayer of the people and the ordination prayer is found in the so-called *Apostolic Tradition* attributed to Hippolytus of Rome:

> 2. Let him be ordained bishop who has been chosen by all the people; and when he has been named and accepted by all, let the people assemble, together with the presbytery and those bishops who are present, on the Lord's day. When all give consent, they shall lay hands on him, and the presbytery shall stand by and be still. And all shall keep silence, praying in their hearts for the descent of the Spirit; after which one of the bishops present, being asked by all, shall lay his hand on him who is being ordained bishop, and pray ...[4]

---

2. Acts 6:5-6 (*New Revised Standard Version*).
3. Acts 13:3.
4. *Apostolic Tradition* 2 as translated in Geoffrey J. Cuming, *Hippolytus: A Text for Students*, [Grove Liturgical Studies, no 8] (Bramcote, Notts., 1976).

Later similar directions are given for the ordination of a presbyter and of a deacon.[5]

In all three cases the prayer offered by the bishop is directly
preceded by a period of prayer by the entire community. There
are no intervening elements to obscure the continuity between
the prayer of the community and the prayer of the bishop. We
are left with an image of the bishop acting in concert with the
community rather than the community as the bishop's audience.

The Medieval Period

The early Roman liturgical tradition kept the prayer of the people and the prayer of the bishop in relative proximity to each
other. In *Ordo Romanus* XXXIV, a document of the mid-eighth
century, the same pattern applies whether the ordination is of a
deacon, a presbyter or a bishop. After the reading of the epistle
and the singing of the gradual psalm, the litany is of-fered and
the bishop then recites the appropriate prayer over the candi-
date(s).[6]

This close association was obscured as Roman and Gallican
elements were fused into the composite rites of the later medieval period.

> In the Western rites, the prayer of the people was obviously
> intended originally to occur between the biddings and the
> prayers, as is still the case in *Roman Ordo* XXXIV ... However,
> in the fusion of Roman and Gallican material in the Gelasian
> Sacramentary and related sources, the litany was instead
> placed before all prayer texts, including the biddings – prob-
> ably the result of a failure to appreciate the true nature of
> these texts – and there it remained in the later composite rites
> of the West.[7]

The role of the people's prayer was further diminished by the
growing emphasis on the laying on of hands and the delivery of
the symbols of office.[8] The laying on of hands with imperative
formula even came to overshadow the presidential prayer of the
bishop.

In the Sarum Pontifical the sequence of liturgical elements

---

5. *Apostolic Tradition*, 7, 8.
6. Bradshaw 1990, 219-221.
7. Bradshaw 1990, 32.
8. Bradshaw 1990, 23.

demonstrates this disintegration of the unity of the people's prayer, i.e. the litany, with the presidential prayer of the bishop.

Deacon: (i) presentation of candidate, (ii) question as to suitability, (iii) final inquiry of the people, (iv) epistle of the day, (v) *litany with special suffrages,* (vi) instructions of deacons in duties, (vii) *imposition of hands on deacons by bishop,* (viii) *the Roman bidding, collect and ordination prayer for deacons,* (ix) vesting with stole and delivery of gospel book, (x) Gallican bidding and ordination prayer for deacons, (xi) vesting in dalmatic, (xii) gospel of the day.[9]

Even if the only candidates to be ordained were to the presbyterate, the gulf between the litany and the laying on hands for presbyters, already significant because of the numerous ritual accretions caused by the fusion of Roman, Gallican and local elements, would be immense.

Priest: (i) presentation of candidate, (ii) question as to suitability, (iii) final inquiry of the people, (iv) epistle of the day, (v) *litany with special suffrages,* (vi) gospel of the day, (vii) instruction of priests in duties, (viii) *imposition of hands by bishop and priests in silence,* (ix) *Roman bidding, collect and ordination prayer for priests,* (x) vesting in stole and chasuble, (xi) Gallican bidding and ordination prayer for priests, (xii) *Veni Creator,* (xiii) blessing and unction of priests' hands, (xiv) delivery of chalice and paten, (xv) after the resumption of the Eucharist imposition of hands with formula *Accipe Spiritum Sanctum quorum peccata.*[10]

Only the rite for the consecration of a bishop retained some of the older Roman sense of connectedness.

Bishop: (i) presentation, (ii) examination and oath of canonical obedience, (iii) eucharist as far as epistle, (iv) instruction in duties, (v) bidding, (vi) *litany with special suffrages,* (vii) *imposition of hands by all bishops* with imposition of gospel book and hymn *Veni Creator Spiritus,* (viii) collect, (ix) Roman ordination prayer, (x) anointing of head, (xi) Gallican ordination prayer, (xii) English ordination prayer, (xiii) additional rites and resumption of eucharist.[11]

---

9. Bradshaw, 1971, 5. *Italics* added for emphasis.

10. Bradshaw 1971, 5.

11. Bradshaw 1971, 5.

At the dawn of the Reformation it was this complex pattern that influenced the experience of those charged with the reform of the ordinal of the Church of England.

From 1550 to 1662

The ordinal of 1550 demonstrates that Cranmer, as a child of the medieval church, was not so much concerned with the proximity of the prayer of the people to the laying on of hands as with the presence of this 'publique prayer' in the rite itself. Cranmer's liturgical sensibility permitted this separation without sacrificing the efficacy of what the rite was intended to achieve.

Deacon: (i) exhortation regarding the necessity of this office, (ii) presentation, (iii) question as to suitability, (iv) inquiry of the people, (v) *litany with special suffrage,* (vi) proper collect for deacons, (vii) epistle, (viii) oath of the royal supremacy, (ix) examination, (x) *laying on of hands with imperative formula,* (xi) delivery of New Testament with imperative formula, (xii) eucharist resumes with gospel reading.[12]

Presbyter: (i) exhortation regarding the necessity of this office, (ii) eucharist as far as gospel, (iii) *Veni Creator Spiritus,* (iv) presentation, (v) question as to suitability, (vi) inquiry of the people, (vii) *litany with special suffrage,* (viii) proper collect for priests, (ix) oath of the royal supremacy, (x) examination, (xi) silent prayer by all, (xii) *ordination prayer,* (xiii) *laying on of hands with imperative formula,* (xiv) delivery of chalice, paten and Bible with imperative formula, (xv) eucharist resumes with the Nicene Creed.[13]

Bishop: (i) eucharist as far as the Nicene Creed, (ii) presentation, (iii) reading of the royal mandate, (iv) oath of the royal supremacy, (v) oath of due obedience to metropolitan, (vi) bidding, (vii) *litany with special suffrage,* (viii) proper collect for bishops, (ix) examination, (x) *Veni Creator Spiritus,* (xi) *ordination prayer,* (xii) *laying on of hands with imperative formula,* (xiii) imposition of Bible, (xiv) delivery of pastoral staff, (xv) eucharist resumes.[14]

Within two years of the publication of the ordinal, changes in the religious sentiment of the government led to revisions both

---

12. First ... *BCP* 293-302.
13. First ... *BCP* 303-312.
14. First ... *BCP* 313-317.

to the prayer book and to the ordinal.[15] Although the ordinal was edited and some liturgical elements omitted, the structure of the three rites remained unchanged. This new ordinal remained in effect, with the exception of the Commonwealth period, until the promulgation of the 1662 prayer book.

The ordinal of 1552, however, was not without its critics both within and without the Church of England.[16] By the time of the restoration of the monarchy and the prayer book, these criticisms gave rise to significant revision to the ordination rites. The only structural revision occurred in the rite for the ordination of presbyters. The *Veni Creator Spiritus* was moved from its position following the gospel into closer proximity to the ordination prayer, creating a new sequence: (a) bidding, (b) silent prayer, (c) *Veni Creator Spiritus*, (d) ordination prayer and (e) laying on of hands with imperative formula.[17]

The structure of the 1662 ordinal became the model for the ordinals of the churches that came to form the Anglican Communion. In this model the litany with its special suffrage and collect continued to be separated from the ordination prayer and laying on of hands. The *Veni Creator Spiritus* as an invocation of the Holy Spirit came to be associated with the rites for presbyters and bishops but not deacons. This distinction expressed the ambivalence to the diaconate as a full and equal order that characterises Anglicanism to the present day.[18]

From 1662 to the present
Significant revision of the structure of Anglican ordination rites, whether in England or elsewhere, would await the twentieth and twenty-first centuries. Revision in England, the United States and Scotland in the 1920s focused on the length and content of the litany rather than the structure of the rite itself and will be discussed later in this essay.

A significant structural proposal emerged with the publication of the liturgical rites of the Church of South India.[19] All

---

15. See F. E. Brightman, *The English Rite*, 2 vv. (London, 1912) 2:928-1017.
16. Bradshaw 1971, 37-86.
17. Brightman 1921, 2:989, 991, 993.
18. Bradshaw 1971, 34-36.
19. Church of South India, *The Book of Common Worship as authorised by the Synod 1962* (London, 1962).

three rites share a common structure with the presentation of the candidates interpolated into the gathering and the remainder of the elements proper to the ordination following the proclamation of the word.[20] In a section entitled 'The Ordination' the sequence is (a) silent prayer, (b) the hymn 'Come, Holy Ghost' and (c) the ordination prayer with the laying on of hands.[21] Given that there is no provision for the litany, the silent prayer and hymn invoking the Holy Spirit have become the prayer of the people. Thus, a reunion of the prayer elements has been achieved with the prayer of the people now directly preceding the presidential prayer of the bishop.

Subsequent revisions of the ordination rites of the Anglican provinces have followed three patterns. Some rites have continued the practice of interpolating the presentation into the gathering of the community and have included the litany as part of that process. Other rites have interpolated all the liturgical elements proper to the ordination within the prayer of the faithful following the proclamation of the word. A smaller group do not easily fall into either group.

Chief among the ordinals that continue to integrate the presentation into the gathering of the community is the American ordinal of 1979.[22] The litany follows the presentation and precedes the proclamation of the word. After the proclamation the remaining elements of the ordination take the following sequence: (a) examination, (b) *Veni Creator Spiritus* or *Veni Sancte Spiritus*, (c) silent prayer and (d) ordination prayer with the laying on of hands.[23] The decision to incorporate the litany into the gathering was a practical rather than theological decision, a balancing of texts so as to avoid a liturgical overload in the later sections of the rite.[24] Consequently, the prayer of the people is divided between the gathering of the community and the prayer of the faithful.

The South African ordinal of 1989 follows the American pattern of the litany being incorporated into the gathering of the

20. South India 1962, 161-162, 166-167, 173.

21. South India 1962, 164-165, 170-172, 177-178.

22. The Episcopal Church in the United States of America, *Book of Common Prayer* 1979, 509-555.

23. USA 1979, 517-521, 531-534, 543-545.

24. The Standing Liturgical Commission of The Episcopal Church, *The Ordination of Bishops, Priests, and Deacons* [Prayer Book Studies, no 20] (New York, 1970) 24.

community and the remaining ordination elements incorporated after the proclamation of the word.[25] Similar in structure to the American ordinal of 1979 is the New Zealand ordinal of 1989. The presentation occurs before the proclamation of the word and the remaining elements come after the proclamation: (a) examination, (b) bidding, (c) silent prayer, (d) option of a hymn invoking the Holy Spirit, (e) versicles and responses and (f) the ordination prayer.[26]

The *Alternative Service Book* 1980 represents those rites that have integrated all the elements proper to the ordination into the prayer of the faithful.[27] When the proclamation is completed, the rite continues with (a) presentation, (b) examination, (c) silent prayer, (d) *Veni Creator Spiritus* (for presbyters or bishops), (e) litany and (f) ordination prayer with laying on of hands.[28] Here we have joined together what time had rent asunder, the prayer of the people and the presidential prayer of the bishop. The 2005 revision of the ordinal maintains the 1980 pattern but includes the option of using the *Veni Creator Spiritus* or some other hymn at the ordination of deacons and suitable invocations of the Holy Spirit during the ordination prayers in all three rites.

The Welsh ordinal of 1984 follows the model of the English ordinal of 1980 but omits the *Veni Creator Spiritus* in all three rites and has a slightly different sequence: (a) litany, (b) silent prayer and (c) ordination prayer with the laying on of hands.[30] *The Book of Alternative Services of The Anglican Church of Canada* also follows the model of the English rite but also varies the sequence of elements: (a) bidding, (b) litany, (c) *Veni Creator Spiritus* or *Veni Sancte Spiritus* (in all three rites), (d) silent prayer

25. Church of the Province of South Africa, *An Anglican Prayer Book* 1989 (London, 1989) 576, 595.

26. The Church of the Province of New Zealand, *A New Zealand Prayer Book* (London, 1989) 887-921.

27. The Church of England, *The Alternative Service Book 1980: Services authorized for use in the Church of England in conjunction with The Book of Common Prayer* (Oxford, 1980) 337-396.

28. England 1980, 344-349, 355-363, 387-394.

29. The Liturgical Commission of The Church of England, *Ordination Services: The Ordination of Bishops, Priests and Deacons* (London, 2005) 6-12, 18, 19, 28-35, 43, 53-61, 69.

30. The Church in Wales, *The Book of Common Prayer for use in The Church in Wales*, 2 vols (Penarth, 1984) 2:716-717, 724-725, 731-732.

and (e) ordination prayer with the laying on of hands.[31] The most recent Australian ordinal also is modelled after England 1980 but with variation in sequence: (a) presentation, (b) silent prayer and litany (either here or before the hymn invoking the Holy Spirit), (c) examination, (d) hymn invoking the Holy Spirit and (e) ordination prayer with the laying on of hands.[32]

In 2004 the Church of Ireland issued its new prayer book with two ordinals, one traditional, the other contemporary.[33] The contemporary rite follows the model of the English rite of 1980 with the elements proper to the ordination occurring after the proclamation of the word. The ordination prayer with the laying on of hands is preceded by (a) bidding, (b) litany, (c) silent prayer and (d) a hymn invoking the Holy Spirit.[34] Another feature of the Irish rites is the option of using one of two ordination prayers in each rite, the second containing congregational responses.[35]

A representative of the third group of ordinals is the *Scottish Ordinal* 1984.[36] Although the elements proper to an ordination follow the proclamation of the word of God, they are distributed in a unique fashion: (a) presentation, (b) response by the bishop, (c) silent prayer, (d) *Veni Creator Spiritus* (for presbyters and bishops), (e) examination, (f) litany or silent prayer and (g) ordination prayer with laying on of hands.[37] The new Kenyan rite is also a unique blend of old and new in terms of content and structure.[38] The litany, however, continues to be separated from the other prayer texts, either by the proclamation in the ordin-

---

31 The Anglican Church of Canada, *The Book of Alternative Services of the Anglican Church of Canada* (Toronto, 1985) 638-639, 648-649, 656-657.

32. The Anglican Church of Australia, *A Prayer Book for Australia for use together with The Book of Common Prayer* (1662) (Sydney, 1995) 784-788, 792-796, 800-805.

33. The Church of Ireland, *The Book of Common Prayer and Administration of the Sacraments and Other Rites and Ceremonies of the Church according to the Use of The Church of Ireland* (Dublin, 2004).

34. Ireland 2004, 557-560, 567-571, 578-582.

35. Ireland 2004, 559-560, 569-571, 580-582.

36. The Episcopal Church of Scotland, *Scottish Ordinal 1984* (Edinburgh, 1984).

37. Scotland 1984, 2-7, 9-13, 16-19. The heading introducing the litany or silent prayer is 'The Prayer of the People'.

38.The Anglican Church of Kenya, *Our Modern Services* (Nairobi, 2003).

ation of deacons and of presbyters or by the examination in the ordination of bishops.[39]

Recent revision reveals several common threads. With some exceptions, a common liturgical structure is used for all three rites. Second, although some ordinals continue to interpolate the litany into the gathering of the community, the ordination prayers of these rites are preceded by opportunities for the prayer of the people, whether silent prayer, invocation of the Holy Spirit or both. Finally, a significant number of recent rites have integrated all the liturgical elements proper to ordination within the prayer of the faithful following the proclamation of the word.

CONTENT

Paul Bradshaw has argued in his study of the development of the Anglican ordination that for Cranmer, '... the essential parts of the three rites of the Ordinal were the litany, with its suffrage and collect, and the imposition of hands.'[40] The litany that Cranmer chose was the English litany of 1544, subsequently incorporated into the 1549 prayer book. This is a lengthy litany with numerous thanksgivings, intercessions and petitions. For the purposes of ordination Cranmer incorporated two new suffrages, one for the ordination of deacons and presbyters, the other for the consecration of bishops, following the general suffrage for the clergy:

> That it may please thee, to blesse these men, and send thy grace upon them, that they maye duelye execute the offyce nowe to bee commytted unto them, to the edifyinge of thy Churche, and to thy honoure, prayse, and glorye.[41]

> That it maye please thee to blesse this our brother elected, and to sende thy grace upon him, [that] he may duely execute the office wherunto he is called, to the edifying of thy Churche, and to the honour, prayse and glory of thy name.[42]

In all three rites the litany concludes with a collect proper to the order being conferred.[43]

---

39. Kenya 2002, 91-94, 105-109, 119-123.
40. Bradshaw 1971, 29.
41. First ... *BCP* 295, 307.
42. First ... *BCP* 314.
43. First ... *BCP* 298, 307, 314.

Bradshaw has argued that the litany with its special suffrage and concluding collect constitute for Cranmer the essential public prayer that precedes the laying on of hands.[44] Bradshaw's argument would seem to be correct given at least three factors:

- the *Veni Creator Spiritus* only appears in the rites for the presbyterate and episcopate
- a period of silent prayer is mandated only in the rite for the presbyterate
- the special suffrage is epicletic in content, i.e. 'send thy grace'.

The content of the two suffrages and three collects remained constant throughout the reigns of Edward VI, Elizabeth I, James I and Charles I.[46] The 1662 ordinal made some revision to the suffrage for deacons and presbyters emphasising the distinctiveness of the offices being conferred and changing 'send' to 'pour'.

That it may please thee to bless these *thy servants*, now to be *admitted to the order of Deacons, [or Priests]* and *to pour* thy grace vpon them, that they may duly execute the*ir* office to the edifying of thy Church and *the* glory *of* thy *holy Name*.[47]

No change was made in 1662 to the special suffrage for the ordination of a bishop.

In the early decades of the twentieth century proposals were made to revise the content of the litany. The proposed English prayer book of 1928 provided rubrical direction for the shortening of the litany when incorporated as part of the Eucharist and provided the option of omitting the litany at the ordination of a bishop in favour of a period of silent prayer.[48] In a break with long-standing tradition, the American prayer book of 1928 provided a shorter litany for ordinations that focused on the ordained ministry and '[its] obvious merits, both in length and in content' led to its supplanting the traditional litany.[49]

Although the South Indian rite of 1962 did not include a

44. Bradshaw 1971, 25-29.

45. First ... *BCP* 306-307, 311, 316.

46. Brightman, *The English Rite*, 2:938-939, 979, 1006-1007.

47. Brightman, *The English Rite*, 2:939. Italics indicate changes to the text of 1552.

48. The Church of England, *The Book of Common Prayer with the Additions and Deviations proposed in 1928* (Cambridge, 1928) 120, 638-639.

49. The Protestant Episcopal Church in the United States of America, *Book of Common Prayer*, 1928, 560-562; Massey H. Shepherd, Jr., *The Oxford American Prayer Book Commentary* (New York, 1950) 560.

litany, its structure brought into focus the role of silent prayer and the invocation of the Holy Spirit as a form of public prayer. Just as the litany with its special suffrage and concluding collect was a common element of all three rites in the 1662 tradition, silent prayer and a hymn invoking the Holy Spirit were common to all three South Indian rites.[50] God ordains '… in response to the prayers of His Church' which offers '… prayer for those about to be ordained or consecrated, that they may receive the gift of the Holy Spirit for their ministry'.[51] The structure and content of the South Indian ordination prayers, i.e. (a) thanksgiving to God, (b) invocation of the Holy Spirit with the laying on of hands and (c) concluding petitions for the ordinand, also had consequences for the role of the litany in the ordination rites.

With some exceptions all contemporary Anglican ordinals have adopted the South Indian structure for the ordination prayers. This changes the role that the traditional litany with its special suffrage and collect played in the ordination rite. Likewise most contemporary Anglican ordinals have reconsidered the place of silent prayer and a hymn invoking the Holy Spirit in all three rites. These structural changes and additions have necessitated a re-thinking of the content of the 'public prayer' of the people.

Where the litany has been retained in a contemporary ordinal, the tendency has been to provide shorter compositions that focus more clearly on the ministry of the whole church. Both the American ordinal of 1979 and the English ordinal of 1980 include such compositions.[52] Some ordinals have chosen to adopt and adapt the American or English compositions.[53] Other ordinals have produced litanies that are unique to their province.[54]

In addition to the litany many provinces have reconsidered the omission of silent prayer in the rites for the diaconate and the episcopate and have chosen to incorporate this element.[55]

---

50. South India 1962, 164-165, 170-172, 177-178.

51. South India 1962, 160, 161.

52. USA 1979, 548-551; England 1980, 346, 375-377, 391-393.

53. Scotland 1984, 23-27; Canada 1985, 661-664; South Africa 1989, 576-578, 595-597.

54. Scotland 1984, 21-23; Australia 1995, 192-193; Ireland 2004, 585-590.

55. USA 1979, 520, 544; England 1980, 346, 390; Scotland 1984, 3, 6, 17, 19; Wales 1984, II:716, 731; Canada 1985, 638, 656; New Zealand 1989, 896, 920; South Africa 1989, 585, 600; Australia 1995, 784, 802; Ireland 2004, 557, 579.

For over four centuries the *Veni Creator Spiritus* or *Veni Sancte Spiritus* were considered proper only to the rites for the presbyterate and episcopate, yet some recent revisions have responded to the recovery of the diaconate by the inclusion of this hymn or some similar invocation of the Holy Spirit in the rite for deacons.[56]

Whither the Future?

In 2001 the International Anglican Liturgical Consultation met and prepared the Berkeley Statement *To Equip the Saints* on ordination. The question of the relationship between the prayer of the people and the ordination was specifically addressed.

Ordination prayer involves the prayer of the whole community. This raises the question as to how continuity between the prayer of all the faithful and the presidential prayer with the laying on of hands may be best achieved. Should the prayer of all the faithful be in silence or in the form of prayers of intercession led by a deacon or lay person – or both? If the second, then it should be a responsive form but not necessarily a standard litany, and whatever form is chosen should contain petitions for the ministry of the whole people of God, as well as prayers for the world, for peace, justice, reconciliation and creation. A hymn or song invoking the Holy Spirit and musical settings of any litany should be suitable for singing by the whole assembly.[57]

The Berkeley Statement also emphasises the importance of gesture in prayer, both of the community and of the presider:

The particular posture adopted by those involved – both the community offering prayer and those for whom the prayer is being offered – is significant. For example:

- if the bishop adopts the same posture as the rest of the assembly for the intercessory prayer and invocation of the Holy Spirit, the bishop is identified as praying with the whole community;
- if the candidates kneel while others stand, it is more clearly indicated that they are being prayed for;
- if both the presider and assembly stand for the presiden-

---

56. USA 1979, 544; Canada 1985, 656; New Zealand 1989, 896; South Africa 1989, 585; Australia 1995, 787; England 2005, 18; Ireland 2004, 557.

57. *To Equip the Saints*, Part II: *Prayer with the Laying on of Hands*, p 231.

tial prayer, it is clearer that the act is that of the whole assembly and not just of the president alone;

- if those who are associated with the presidential imposition of hands (i.e. presbyters at the ordination of presbyters, and bishops at episcopal ordinations) join in any other manual gestures with the president throughout the entire prayer, its unity is more clearly demonstrated.[58]

Given the review of the history of the structure and content of the prayer of the people and the ordination prayer in the Anglican ordinal and the trajectory evident in recent revision and liturgical consultation, a partial agenda for future revision emerges.

- Future revisions should ensure that the prayer of the people, regardless of its elements, be in structural proximity to the presidential prayer and the laying on of hands.
- If a litany is to be used in the rite, it should 'contain petitions for the ministry of the whole people of God, as well as prayers for the world, for peace, justice, reconciliation and creation' rather than a lengthier and more general form'.[59]
- Despite the antiquity of the practice, rites for the diaconate should not be characterised by the omission of a hymn invoking the Holy Spirit if such a hymn is used in the rites for the presbyterate and episcopate.
- Both the postures adopted during the prayers and the content of such prayers must make evident the unity of the prayer of the people with the presidential prayer of the bishop. Whether this is accomplished by the assembly joining the bishop in a common posture or by presidential prayers with congregational responses or both is a matter of local concern.

In short we need to re-define our understanding of 'ordination prayer'. Our history has led us to focus primarily on the presidential prayer of the bishop rather than understand that 'ordination prayer' describes a *liturgical unit* not a *liturgical element*. A liturgical unit brings together various elements intimately related to each other by juxtaposition and the complementary actions of presider and assembly. In so doing the corporate action of the church in ordination is made more evident.

---

58. *To Equip the Saints*, Part II: *Prayer with the Laying on of Hands*, p 232.
59. *To Equip the Saints*, Part II: *Prayer with the Laying on of Hands*, p 231.

Considering the Possibility of Direct Ordination

John St H. Gibaut

Introduction

The 2001 International Anglican Liturgical Consultation, with its published findings, the Berkeley Statement: *To Equip the Saints*, reflects a significant moment in over a century of profound reflection on ministry within the Anglican tradition. Within the dual ecumenical contexts of Anglican relationships with the Roman Catholic and Orthodox churches on the one hand, and the diversity of non-episcopal churches on the other, there has been a sustained theological reflection on the nature of episcopacy, priesthood, and ordination. This vast array of scholarly research has borne fruit in agreed ecumenical statements, plans of union, in contemporary revisions of Anglican ordination rites, and beyond. Ministry has experienced a healthy renewal through its engagement with the social sciences, and in revised structures and models of theological education. A sharper perception of the distinctions between the ministries that emerge by virtue of baptism and ordained ministries has contributed to a less clerically defined understanding of both the church and its ministries. The restoration of the ministry of deacon as a distinctive order has been a consistent strand throughout the last century.

One area which has not received any concrete plans for change or reform is the actual structuring of the threefold ministry, namely the process by which candidates are ordained sequentially through the orders of ministry: deacon, priest, and bishop. Significantly, one of the proposals from the Berkeley Statement suggests such a change.

A Brief History of Sequential and Direct Ordination

This is not the place for a detailed chronicle of the historical development of what would come to be known classically as the *cursus honorum*, or simply, 'sequential ordination'.[1] Even so, it is

---

1. For a fuller account, please see John St H. Gibaut, *The Cursus Honorum: A Study of the Origins and Evolution of Sequential Ordination* (New York, 2000). For a briefer account, see also my *Sequential or Direct*

important to sketch out here some of the main lines of its development. While there is some evidence in the pre-Nicene period, the practice of sequential ordination emerged as a canonical tradition in the mid-fourth century and reached its final form in the late eleventh century. It is essentially an ordinance of canon law, whose intent is entirely pastoral: to test and train the clergy by service in the lower ministries, before (s)election to the higher. Christian ministers began with appointments to the minor orders of doorkeeper, lector, exorcist, and acolyte, then a subdeacon (which by the late medieval period was considered a major order), followed by ordination to the major orders of deacon and priest, and finally, the episcopate. Within the medieval period, the *cursus honorum* had undergone a significant development, not only in terms of the sequence of orders, but especially in regards to the time to be spent in them. For example, instead of spending many years in the minor orders, the time was often reduced to days; instead of the traditional five-year period in the diaconate, the time could be as little as a day, though normally a matter of months. The connection between sequential ordination and testing and training had been lost in practice.

From the fourth century onwards, the *cursus honorum* or sequential ordination began to replace the more common practice of the first three centuries of ordaining candidates directly to the orders of ministry to which they were called, without any other intervening ordinations to other ministries. This meant, in effect, that if one was called to be a bishop, one was ordained directly to the episcopate; if one was called to be a subdeacon, one was ordained directly to the subdiaconate; if one was called to be a presbyter, one was ordained directly to the presbyterate, and so forth. Known in medieval canon law as *per saltum* ('by a leap') ordination, 'direct ordination' was a common practice well into the eleventh century, although canon law was increasingly insisting on the observance of the *cursus honorum*. For instance, medieval biographical and liturgical sources from Rome such as the *Liber pontificalis* and the *Ordines romani* 34 and 35 make it abundantly clear that many presbyters were never deacons but were ordained directly from the subdiaconate, and many bishops were never presbyters but had been ordained directly from

---

Ordination? A Return to the Sources (Cambridge, 2003). For an even briefer introduction, see my chapter, 'Sequential and Direct Ordination,' in *Järvenpää* 36-40.

the diaconate.[2] Roman canonistic collections from the late patristic *Dionysiana* well into to the later medieval collections of Ivo of Chartres and Gratian, also reflect the eventuality that deacons or presbyters could be ordained bishops.[3] *Per saltum* or direct ordination was simply a fact of life throughout most of the Middle Ages, though it must be pointed out that what was being omitted was an order or two, such as the diaconate or the presbyterate, rather than all the orders as would have been the case in the pre-Nicene period. Sequential ordination through all the orders was more a feature of Gallican Christianity from the ninth century, and became a uniform feature of Western ordination practice in the wake of the Gregorian reforms of the eleventh century.

The English Reformation and Sequential Ordination
The *cursus honorum* was significantly altered by the sixteenth-century English Reformers, who abolished the minor orders and the subdiaconate, retaining only what was considered to be the biblical and apostolic ministries of bishop, priest, and deacon, as evidenced in the Ordinal of 1550. In retaining the threefold ministry, the Church of England maintained the practice of sequential ordination. And yet by abolishing the minor orders, particularly the subdiaconate which since the eleventh century had been held to be indispensable in the Western church, the English Reformers demonstrated their conviction that sequential ordination is certainly adaptable.

The English Reformers also demonstrated their awareness of the historic reasons behind sequential ordination, namely, pro-

2. Louis Duchesne, ed, *Liber Pontificalis: Texte, Introduction, et Commentaire*, 2 vols. (Paris, 1886[2]). Michel Andrieu, *Les Ordines Romani du haut moyen age*, vols 3 & 4 (Louvain, 1951/1956). See also, Andrieu, 'La carrière ecclésiastique des papes et les documents liturgiques du moyen âge,' *Revue des sciences religieuses* 21 (1947) 90-120.
3. A particular case in point is how the earliest canon enjoining sequential ordination, Canon 13 of the Council of Sardica, AD 343 with its sequence – deacon and presbyter then bishop – was actually changed by the Roman canonists to reflect their historic pattern – deacon or presbyter, then bishop – and then likely changed back to the original by the Gallican canonists to reflect an entirely new understanding of squential ordination by the ninth century. See my chapter, 'The Peregrinations of Canon 13 of the Council of Sardica,' in Kathleen G. Kushing & Richard F. Gyug eds, *Ritual, Text and Law: Studies in Medieval Canon Law and Liturgy Presented to Roger E. Reynolds* (Aldershot, 2004) 141-160.

bation and preparation. The final prayer in the Making of a
Deacon in the Ordinal of 1550, for instance, contains the petition:
'[that they] ... may so well behave themselves in this inferior office, that they may be found worthy to be called unto the higher
ministries in thy church; through the same ...'[4] Clearly the intent
is testing or probation. On the other hand, the rubric at the conclusion of the rite indicates training and preparation:

> And here it must be declared unto the Deacon that he must
> continue in that office of a Deacon the space of a whole year
> (except for reasonable causes it shall otherwise seem good
> unto the Bishop) to the intent he may be perfect, and well ex-
> pert in the things pertaining to the Ecclesiastical Admin-
> istration. If he has been found faithful and diligent, and has
> satisfied the Bishop that he is sufficiently experienced in the
> things belonging to the Ministry, he may be admitted by his
> Diocesan to the Order of Priesthood at the Ember Seasons, or
> on any Sunday or Holy Day.[5]

The same historic rationales are also reflected in the earliest
post-Reformation canonical collection, the *Constitutions and
Canons Ecclesiastical* of 1604, but with a deep 'genetic' inconsist-
ency received from the Church of England's medieval heritage.

> XXXII. The office of deacon being a step or degree to the min-
> istry, according to the judgement of the ancient fathers, and
> the practice of the primitive church; we do ordain and ap-
> point, that hereafter no bishop shall make any person, of
> what qualities or gifts soever, a deacon and a minister both
> together upon one day; but that the order in that behalf pre-
> scribed book of making and consecrating bishops, priests,
> and deacons, be strictly observed. Not that always every dea-
> con shall be kept from the ministry for a whole year, when
> the bishop shall find good cause to the contrary; but that
> there being now four times appointed in every year for the
> ordination of deacons and ministers, there may ever be some
> trial of their behaviour in the office of deacon, before they be
> admitted to the order of priesthood.[6]

---

4. First ... *BCP*, 302; The Church of England in the Dominion of Canada,
The Book of Common Prayer (Cambridge, 1918) 622; Protestant Episcopal
Church in the United States of America, *The Book of Common Prayer*
(1928) 534-5.
5. First ... *BCP* 302.
6. G. R. Evans, and J. Robert Wright, eds, *The Anglican Tradition: A
Handbook of Sources* (London, 1991) 192.

While the intent of Canon XXXII is to prohibit a candidate from being ordained a deacon and a presbyter on the same day, it describes the traditional Anglican understanding of the order of deacon: a 'step or degree to the Ministry' (i.e. the presbyterate) for the purpose of preparation and probation. The canon does, however, implicitly admit the possibility of ordination to the diaconate and priesthood in two days, and explicitly within three months 'when the bishop shall find good cause'. Here, the medieval practice of shortening the period of time served in the diaconate resurfaces in an Anglican guise. If not for training and testing, what purpose, then, does such a short time in the diaconate serve? What does 'good cause' mean? Does it mean that testing and training have been met in some other venue? Is there another, ulterior purpose to sequential ordination not mentioned in the canon, nor in the Ordinal for that matter? The canonical possibility of sequential ordination in two days or even three months betrays the patristic design of the practice, reflected in the rites of ordination themselves, namely serious 'on the job' testing and training,[7] and allows for the abuses of the Middle Ages.

A Loss of Rationale for Sequential Ordination

The practice of sequential ordination arguably served a practical and pastoral purpose from late antiquity and the early medieval period – when the specified lengthy intervals of times within the orders were observed – namely, the preparation and probation of the clergy in the absence of any formal theological education or pastoral formation. At various times in the Middle Ages, insistence on sequential ordination with the prescribed intervals, was used to curb the abuse of simony.

From the sixteenth-century English Reformation it is difficult to maintain that a period of time ranging from forty-eight hours to twelve months is either adequate preparation or probation for the weighty nature of priestly ministry, as understood by the reformed Church of England. But what about the modern period from the nineteenth century onwards, when theological form-

---

7. It is interesting to note that in the late twentieth century, at least, it was possible to be ordained deacon and priest on the same day in the Church of England, with a faculty from the Archbishop of Canterbury. See Canon 3.7, *The Canons of the Church of England*, 4th ed., 5th supp. (London, 1986/1991) 59.

ation, testing and preparation prior to ordination, and even
prior formal studies themselves, have become extended and
much more comprehensive? With the advent of seminaries and
theological colleges across the Anglican Communion from the
nineteenth century onwards, it becomes increasingly difficult to
identify a transitional period in the diaconate as the period of
preparation and probation for priesthood that it once was, in
light of an increasingly sophisticated process of theological
education. In the contemporary church, the standards for discernment, training, and testing are met by institutions such as
ecclesiastical selection processes, diocesan candidates' committees, canonical examinations, various forms of clinical pastoral
education, psychological testing, and the like, rather than by the
canonical requirement of sequential ordination. If, after a rigorous selection process and at least three years of such seminary
formation, a bishop is still unsure whether a candidate ought to
be ordained to the priesthood, it is highly questionable whether
he or she should be ordained to the diaconate either! If the explicitly stated reasons for sequential ordination, at least between
deacon and presbyter, are no longer pertinent in some parts of
the Anglican Communion, then another rationale has to be either
sought, or more often, invented, to justify its continued existence.[8]

The Restoration of the Diaconate and Direct Ordination
Since the 1840s there have been serious efforts within the
Anglican tradition to restore the diaconate as a distinctive and
lifelong order as described in the ordination liturgies and in ancient tradition. Part of this vision of a restored diaconate included
the possibility that for some it would not lead to ordination to
the priesthood. Yet by the late twentieth century, it was the experience of some parts of the Anglican Communion that a vision
and exercise of a so-called 'permanent' diaconate are impossible
to maintain when the practice of the so-called 'transitional' diaconate is maintained along side of it.

From the 1970s, challenges to the practice of sequential
ordination have been raised by proponents of the restoration of
the diaconate as a distinct order, particularly in North America.
More recently, some American and Canadian Anglicans have

---

8. Sermons preached at the ordinations of deacons, in my experience,
are wondrous examples of such inventiveness.

argued that as long as candidates for the presbyterate must first be ordained deacons, the diaconate can hardly be a distinct order with its own integrity, but will never be much more than, in the words of Canon XXXII, 'a step or degree to the Ministry'. Consequently they argue for direct ordination to the priesthood for those called to that order without an anterior ordination to the diaconate. Some years ago, the problem was stated succinctly (with, albeit, some vitriol) in an editorial of *Diakoneo*, the journal of the North American Association for the Diaconate:

> The issue of transitional deacons refuses to go away. Every ordination as deacon of one intended for priest forces the issue upon the church. The use of one order as preparation for another is neither biblical nor patristic. Yet the church continues it as a discipline, by providing [for] it in canon law, as if it were a pearl of great price.
>
> What does the transitional diaconate mean? At best it is polite fiction, at worst pious fraud. In almost every ordination of a person in transit, there exists a defect of intention. Ask any bishop or priest whether he or she intended to become a deacon. Ask also how long the bishop or priest remained a deacon. The answer is clear. Transitional deacons don't intend to be deacons. They intend to be priests. Nor does the church intend them to be deacons. Their ordination as deacon takes place only as a legal game, in which the participants speak empty words and perform empty gestures. The game has no reality in life, and no validity.[9]

Lambeth Conferences have given special attention to the restoration of the diaconate. The 1958 Lambeth Conference, in its report 'The Order of Deacon,' submitted that the time had come when Anglicans must conclude that either there is no place for the order of deacon, or else begin to restore the office of deacon in the worship and witness of the church.[10] The bishops strongly endorsed the latter position. Consequently, in what appears to be an implicit proposition for direct ordination to the priesthood, Resolution 88 of the 1958 Conference states:

> The Conference recommends that each province of the Anglican Communion shall consider whether the office of

9. 'Getting our orders straight: a defect of intention,' *Diakoneo* 10, 1 (January, 1988) 1.
10. 'The Order of Deacon', The Lambeth Conference, 1958 (London, 1958), Sec 2, 106.

deacon shall be restored to its place as a distinctive order in the Church, *instead of being regarded as a probationary period for the priesthood*.[11]

The 1968 Lambeth Conference also dealt with the restoration of the diaconate. In Resolution 32 the bishops recommended that the diaconate be open to men and women, to full time church workers, as well as to candidates for the priesthood. The same resolution also directed that the ordination rites of the Anglican Communion be revised to take into account the new role of the diaconate, to remove references to the diaconate as an 'inferior office', and to emphasise the continuing element of *diakonia* in the ministries of presbyters and bishops.[12]

Resolution 32 of the 1968 Lambeth Conference was dealt with by the Anglican Consultative Council meeting in April 1976. In Resolution 10a) in the Section on Ministry, the council cautiously recommended:

... that the use of the Diaconate as a period of preparation for the priesthood be retained: and that every church should review its practice to ensure that this period is one of continued training and further testing of vocation; but that it is not to be regarded as necessarily leading to the priesthood.[13]

One of the strongest statements from the Lambeth Conference on the restored diaconate appears in the section reports of the 1988 Conference. A section of the report on 'Ministry and Mission,' entitled 'The Distinctive Diaconate', stressed that:

We need to rediscover the diaconate as an order complementing the order of priesthood rather than as a merely transitional order which it is at present. We should ensure that such a diaconate does not threaten the ministry of the laity but seeks to equip and further it. Such a diaconate, furthermore, would serve to renew the *diakonia* of the whole church; laity, deacons, priests, and bishops ...

Similarly the long-standing tradition that the diaconate is an 'inferior' order (cf the old ordinals) through which you

---

11. Roger Coleman, ed., *Resolutions of the Twelve Lambeth Conferences: 1867-1988* (Toronto, 1992), 140. [Emphasis added.]

12. Coleman, *Resolutions*, 162-163.

13. *ACC-3. Anglican Consultative Council. Report of Third Meeting: Trinidad, 23 March-2 April 1976* (Coventry, 1976) 44.

pass on the way to the priesthood is also an obstacle to the emergence of a distinctive diaconate.[14]

The report is clearly critical of the practice of sequential ordination and cites it as an obstacle to the emergence of a distinctive diaconate. For all that, it does not explicitly propose its alternative, namely, direct ordination.

The Distinctiveness of the Presbyterate and Episcopate, and Direct Ordination

The restoration of the diaconate may be the premier context for the current calls for a re-examination of the practice of sequential ordination, but it is not the only one. Other Anglicans argue that the practice of sequential ordination threatens the distinctiveness of the presbyterate. What does it mean to require prior diaconal ordination for a lay reader who has been the pastoral leader of a parish community for years before the church has discerned a vocation to the presbyterate? What does it mean in a monastic setting, for instance, to ordain a lay abbot or abbess to the diaconate before he or she is ordained to presbyterate to which the wider church and their particular community have called them? What does it mean to ordain a minister from a non-episcopal tradition, who already has requisite presbyteral formation and experience, an Anglican deacon for a period of days, weeks, or months before ordination as a priest? When the exercise of the diaconate is neither intended nor discerned, in what ways is the presbyterate a distinct ministry if it relies so clearly on a previous ordination to the diaconate?

At a time when lay people can be as theologically well educated as the clergy, when their faith, spirituality and mission are as profound as that of the clergy, and when they often have much more sophisticated skills and experience of theological education, leadership, conflict resolution, communication, pastoral care, administration, and the like, what does it mean to restrict candidature to the episcopal office to presbyters alone? Is the episcopate a distinct office which calls forth the best candidates – lay and ordained – or is it some sort of completion of the presbyterate? Even beyond the first three centuries of the life of the church, the elections and ordinations of lay people in times of

---

14. Secs. 121, 122, 'Ministry and Mission,' *The Lambeth Conference, 1988* (London, 1988) 56.

crisis, such as Ambrose of Milan and Nectarius of Constantinople, suggest that the Spirit may raise up, and the Christian
community may discern, episcopal leadership amongst the
laity. There are churches in crisis in the Anglican Communion
where the inherited canonical tradition cannot provide the same
degree of insight and possibility today. While the language of
'distinctiveness' of ministry may surface in the more Western
provinces of the Anglican Communion, to what extent does the
practice of sequential ordination hinder the mission of those
provinces who struggle to maintain the life and mission of the
church? Is leadership of local and wider communities enhanced
or diminished when only deacons can be presbyters, and only
presbyters can be bishops? For Anglicans around the world, it
may well be that the inherited European canonical tradition of
sequential ordination limits our ability to discern and hear with
the Spirit those who have the gifts and calling for pastoral leadership.

IALC, IASCER and Direct Ordination
It is within the context of the restoration of the diaconate, and
within a serious scholarly engagement with the historical roots
and rationale for the origins of sequential ordination, that the
2001 statement of the International Anglican Liturgical Consultation (IALC) – *Anglican Ordination Rites, The Berkeley Statement:
'To Equip the Saints'* – included a brief paragraph with the heading 'Direct Ordination':

> Because the three orders are viewed as distinct ministries,
> direct ordination to the presbyterate, and even the possibility
> of direct ordination to the episcopate, are being advocated by
> some in the Anglican Communion. There is historical prece-
> dent for both sequential and direct ordination. In the pre-
> Nicene church, direct ordination was commonly practised,
> and sequential ordination did not become universal until the
> eleventh century. *Provinces may therefore wish to consider the
> possibility of direct ordination to the episcopate and to the pres-
> byterate.*[15]

This particular paragraph, which appears in the section entitled 'The Ordered Nature of the Church,' is arguably the most
radical of the entire document: lay people could be ordained

---

15. *To Equip the Saints*, Part 1: *Direct Ordination* [emphasis added].

directly to the priesthood; deacons or lay people could be elected and ordained as bishops.

Of the nearly seventeen pages of succinct, and profound theological and pastoral reflection on the nature of orders and ordination in the Anglican tradition, it is this particular paragraph, with its final 'offending' sentence, which appears to have garnered the harshest international attention, and from a most unlikely source. The members of the International Anglican Standing Committee on Ecumenical Relations (IASCER) have expressed concern about the IALC statement on direct ordination at their December meetings in both 2001 and 2002. While there were a number of issues from *Anglican Ordination Rites* which were discussed by IASCER, apparently its members have had the greatest difficulty with the section on direct ordination.[16] At the December 2003 meeting, IASCER passed the following resolution:

Resolution 2.03: Ongoing Studies - Direct Ordination

IASCER: Notes with concern the suggestion in the IALC statement *Anglican Ordination Rites* that 'provinces may wish to consider the possibility of direct ordination';

Observes that the invariable practice of Anglican churches has been sequential ordination and that this is presupposed in the ecumenical agreements.

This is a very odd resolution, indeed. Firstly, there has been a long conversation in Anglican tradition about direct ordination, under the medieval canonical terminology of *per saltum* ordination, and the context has been entirely ecumenical. Furthermore, in ecumenical agreements with non-episcopal churches in the first half of the twentieth century (and beyond), and in virtually all ecumenical agreements with Lutheran churches in the latter part of the twentieth century (and beyond), some measure of *per saltum* or direct ordination has been very much presupposed. In fact, 'Holy Order in Ecumenical Dialogue,' a report prepared for IASCER by Canon J. Robert Wright and Dr William Crockett, notes without apparent worry or criticism a reference to direct ordination in a recent Anglican-Lutheran document. *The Diaconate as Ecumenical Opportunity: The Hanover Report of The Anglican-Lutheran International Commission* challenges Anglicans to restore the diaconate as a lifelong and distinct form

16. From the Report to IALC by the Revd Dr William Crockett, IALC Consultant on IASCER, August, 2003.

of ordained ministry, pointing to the possibility of direct ordination to the presbyterate for those who have a vocation to this
order rather than to the diaconate.

Anglican Ecumenism and Direct Ordination

The first instance of 'direct ordination' in an Anglican ecumenical
context occurred in the early seventeenth century, through an
attempt to restore episcopacy to the Scottish church during the
reign of James I. In 1610, the king ordered three Presbyterian
ministers, John Spottiswoode, Gaven Hamilton, and Andrew
Laws to be consecrated to the episcopate by bishops of the
Church of England, and then to return to Scotland. The consecrations took place on 21 October 1610.

The original account of the incident, recorded by the Scottish
historian John Spottiswoode (one of the candidates), relates that
Lancelot Andrewes, Bishop of Ely, felt unable to take part in the
consecrations since the three Presbyterians had never been ordained priests. Andrewes was simply adhering to the rules of
the *cursus honorum*. According to Spottiswoode, Richard Bancroft,
Archbishop of Canterbury, intervened and supported the
consecrations on the grounds that in countries where no bishops
could be found, presbyteral ordination was counted as sufficient:

> A question in the mean time was moved by Dr Andrewes
> Bishop of Ely touching the consecration of the Scottish
> Bishops, who, as he said 'must first be ordained Presbyters,
> as having no ordination from a Bishop', the Archbishop of
> Canterbury Dr Bancroft who was by, maintained 'That there-
> of there was no necessity, seeing where no bishop could be
> had, the Ordination given by Presbyters must be esteemed
> lawful; otherwise that it might be doubted, if there were any
> lawful vocation in most reformed churches.' [...] This ap-
> plauded to by the other Bishops, Ely acquiesced, and at that
> day, and in the place appointed the three Scottish Bishops
> were consecrated.[17]

Since the orders of the Presbyterians were recognised,
Andrewes and the others would be ordaining presbyters to the
episcopate according to the Church of England's practice of
sequential ordination after all.

17. John Spottiswoode, *The History of the Church of Scotland*, Bk VII, 1655
(Facsimile; Menston Yorkshire, 1972) 514.

A subsequent account of the same event was recorded by Peter Heylyn (1600-1668) in a post-Restoration work entitled *Aërius Redivivus, Or the History of the Presbyterians*. Heylyn's account corresponds to Spottiswoode's on most points. Both agree that Andrewes was unable to take part in the consecrations because the Presbyterians had not been ordained to the priesthood. Both agree that Archbishop Bancroft intervened and successfully persuaded Andrewes to participate. Heylyn's outstanding departure from Spottiswoode's account lies in his alternate version of Bancroft's reasons for supporting the consecrations:

> But first a scruple had been moved by the Bishop of Ely, concerning the capacity of the persons nominated for receiving Episcopal Consecration, in regard that none of them had formerly been ordained Priests: which scruple was removed by Archbishop Bancroft, alleging that there was no such necessity of receiving the Order of Priesthood, but that Episcopal Consecration might be given without it; as might have been exemplified in the cases of Ambrose and Nectarius of which the first was made Archbishop of Millain [*sic*], and the other Patriarch of Constantinople, without receiving any intermediary Orders, whether of Priest, or Deacon, or any other (if there were any other) at that time in the Church.[18]

According to Heylyn – in the acrimonious anti-Presbyterian spirit of the Restoration – Bancroft said that the consecrations were to be thought of as effectively 'direct ordination' in nature, following the examples of Ambrose of Milan and Nectarius of Constantinople in the late fourth century, so that in effect, three lay men were being ordained directly to the episcopate.

Plainly, Spottiswoode and Heylyn are irreconcilable in terms of Bancroft's response to Andrewes. There are historians who can be found in support of either version. In *Old Priest and New Presbyter* Norman Sykes, for instance, suggests that Spottiswoode was probably right.[19] For one thing, Sykes argues, Spottiswoode was an eye witness; for another thing, the Church of England was much more flexible in matters of order in the seventeenth century prior to the Restoration than in subsequent centuries. It is interesting to note, however, that when Charles II attempted to re-establish episcopacy in Scotland in 1662, the

---

18. Peter Heylyn, *Aërius Redivivus, Or the History of the Presbyterians* (London, 1672 2) 382.
19. Norman Sykes, *Old Priest and New Presbyter* (Cambridge, 1956) 101.

four Presbyterian ministers nominated at that time were sequentially ordained deacon, priest, and bishop in a day,[20] contrary to
Canon XXXII.

While Heylyn's explanation is likely an instance of post-
Restoration polemic against the validity of the ministries of the
non-episcopal churches, it nevertheless reflects an Anglican perception that while unusual, direct ordination is not only possible, but in some instances, useful. This admission of the validity
of *per saltum* or direct ordination, with respect to the episcopate,
is evidence of an Anglican position which understands the practice of sequential ordination as dispensable, and certainly not of
a theological priority: direct ordination is true ordination.

In the end, the most important point about Peter Heylyn's account is that it is his, and not Spottiswoode's, which is the one
remembered by later generations of Anglicans.[21] The use of the
1610 consecrations, according to Peter Heylyn's interpretation,
has been applied by various Lambeth Conferences as precedent
for the consecration of non-episcopally ordained ministers to the
episcopate in plans of organic union between Anglican and non-
episcopal churches. The Lambeth Conference of 1908 is the first
to cite the 1610 consecrations as such a precedent. In Resolution
75 the bishops state:

> The Conference … is of the opinion that, in the welcome
> event of any project of reunion between any Church of the
> Anglican Communion and any Presbyterian or other non-
> episcopal Church, which, while preserving the Faith in its in-
> tegrity and purity, has also exhibited care as to the form and
> intention of ordination to the ministry, reaching the stage of
> responsible negotiation, it might be possible to make an ap-
> proach to reunion on the basis of consecrations to the episco-
> pate on lines suggested by such precedents as those of 1610.[22]

---

20. Norman Sykes, *The Church of England and the non-episcopal Churches
in the sixteenth and seventeenth centuries* (London, 1949) 27.

21. For example, the entry for 'Spottiswoode' in the *Oxford Dictionary of
the Christian Church* records that he 'did not receive episcopal consecration, however, until 1610, when, with two other Scottish bishops, he
was consecrated (*per saltum*, on High Anglican principles) at London
House.' *Oxford Dictionary of the Christian Church*, F. L. Cross and E. A.
Livingstone, eds, (Oxford, 1990 2) 1303.

22. Coleman, *Resolutions* 43; R. T. Davidson, ed, *The Six Lambeth
Conferences: 1867-1920* (London, 1929) 336.

A note within the body of the report (in Archbishop Davidson's edition) adds the following commentary: 'In so far as these precedents involve consecration to the Episcopate *per saltum*, the conditions of such consecrations would require careful investigation and statement.'[23]

Although *per saltum* terminology is absent in the reports and resolutions of the 1920 Lambeth Conference, it reappears in the 1930 conference. In the report 'The Unity of the Church,' the conference commended the mutual commissioning by Anglican ministers and others in the inaugurations of united churches. This gesture would satisfy the Anglican requirement that all ministers receive episcopal ordination. Such a 'commissioning' from the hands of an Anglican bishop is regarded, however, as ordination *per saltum:*

> On the question of Consecration *per saltum* [a footnote in the text elaborates: 'i.e. Consecration to the Episcopate without previous ordination by a Bishop to the diaconate and priesthood'] our view is that while undesirable in the normal course of the Church's life, such Consecration is valid and in the special circumstances of the inauguration of the united Church is justifiable.[24]

While this cautious statement upholds the desirability of the sequential ordination, it acknowledges that it is not an absolute necessity and may be abrogated in the interest of Christian unity. Presumably in the eyes of the 1930 Lambeth Fathers, bishops consecrated in united churches from non-Anglican traditions would have no less a claim to the ascription 'historic' than they themselves. Nor has there been any question of the broader recognition of the orders of presbyters and deacons ordained by such bishops (e.g. the Church of South India), not withstanding fears to the contrary.

The advisability of using the 1610 consecrations – with Peter Heylyn's interpretation of the same – as a model and precedent in plans of union between Anglicans and non-episcopal churches is debatable. Be that as it may, two Lambeth Conferences have replied that the consecrations of Presbyterian ministers and others to the episcopate in plans of church unions involving Anglicans would not be according to the rules of sequential ordination but would be instances of direct ordination. Hence, from an

---

23. Davidson, *Lambeth Conferences* 432 n 2.
24. 'The Unity of the Church,' *Lambeth 1930* (London: SPCK, 1930) 128.

Anglican point of view it cannot be maintained that sequential ordination is a theological or sacramental priority.

Moreover, the Lambeth resolutions concerning *per saltum* ordination made possible Anglican participation in uniting churches, such as the Church of South India, and the Church of North India, which are now members of the Anglican Communion. While the language of direct or *per saltum* ordination has been perhaps helpfully absent from Anglican-Lutheran dialogue, it remains that Lutheran pastors who have never been ordained as deacons, are exercising presbyteral ministries in Anglican churches, and that Lutheran bishops, in traditions which until recently were not in historic episcopal succession, are being ordained as bishops without anterior ordination as deacons (and presbyters) by Anglican bishops. While Anglicans have invariably insisted on the historic episcopate, we have not insisted that Lutheran churches restore the diaconate as part of renewed *cursus honorum*. In that Anglicans are in full communion with churches who do not practice sequential ordination as we do, it is hard to argue, as IASCER seems to do, that the 'invariable practice of Anglicanism has been sequential ordination.' It is even more difficult to maintain that, without massive qualification, sequential ordination 'is presupposed in the ecumenical agreements that they have made.'

The Diaconate and Sequential Ordination?
There is a recent trend within the Anglican Communion which intrinsically links the diaconate and sequential ordination. This particular view identifies the diaconate as the basis of all *diakonia*, and the ongoing source of servant-hood for presbyters and bishops; as such, it is unimaginable without sequential ordination. Especially popular within the Church of England during recent decades, it is reflected in the recent 2001 working report of the House of Bishops to the General Synod, *For Such a Time as This: A Renewed Diaconate in the Church of England*.[25] The roots of the 2001 document are reflected in a 1988 report also commissioned by the General Synod, *Deacons in the Ministry of the Church:*

> Although those who are called to the priesthood legitimately spend time as transitional deacons (and need to be encouraged

---

25. *For Such a Time as This: A Renewed Diaconate in the Church of England.* A Report to the General Synod of the Church of England of a Working Party of the House of Bishops (GS 1407) (London, 2001).

to make the best use of their opportunities in that ministry) the use of the distinctive diaconate as the first step towards priesthood is not to be discouraged.[26]

As part of the process of rediscovery, those who are preparing for priesthood will need to be helped in the understanding and use of their time in the diaconate. For not only might they work subsequently with distinctive deacons, but their priestly ministry is necessarily based upon *diakonia*.[27]

It is somewhat ironic to note, however, that a 1974 report of the Advisory Council for the Church's Ministry of the Church of England, *Deacons in the Church*, actually proposed the abolition of the diaconate as a distinct order of ministry within the church.[28] While its authors favoured the demise of the diaconate altogether, they admitted that it would be simpler to 'let sleeping dogs lie' and retain the diaconate 'as a short probationary and intermediate stage through which pass all candidates for priesthood.'[29] Although in the end the authors of *Deacons in the Church* advocated the traditional place of the diaconate within the process of sequential ordination, they did acknowledge that candidates for the priesthood need not necessarily receive prior ordination to deacon's orders. Ultimately, the Church of England accepted neither proposal from this document.

There are a number of questions which need to be posed to *For Such a Time as This: A Renewed Diaconate in the Church of England* and similar texts which understand diaconate as the fundamental stratum of ordained ministry, whatever else is added to it. From an ecumenical perspective, does such an understanding of the diaconate bear theological, liturgical, and canonical resonances with other traditions which have maintained the threefold ministry, especially the Roman Catholic and Orthodox Churches, and with whom Anglicans are engaged in serious ecumenical dialogue on questions of ordained ministry? Or, do Anglicans run the danger of a sort of catholic idiosyncrasy on this point? What are the consequences of such a theology

---

26. *Deacons in the Ministry of the Church*. A Report to the General Synod of the Church of England (Westminster, 1988) 105-106.

27. *Deacons in the Ministry*, 108.

28. *Deacons in the Church*, Advisory Council for the Church's Ministry (Westminster, 1974) 22-25.

29. *Deacons* (1974), 23.

of ministry for our historic and ongoing ecumenical relationships with the non-episcopal churches, and those episcopal
churches which either do not retain the diaconate as Anglicans
understand the order, or do not insist on the sequence between
deacon and presbyter? Is a lack of diaconal ordination some sort
of new form of 'invalid ordination'? In the last century we spoke
of the non-episcopal churches; now will we be speaking of the
non-diaconal churches? A theological insistence on anterior diaconal ordination for priestly and episcopal ordination appears
to introduce a new category into Anglican sacramental theology,
parallelling the medieval scholastic conviction which understood episcopal consecration without anterior presbyteral ordination as a theological impossibility.[30]

Secondly, do the assumptions of *For Such a Time as This*
around the diaconate and sequential ordination bear the weight
of history? Unless one posits that the Gregorian Reforms of the
eleventh century mark the authoritative period for the practice
of sequential ordination – and explain why – one must conclude
that it does not. What does one make of the countless pre-Nicene
and patristic bishops and presbyters who were never deacons?[31]
Or the medieval presbyters and bishops who were likewise
never deacons?[32] Or of modern bishops such as Leslie Newbigin

30. Interestingly, while Thomas Aquinas was certainly among these
scholastic theologians, he did teach that it was theologically possible to
ordain someone directly to the presbyterate without ordination to the
diaconate. Such an ordination, he concludes, would be illicit, though
valid. *Summa Theologiae*, Pars IIIa et Supplementum, Billuart De Rubeis
and P. Faucher, eds. (Rome, 1953) 758.
31. E.g. Bishop Fabian of Rome was a lay person when ordained bishop
in 236. Cornelius of Rome was a lay person when ordained presbyter,
and then bishop of Rome in 251. Origen was a lay person before ordination to the presbyterate in 229. None of the three Cappadocian fathers
were ever ordained deacons. Ambrose of Milan was a lay person at his
ordination as a bishop in 374. Augustine of Hippo was a lay person
when he was ordained a presbyter in 391. Theodore of Tarsus was a
subdeacon before ordination as Archbishop of Canterbury in 668.
32. The *Liber pontificalis* reports on the following bishops of Rome: Leo
III was a subdeacon, presbyter, then bishop (795). Paschal I was likewise subdeacon, presbyter, then bishop ((817). So was Gregory IV,
(827). Sergius II was subdeacon, archpresbyter, then bishop (844). Leo
IV was subdeacon, presbyter, bishop (847), as was Benedict III (855).
Hadrian II and Stephen V were both subdeacons, presbyters, then bishops (867, 885).

or Nathan Söderblom who were likewise never deacons? One must also return to the historically articulated reasons for sequential ordination, as evidenced from the canonical tradition from the fourth century through the medieval canonistic collections to the Canons of 1604, as well as the precepts of the Ordinal: namely, that the purpose of the sequence from deacon to priest is for training and testing.

The Alternatives from Tradition: Sequential and Direct Ordination
If the case can be made that *diakonia* of bishops and presbyters is somehow rooted in the diaconate, it cannot be located in ordination to the diaconate as an isolated event, but rather in the lived experience of ministry as a deacon. One must question whether current Anglican canonical and pastoral practice which permits ordination to the priesthood anywhere from one day to one year after ordination as a deacon can in anyway be an authentic exercise of the diaconate, upon which the habits and identity of *diakonia* for a lifetime of presbyteral or even episcopal ministry are to be founded. One solution from the tradition, which respects the historic integrity of sequential ordination, is to return to the ancient interval of a minimal five-year diaconate. From amongst those who had served well as deacons for five years, some might be (s)elected to the presbyterate, while others might not, as is currently the case regarding the presbyterate and the episcopate. The restoration of the classic interval between the diaconate and the presbyterate would doubtless incense those who reject the practice of using one order in preparation for another; it could be accused of being oppressively anachronistic and impractical. It does, nevertheless, remain consistent with classic Anglican, medieval and patristic understandings of the purpose of sequential ordination, and provides a pragmatic opportunity for the said purpose. It may even offer such a faithful exercise of diaconal ministry that many deacons might well discover their true vocation lies in this order rather than in another, and decide not to be ordained priests (or bishops).

The second alternative is to return to the equally historic practice of ordaining people directly to the priesthood. Since the fundamental purpose of sequential ordination is preparation and testing, these categories must be part of the criterion for a consideration of its continuance, modification, or abolition. If these criteria are truly being met elsewhere in contemporary Anglican provincial churches in a proper and extended process of discernment, professional, pastoral and spiritual formation, theological education, field placements, and the like, the second option may certainly be viable. Moreover, if these conditions are met, the classic reasons behind sequential ordination are simply made redundant. Once again, if certain bishops are not convinced whether candidates should be ordained as priests, they should not be ordaining them as deacons to test and train them further! Since the pastoral reasons for retaining sequential ordination may no longer be relevant in parts of the Anglican Communion, there may be 'good cause' and compelling reasons for amending the canons on ordination in provincial churches of the Anglican communion to permit direct ordination.

In a church with a thoroughly renewed diaconate, there is no reason to suppose that deacons would not be as eligible as presbyters for election and ordination to the episcopate. Similarly, there is no compelling theological reason against the election and ordination of a lay person to the episcopate. In both cases the primary consideration is whether such candidates have been truly called, and adequately tested and prepared for episcopal ministry. After all, the lessons from the history of ordained ministry demonstrate instances where direct ordination has been of benefit to the whole church, as Anglicans have discovered in the modern ecumenical context. It is possible that in the future, at times the church may find the best candidates for the episcopate amongst the deacons or laity. Or, at times the church may continue to find that the priestly, prophetic, and pastoral gifts it seeks in candidates for the episcopate are most effectively tested and discerned in those who have already exercised them as presbyters.

Lastly, the history of ordination rites demonstrates that canonical traditions and pastoral practices are subject to change. There is no compelling reason to suppose that the practice of sequential ordination is past the point of further adaptation. As it happened, the Reformation Church of England altered significantly the received practice of sequential ordination. Twentieth-century Anglican ecumenical thought permitted *per saltum* or direct ordination, in certain situations.

Perhaps the movement for the restoration of the diaconate challenges Anglicans to consider further adaptations today. Reasonably, as the present IALC document so tentatively puts it: 'Provinces may therefore wish to consider the possibility of direct ordination to the episcopate and to the presbyterate.'

The Place of Symbols and Vesting in Ordination Rites

Lizette Larson-Miller

In the Berkeley Statement on Anglican ordination rites, *To Equip the Saints*, several theological contexts are presumed as foundational, and thus function as starting points for any discussion on the rites of ordination. The first is the centrality of baptism as 'the foundation of the life and ministry of the church,'[1] based on a baptismal ecclesiology that presumes a commonality in ministerial call to all Christians before acknowledging the necessity of differentiated ministries. The second presumption is that all ministry is 'in service of the ministry of the whole people of God,'[2] and exists for the building up of the Body of Christ and for the good of the whole world, not for individual privilege or gain. The third is the historical tradition and ecclesial advantage of the threefold order of bishop, priest, and deacon, which best expresses the variety of charisms in leadership and maintains the local and universal realities of the Body of Christ. The actual rites of ordination should ideally be expressive of these theological realities as well as symbolically capable of being the source of theological insight, of representing 'the whole of the world to which it belongs.'[3]

This essay will look at some of the symbols used in the ordination rites as they are related to the theological priorities stated above, primarily in presbyteral ordination rites, (diaconal and episcopal practices are covered elsewhere in this volume). The guiding questions will be: What have these actions meant and what are their meanings today? Why were they added? Do they contribute to or hinder the expression of the primary theological perspectives on which the Berkeley Statement is grounded? If the ecumenical agreement on the shape of ordination has as its primary moments the recognition and election of the candidate for ordination, the laying on of hands and accompanying

---

1. *To Equip the Saints*, Part I: The Calling of the People of God.
2. Ibid., Part I: Cultural Shaping of Ministry.
3. Louis-Marie Chauvet, *The Sacraments: The Word of God at the Mercy of the Body* (Collegeville, 2001) 72.

prayer, and the invitation into the particular commitments of the ordained ministry as named – all within the context of the eucharist[4] – many of the symbolic actions and things mentioned below are clearly of a secondary nature. The question, however, is not to ask what the minimal requirements might be, with extras added or deleted according to cultural preferences, but what is the best expression of the rich plurality of meanings associated with ordination understood as having both particular moments and a lifelong trajectory through the varied process of call, recognition, preparation, ordination, and a living into the reality of ordained ministry in the church.[5] As with the process of initiation gathered within the catechumenate, the many related symbolic actions of the ordination rite express a multiplicity of meanings and represent the breadth of the process, building on 'the order of recognition'[6] unfolding in the experiences of those engaged in the process. Following on this assumption of a series of ritual actions and things with related symbolic meaning, this essay begins with the central symbolic action of the laying on of hands and moves from there to the actions which flow out of that primary gesture, focusing on those symbols which have an extended historical trajectory.

The Laying on of Hands
In spite of its varied meanings, and varied status within the rituals surrounding the recognition of appointed Christian leaders, the imposition of hands has remained a constant trajectory in the history of the rites, and its centrality in contemporary and ecumenically diverse practices is due both to historical longevity and universal indication.

   Biblical and early church accounts of the laying on of hands have been researched for many decades now, with extensive, and sometimes, differing conclusions. The Old and New Testament accounts of the imposition of hands are diverse, sometimes with continuity of form more evident than continuity

---

4. *BEM*, Ministry, B: The Act of Ordination.
5. 'We need to regard ordination as essentially a process and not merely a rite, a process accomplished over time and not just in a brief sacramental moment ...' Paul Bradshaw, 'Ordination as God's Action through the Church,' *Järvenpää* 9.
6. '... symbol belongs to the order of recognition, therefore to the order of the relation between subjects as such.' Chauvet, *Sacraments* 74.

of meaning.[7] Building on the gospel accounts of Jesus blessing, healing, and freeing 'through the imposition of hands',[8] and the related use of the gesture by the disciples, Jim Puglisi summarises the ordination rite inheritance from the New Testament with the following five points:

1) It is difficult to conclude from the New Testament texts alone … that this was fixed and stable rite;

2) The meaning of the gesture varies …;

3) In all the texts (except 1 Timothy 5:22) there is a link between the gesture meaning the Spirit and the gesture when it signifies the gift of God;

4) When it refers to the gift, this latter is never conferred for the sole benefit of the person, but in view of service towards others; and

5) This gesture is always performed in a context of prayer.[9]

The key liturgical document which links the ambiguous information of the New Testament through the several second and third century references to centuries of later ordination rituals is the disputed *Apostolic Tradition*.[10] Setting aside the known controversies over identity and dating of authorship and layers of editing, The *Apostolic Tradition* reveals what Godfrey Diekmann wrote many years ago, that the AT reveals the imposition of hands as the basic sacramental rite,

the basic liturgical rite common to all the sacraments mentioned – the ordination of bishop, of presbyter, of deacon; the Eucharist; and baptism and its complementary rite which we call confirmation – seems to me to be beyond dispute. That

---

7. Everett Ferguson, 'Laying on of Hands: Its Significance in Ordination', *Journal of Theological Studies* 26 (1975) 1-12. Primarily the differences are based in the two etymological sources of the gesture, *samakh* – to lean upon ('to create a substitute'), and *sim* – to touch ('an act of benediction'). Rather than a continuation of *samakh* from Jewish to Christian sources, the semitic Christian usage preferred *sim*, with its alternative interpretations (and differences of artistic reconstruction – namely the crossing of the arms in blessing). See also David Daube, *The New Testament and Rabbinic Judaism*, (London, 1956) 224-246.

8. James F. Puglisi, *The Process of Admission to Ordained Ministry: A Comparative Study* (Collegeville, 1996) 1:34.

9. Ibid., 34-5.

10. The best contemporary edition is by Paul F. Bradshaw, Maxwell E. Johnson, and L. Edward Phillips, *The Apostolic Tradition* (Minneapolis, 2002).

this laying on of hands was meant to signify the conferral of the Holy Spirit is also clearly expressed in all these instances, except in the case of the baptismal rite, where it is however (to my thinking) unmistakably implied.[11]

The continuity of the imposition of hands has been traced through the ancient church rites East and West and through the Western rites into the Anglican rites in their various histories while still clearly exhibiting differences in the interpretive words accompanying the gesture; who was imposing hands (the bishop alone, several bishops, bishops and presbyters); and the perceived centrality of the rite. This latter point is an interesting shift in Western history, most notably articulated in the scholastic period in the theological reflection of Thomas Aquinas, who saw the matter and form of the sacrament not in the laying on of hands and accompanying prayer of consecration, but in the handing over of the chalice and paten (*traditio instrumentorum*).[12] It is interesting to trace the parallel decline of the centrality of the laying on of hands and of pneumotological awareness in the medieval Western Church in light of the close association of epicletic meaning to the gesture.[14]

The Anglican inheritance, in its usual tug of war between

---

11. Godfrey Diekmann, 'The Laying on of Hands: The Basic Sacramental Rite,' *Proceedings of the Catholic Theological Society of America* 29 (1974) 340.

12. See Bradshaw 1971, 1990; John Gibaut, 'Amalarius of Metz and the Laying on of Hands in the Ordination of a Deacon,' *Harvard Theological Review* 82 (1989) 233-240; Cyrille Vogel, 'L'imposition des mains dans les rites d'ordination en Orient et en Occident,' *La Maison-Dieu* 102 (1970) 57-72; Puglisi, *The Process of Admission to Ordained Ministry*, volumes I, II, III.

13. 'The conferring of power is effected by giving something pertaining to their proper act. And since the principal act of a priest is to consecrate the body and blood of Christ, the priestly character is imprinted at the very giving of the chalice under the prescribed form of words.' *Summa Theologiae*, Supp., q.37, a.5. Cited in Louis Weil 'The Practice of Ordination: Distinguishing Secondary Elements from Primary,' *Järvenpää* 47.

14. Elsewhere in this collection is an essay on the consecratory prayer and its shifting emphases. Suffice it to say that the epicletic interpretation has been a dominant one, although for an alternative interpretation, see J. Kevin Coyle, 'The Laying on of Hands as Conferral of the Spirit: Some Problems and a Possible Solution,' *Studia Patristica* 18 (1989) 339-353.

puritans and catholics, generally retained the imposition of hands, the notable exception being Knox's influence in his rite for superintendents that favoured a handshake. But even there it was gradually replaced by a return to the imposition of hands,[15] and by the revisions of 1661 the imposition of hands as an epicletic gesture was clarified by the 'relocation of the hymn to the Holy Spirit [that] calls attention to the action of the Spirit in the conferral of ordination' and by the clarity of the sentence 'Receive the Holy Ghost, for the Office, and the work of a Priest, in the Church of God, now committed unto thee by the imposition of our hands.'[16]

A survey of contemporary ordination rites around the Anglican Communion reveals a great deal of uniformity of gesture in the symbolic act of laying on of hands. For bishops, the imposition of hands and prayer of consecration is done by bishops (often noted as a minimum of three); for presbyters, the imposition of hands is by the bishop and the college of presbyters (actually executed in several different forms), and for deacons by the bishop alone. All three orders have generally restored epicletic language in the prayer with some specificity for which gifts of the Spirit are most associated with each order,[17] and while variations about the arrangement and the juxtaposition of silence, prayer and laying on of hands varies, there is outwardly, at least, much agreement on the centrality of this gesture and its spectrum of meanings.

Vesture and Vesting

In many of the ordination rites of the Anglican Communion, the laying on of hands and the prayer of consecration are followed by the rubric: 'The new priest (the new bishop, the new deacon) is now vested according to the order of priests (bishops, deacons).'[18] Although not as universal as the primary gesture of the laying on of hands, the putting on of clothing associated with a particular appointed ministry has a long and rich history of meanings

---

15. See Bradshaw 1971, 52-53; 56.

16. Puglisi, *The Process of Admission*, 2:138, and Bradshaw 1971, 90.

17. H. Boone Porter, 'The Theology of Ordination and the New Rites,' *Anglican Theological Review* 54 (1972) 75.

18. The wording of *The Book of Common Prayer* 1979 of the Episcopal Church, USA and *The Book of Alternative Services of The Anglican Church of Canada*. Other BCP rubrics are less direct, hence in *A New Zealand Prayer Book*, the rubric states: 'The new priests may now be vested ...'

and associations. Behind the cultural and religious associations of vestments with function, office and ministry, however, is the more foundational link to the clothing metaphor as a favoured Christian symbol for having put on Christ in baptism. ('As many of you as were baptised into Christ have clothed yourselves with Christ.' Galatians 3:27) As a metaphor for both the incarnation of Christ (putting on humanity) and for baptised Christians (putting on Christ), the clothing metaphor was a particularly cherished one in semitic Christianity, as well as other cultural and linguistic branches of early Christianity[19] in which what we are by nature is symbolically augmented by what we have put on.

The vestments associated with particular ministries may find their specifics in time-bound cultural associations of clothing and their primary contemporary value in their uniqueness which allows them to be vehicles of historical tradition, but theologically they are rooted in baptism alone.

Unlike the imposition of hands, the vesting of elect or ordained persons is not mentioned in *The Apostolic Tradition*. Aside from cultural references to symbols of office, it is not until after the collection of texts known as the *Sacramentarium Veronense*,[20] and in the related *ordines* of Roman and mixed Roman-Gallican origin, that we begin to see detailed descriptions of ordination vesting. In *OR 39* we learn of a series of public rituals, beginning with a public oath, followed by two stational masses at which the elect

> already dressed in their vestments, stood in the presbyterium, in the presence of the assembly while the list of their names and of the titles for which they were to be ordained was read to see if there were any objections on the part of the faithful to their nomination.[21]

The ordination liturgy proper follows these events. The emphasis is on the election and recognition by the whole church and, through a number of ritual events before and after the

19. For example, see Sebastian Brock's commentary on the importance of the baptismal garment as the 'robe of glory ... woven of fire and Spirit,' (336) in 'Baptismal Themes in the Writings of Jacob of Serugh,' *Symposium Syriacum 1976* (Rome, 1978) 325-347.

20. See Vogel, Cyrille, *Medieval Liturgy: An Introduction to the Sources* (Washington, DC, 1986) 38-46

21. Puglisi, *The Process of Admission*, 1:102.

ordination, on the close relationship between the bishop (pope) and his presbyters. As with many rites that began as a process, however, *Ordo 34* points to the conflation of these separate rites into one, in which the presbyter is vested in a chasuble just prior to the prayer of consecration, apparently within a single rite.[22]

The expansion of the rituals of vesting with accompanying prayers comes from the Gallican (and presumably Eastern) ordination rites,[23] along with the placement of the vesting following the laying on of hands and prayer of consecration. It seems likely, however, that a contributing factor in the elaboration of this particular ritual is the loss of association of stole, chasuble and dalmatic with everyday clothes, moving the attire itself from the realm of the every day to the sacral, and thus, to the holy function of setting the individual apart from others.[24] Within the Latin-speaking Carolingian synthesis, liturgical investiture became another outward expression of what was spoken in the prayers, prayers which 'had become inaccessible to the faithful due to the language problem.'[25] Certainly the sense of putting on the virtues described in Colossians ('clothe yourselves with compassion, kindness, humility, meekness, and patience ...' [Colossians 3:14])[26] was already evident in the consecration prayers, but the literal action made cultural sense and heightened the drama of the occasion. The fixing of investiture rituals in the centuries leading up to the Reformation, later concretised in the Roman Pontifical of 1596, contributed to a web of secondary elements generally understood to be expressive of the sacralisation of the office and the personal sanctification of the priest.[27]

The mixed inheritance from medieval Catholic and continental reformers in the Anglican ordinals took the investiture rituals in general, and vestments specifically, to extraordinary heights

22. Cited and translated in Bradshaw 1990, 220. The practice of vesting prior to ordination is still found in the eleventh century in Spain, *Liber Ordinum*. See Porter, *Ordination Prayers*, 63.

23. Most of the Eastern ordination rites include the vesting following the prayer and laying on of hands, but the exact trajectory is difficult to trace due to the late manuscript tradition of Byzantine, Armenian and Coptic rites. See the descriptions in Bradshaw 1990, 127-212.

24. See H. Boone Porter, *The Ordination Prayers of the Ancient Western Churches* (London, 1967) 79, for the same line of thinking.

25. Puglisi, *The Process of Admission*, 1:155.

26. Ibid., 158.

27. See Bruno Kleinheyer, *Die Priesterweihe im römischen Ritus: eine liturgiehistorische Studie* (Trier, 1962) esp. 74-84; 128-134; 154-159.

of controversy. The arguments were not, of course, primarily about clothes but what the vestments were thought to represent. Michael Perham describes these ecclesiological differences as

> ... the precise reason why some have wanted to abandon the use of the traditional eucharistic vestments of Western Christianity. They would want to say that what the church did at the Reformation was to make a break with medieval doctrine, and the vestments were part of the way that doctrine was expressed.[28]

The relation of the vestments controversy in general to ordination rituals is a direct one, as what is symbolised in the ordination rite is presumably a reality of ministerial practice. The gradual return of suggested or direct rubrics for vesting the newly ordained in the new ordinations rites of various members of the Anglican Communion seems to be an acknowledgement of the symbolic power of clothing still present in many societies, while symbolic polyvalence is maintained by a lack of accompanying text.[29] Putting on the stole of office and therefore of service, and putting on the garment representing a particular liturgical role would seem to outwardly signify the universal and local dimensions of ministry ('Not only does dress identify a person's function and office in the *local* celebration but it serves also as a kind of sign of the way in which the ministerial order of the *wider* church is represented at the local level...')[30] as well as symbolise the necessary *kenosis* of self for just and authentic liturgical leadership ('Like the redemptive work of Christ which it memorialises and represents, the liturgy is celebrated for the life of the world, not for the personal convenience and consolation of the participants.').[31] Its placement after the imposition of

---

28. Michael Perham, *Lively Sacrifice: The Eucharist in the Church of England Today* (London, 1992) 82-3. Cited in Dick Hines, *Dressing for Worship: A Fresh Look at What Christians Wear in Church* (Cambridge, 1996) 13-14.

29. In addition, while which vestments are the 'correct' vestments has many interpretations, the restoration of ordination candidates coming to the ordination 'each of them being properly vested' in the Ordinal of 1662 points to a long Anglican tradition of the symbol of clothing without the specificity of accompanying formulae. See Puglisi, *The Process of Admission*, 2:137.

30. Hines, *Dressing for Worship*, 14-15.

31. Mark Searle, 'Private Religion, Individualistic Society, Common Worship,' in Eleanor Bernstein, ed. *Liturgy and Spirituality in Context: Perspectives on Prayer and Culture* (Collegeville, 1990) 38.

hands and prayer of consecration parallels the restoration of baptismal clothing following the water bath and chrismation – the putting on of Christ symbolised by the white gown.[32] It is striking to see the early medieval parallels in the baptismal ritual of *Ordo Romanus* XI, where, after the actual baptism, the pontiff goes to his throne and '… the infants are carried down before him and he gives to each a stole and over-garment [*stola, casula*] and chrismal cloth and ten coins, and they are robed.'[33]

Finally, while custom rather than rubrics usually dictates who assists with the vesting, when the normative vesters are members of the order to which the individual(s) has/have just been ordained, a plethora of symbolic associations is possible, ranging from a sense of continuity with ancient rites and an emphasis on presbyteral collegiality to an overly-emphasised initiation into a private club.

The Anointing of Hands

Unlike the vesting with its various and cloudy historical associations, the anointing of the hands has a definitive beginning in place and history. Its appearance in the early eighth century *Missale Francorum* without any extant predecessors tells us that it arose in a Gallican context that may or may not have had direct influence from other churches.[34] The two anointing prayer texts are quite different in their focus; the first hallows the hands so that 'whatever they bless may be blessed…'[35] while the sec-

---

32. For example: '*If the newly baptized are clothed with a white robe, a hymn or song may be used, and then a minister may say:* You have been clothed with Christ. As many as are baptized into Christ have put on Christ.' 'The Liturgy of Baptism,' *Common Worship: Services and Prayers for the Church of England* (London, 2000) 357. However, the *ASB* 1980 suggests the vesting after the declaration, before the imposition of hands!

33. '*Et deportantur ipsi infantes ante eum et dat singulis stola, casula et crismale et decem siclos et vestiuntur.*' *OR* XI, 99. *Casula* is also translated as chasuble, so the vesting items are the same for neophytes and presbyters in these early centuries. *Les Ordines Romani*, Michel Andrieu ed. (Louvain, 1948) 2:446.

34. A variety of hypotheses have been put forth, from indigenous to Spanish to Celtic influence. See Porter, *Ordination Prayers*, 37, and Paul A. Jacobson, '*Sicut Samuhel unxit David*: Early Carolingian Royal Anointings Reconsidered,' in Lizette Larson-Miller ed, *Medieval Liturgy: A Book of Essays* (New York, 1997) 269-70.

35. 'May these hands be consecrated and hallowed by this unction and

ond is much more extended, including references to Samuel anointing David and a probable reflection of the manner of the anointing in the shape of the cross.[36]

The precise source of presbyteral anointing of the hands in the ordination rite has not been found; however, the 'anointing milieu' of the Frankish, Gothic and Gallican worlds was certainly a contributing factor. The parallels between the earliest texts of royal anointing (possibly back to Pippin in 751) and the ordin-ation anointing of the *Missale Francorum* are striking,[37] and point to an inculturated sacralisation of the king as well as a growing monarchical association with priests. But the liturgical source for both of these may well be the rites of initiation as they were inherited and developed within the Merovingian and Frankish churches. This link has been noted by a number of scholars[38] but is worth pointing out in light of the particular task of this essay. The *Bobbio Missal* (c. 700) uses the same text as above for the pre-baptismal anointing: 'I anoint you with sanctified oil, as Samuel anointed David to be king and prophet,'[39] whereas most texts use the related imagery of anointing the baptised priest, prophet and king. The christic association is clear, dependent on various interpretations of 1 Peter and the theological association of the threefold ministry of Christ himself.[40]

our blessing, so that whatever they bless may be blessed and whatever they hallow may he hallowed ...' *Missale Francorum*, L.C. Mohlberg ed., (Rome, 1957); PL 72, 317-340. Cited and translated in Bradshaw 1990, 227.

36. 'May these hands be anointed with hallowed oil and the chrism of holiness. As Samuel anointed David to be king and prophet, so may they be anointed and perfected, in the name of God the Father and the Son and the Holy Spirit, making the image of the holy cross of the Savior our Lord Jesus Christ, who redeemed us from death and leads us to the kingdom of heaven ...' Ibid.

37. From the *Benedictional of Friesing*: 'Unguantur manus istae de oleo sanctificato, unde uncti fuerunt reges et prophetae, sicut unxit Samuhel David in regem ...' *The Benedictionals of Friesing*, Robert Amiet ed. [Henry Bradshaw Society 88] (Maidstone, Kent, 1974) 100-102. From the *Missale Francorum*: 'Unguantur manus istae de oleo sanctificato et cris-mate sanctificationis: sicut uncxit Samuhel David in regem et prophetam ...'

38. See the list of scholars noted in Jacobson, 'Royal Anointings,' 271.

39. The Bobbio Missal at the *effeta*, E.C. Whitaker, *Documents of the Baptismal Liturgy*, Maxwell E. Johnson ed. (London, 2003³) 272.

40. For example, the late sixth century interpretation of Isidore of

Aside from the commonality of all the anointings as symbolic of status change,[41] the baptismal chrismation is linked to baptismal clothing, in that both symbolise putting on Christ.

I anoint you with the chrism of holiness, the garment of immortality which our Lord Jesus Christ first received from the Father, that you may bear it entire and spotless before the judgment seat of Christ and live unto all eternity.[42]

Perhaps the association of the baptismal chrismation text with the anointing of hands in Gallican ordinations also contributed to a physical manifestation of the prayer text which asked that the one to be ordained exhibit the outward qualities of Christ, showing himself 'to be an elder by the dignity of his acts and the righteousness of his life ...'[43]

Regardless of its original association with baptismal chrismation, by the tenth century the ultramontane ritual of anointing the hands had become linked with a formula that clearly set the hands of the anointed apart and made them holy, so that holy hands alone had the power to sanctify.[44] This association of ritual action and text that journeyed to Rome from German lands during the chaos of the eleventh century papacy assured its inclusion in Roman books and from there to the uniformity of the Roman Pontifical of Clement VIII (1596). Not only was the ritual action of anointing the hands made uniform, but also the theo-

---

Seville: 'But according as our Lord was anointed by God the Father, being true king and eternal priest, with a celestial and mystic unguent, so now not only pontiffs and kings, but the whole church is consecrated with the unction of chrism, because it is a member of the eternal king and priest. Therefore, because we are a priestly and royal nation, after baptism we anoint, that we may be called by the name of Christ.' *Concerning the Church's Institutions, Book Two; #26. Concerning the Chrism*, Cited in Whitaker/Johnson, *Documents*, 160.

41. Jacobson, 'Royal Anointings,' 270.

42. *Missale Gothicum*, no 261 at 'When you touch him with chrism you say:' Cited in Jacobson, 'Royal Anointings,' 280. See also the Gelasian Sacramentary, preface for Chrism Mass: '... so that being imbued, as your sacrament shows, with royal and priestly and prophetic honor, they may be clothed with the garment of your perfect gift.' Ibid.

43. Blessing for presbyter (which immediately preceded the anointing of hands) from the *Missale Francorum*. Cited in Bradshaw 1990, 227.

44. The first textual change seems to be in the ninth century Ms B.N. Lat. 2290, See Gerald Ellard, *Ordination Anointings in the Western Church before 1000 A.D.* (Cambridge, MA, 1933) 48.

logical shift from 'putting on Christ' to 'power over the church ... through the power of sanctification.'[45]

In light of this theological shift, it is no surprise that one of the ritual elements missing in the first Anglican Ordinal was the anointing of hands, especially as it had in its contemporary understanding the weight of being a part of the matter and form of ordination.[46] While it is unclear whether Cranmer saw anointing and investiture as permissible ('divers comely ceremonies and solemnities used which be not of necessity')[47] or irrelevant in light of the centrality of the laying on of hands and prayer, the publication of the first ordinal in 1550 did not include anointing, and the Puritan critique of the ordinal made all of the secondary rituals suspect. There were requests during the nineteenth and twentieth centuries for a restoration of 'various medieval ceremonies'[48] from various constituencies, but a quick survey of contemporary Anglican ordinals reveals virtually no official mention of the anointing of hands. Anecdotal and experiential surveys reveal a different story, however, with many presbyteral ordinations including an anointing of hands either before the actual liturgy (a type of 'pre-liturgy liturgy' with bishop and ordinands in private) or an anointing in its traditional 'post-consecration slot' with a variety of accompanying prayer texts. The meaning of a private anointing ('private' as between bishop and ordinands with no congregation) often seems to carry with it a heightened clericalist understanding emerging from a vaguely secret ceremony. The anointings done in the midst of the liturgy are interpreted in a variety of ways depending on what is said as the actual anointing takes place. Additionally, it would appear that in communities where the baptismal chrismation is done visibly and with solemnity the anointing of hands at ordination is capable of functioning within a symbolic relationality, but if

---

45. Puglisi, *The Process of Admission*, 1:156. It would be interesting to trace the parallel developments of this anointing theology with the changed circumstances of parish priests, functioning as 'mini-bishops' in isolated parishes.

46. William Tyndale: 'Last of all, one singular doubt they have; what maketh the priest; the anointing, or putting on of the hands, or what other ceremony, or what words? About which they brawl and scold, one ready to tear out another's throat. One saith this, and another that; but they cannot agree.' Cited in Bradshaw 1971, 7.

47. Thomas Cranmer, responses of 1540. Cited in Bradshaw 1971, 15.

48. Ibid., 161.

there is no referential experience, the representational power of symbol to be 'what it represents'[49] is muted.

The Presentation of Symbols of Office – Traditio Instrumentorum
The handing over of symbols of office associated with a particular order is not present in the earliest rites of ordination. Paul Bradshaw notes that the medieval tradition of the bestowal of symbols of office associated with minor orders is borrowed and added to the ordinations in major orders,[50] gradually assuming more and more importance until arriving at their apex with Thomas Aquinas' opinion that the matter of the sacrament was the *traditio instrumentorum*.[51] The giving of symbols of office for bishops developed the earliest and the most elaborately, linked ritually to the enthronement of the bishop.[52]

The earliest medieval liturgical documents outside of Rome do not mention the *traditio instrumentorum* for the major orders, except to figuratively refer to the gifts of the Spirit received by the ordinand. In the Gallican texts there is a strong emphasis on the charisms of preaching (and evangelisation) for bishops and priests as the primary 'gifts' given.[53] It is in the Carolingian and later texts that the non-Roman emphasis on handing over a 'chalice containing some wine mixed with water, and a paten with some bread'[54] is seen. The emerging formula helps focus the idea of priestly ordination as primarily a reception of power to offer the eucharistic sacrifice: 'Receive the power to offer to God the sacrifice, and to celebrate Mass for the living and the dead. In the name of the Lord.'[55]

Unlike the anointings of priest and bishop and the vesting rituals associated with all three orders, the handing over of the gifts at a presbyteral ordination takes on a distinctive theological emphasis not present in the ordination of a bishop. There the episcopal signs are the staff (from seventh century Spain), signifying local governance, and the ring, signifying authority and

49. Chauvet, *The Sacraments*, 72.
50. Bradshaw 1990, 36.
51. See note 13 above.
52. Already in the Canons of Hippolytus and in the Apostolic Constitutions. Cited in Bradshaw 1990, 111, 114.
53. Puglisi, *The Process of Admission*, 1:144-147.
54. Ibid., 159.
55. Ibid.

jurisdiction.[56] The latter are borrowed primarily from secular and imperial associations, the former, for priests, from cultic and vaguely Old Testament associations.

The Pontifical of William Durandus (c.1293-1295) made a few changes of elaboration with regard to the secondary rites of ordinations (primarily those following communion), and his recension carries through to *PR* 1596 with few changes. In the Roman Rite the *porrectio instrumentorum*, 'the symbolic ceremony of handing to the candidate some instrument representative of his function, as an authorisation to exercise that function'[57] was the heart of the ritual for acolyte and subdeacon, and an important secondary ritual for the three major orders. The English Pontificals were no exception, and continued the long tradition of handing over the gospel book to deacons, the chalice and paten to priests and the gloves, staff, ring, mitre and gospel book to bishops.

In the decade between 1540 and 1550, the debate over Anglican theology of ordination would, of course, influence which ritual elements were maintained and which were dropped or altered. Even with the appearance of the first Anglican Ordinal, a mixture of Lutheran and Roman pontifical elements, how the rituals were received and understood is not clear. The *porrectio instrumentorum* was one of the secondary rituals retained but considerably altered.

> Deacons receive the New Testament instead of the Book of Gospels, priests receive the Bible as well as the chalice and bread, and bishops are given only the pastoral staff and no other symbol of their office ...[58]

The new formula maintained the symbolising of handing over authority without the sacrificial imagery. 'Take thou aucthoritie to preache the word of God, and to minister the holy Sacramentes in thys congregacion.'[59] While handing over the chalice and paten was too much for the Puritans, its omission by 1552, and particularly the omission of the formula identifying this as the power received for a sacrificial priesthood, resulted in

56. Ibid., 160-1. The third episcopal gift, the Book of the Gospels, carries with it the image of the great commission and the gift of evangelisation, 167.

57. Bradshaw 1971, 2.

58. Ibid., 21, n 1.

59. First ... *BCP*, 312.

a debate between Roman Catholics and Anglicans on the validity of the ordinations that continues to this day.[60]

The Ordinal of 1662 retained the handing over of the Bible alone, along with the now traditional text (and the addition of congregational specificity '… where thou shall be lawfully appointed thereunto'[61]) as a secondary symbol of authority and jurisdiction, in many ways repeating what was said at the prayers during the imposition of hands. Throughout the liturgical movement of the twentieth century, calls were made for the expansion of things given at the presentation, which has resulted in a mixture of formulae and symbolic things within the contemporary rites. To name three examples, in the *ASB* 1980 of the Church of England, a Bible is handed over right after the ordination proper, with the formula: 'Receive this Book, as a sign of the authority which God has given you this day to preach the gospel of Christ and to minister his Holy Sacraments.'[62] In the *BCP* 1979 of the United States, the presentation of the Bible is given to the newly ordained immediately after the vesting, with the formula: 'Receive this Bible as a sign of the authority given you to preach the Word of God and to administer his holy Sacraments. Do not forget the trust committed to you as a priest of the Church of God.'[63] The last sentence is unique to presbyteral ordination, and the first sentence modified for diaconal ordination ('Receive this Bible as the sign of your authority to proclaim God's Word and to assist in the ministration of his holy Sacraments.'[64]). Finally, in the Canadian *BAS* of 1985, after the ordination proper and the vesting, the new priest is handed a Bible and a chalice and a paten, with the same formula as the US *BCP*, only adding the necessary 'this chalice and paten'.[65]

It would seem that where the formulae and the symbols of office are maintained as unique to each office, the ritual action contributes to both the unique charisms of each office and to the intrinsic worth of each office, while the commonality of ritual placement unites the three orders. Conversely, the repetition of

---

60. Bradshaw 1971, see particularly chapter 5.
61. *BCP* 1662, *The Form of Ordaining or Consecration of an Archbishop of Bishop*; Puglisi, *The Process of Admission*, 2:138.
62. Ibid., 3:143.
63. *BCP* 1979, 'Ordination: Priest,' 534.
64. Ibid., 545.
65. *The Book of Alternative Services of the Anglican Church of Canada*. Ordination: Priest. (Toronto, 1985) 649.

the same symbolic transfer (of a Bible) would seem to minimise
the necessary differences between the three ordinations and present a ritual contrast to the specifics of each proper ordination
prayer.

Other Symbols of Ordination

In addition to the imposition of hands, vesting, anointing and
presentation of symbols of office, there are many other symbolic
items and actions which occur in an ordination liturgy, only two
of which will be mentioned here. One of the most ancient and
sometimes overlooked symbolic actions is the kiss of peace,
which 'seals' the ordination rite, bridges it to the eucharistic rite,
welcomes the newly ordained into the rank of the ordained, and
truly exchanges the peace of Christ. Prominent already in *The
Apostolic Tradition*, the kiss of peace includes this welcome and
acknowledgement of the newly ordained bishop: 'let all salute
him with the kiss of peace, because of his having been made
worthy.'[66] The kiss of peace emerges as a constant feature of ordinations, although increasingly limited to the clergy alone by
the second millennium of Christianity. In many contemporary
ordination rites of the Anglican Communion, 'The Peace' is
often interpreted as the presentation of the newly ordained to
the congregation, but the exchange of the peace first with the ordaining bishop, and the frequent rubric that the 'new Priest then
says to the congregation: "The peace of the Lord be always with
you"' makes the offering of the peace of Christ the first action
that the newly ordained does, and represents a major turning
point in the liturgy, from '*ordinatio*, expressed in the imposition
of hands and the *epiclesis*'[67] to '*missio*', the assuming of the ministries for which the ordination was accomplished.

Finally, the first of the three major components of ordination,
'*electio*, in which the Holy Spirit acts in the process that involves
both faithful and clergy in the choice of their ministers,'[68] has
one of the clearest historical trajectories in liturgical history, although the manner in which the election has been ritualised has
varied tremendously. The glimpse into the early traditions of

---

66. *Apostolic Tradition*, 4. Literally from the Latin Ms: '… let all offer the
mouth of peace, greeting him because he has been made worthy.' *The
Apostolic Tradition*, Bradshaw/Johnson/Phillips eds, 38.
67. Puglisi, *The Process of Admission*, 3:173.
68. Ibid.

the city of Rome afforded by the *ordines Romani* reveals a sequence of opportunities for the whole Christian community to voice their approval of the candidates, as well as for the ordinands themselves to engage in the symbolic act of swearing an oath on the relics of the saints, attesting to their own ethical and moral health and their vocation to ministry.[69] The continuation of ritual presentations and attestations of worthiness continue to mark the opening of ordination liturgies for centuries, but the first Anglican Ordinal of 1550 added an additional oath-taking, 'The Oath of the King's Supremacy.' The oath recognised the royal head of the Church of England, and was later amended to include subscription 'to the Articles of Religion, the Prayer Book, and the ordinal as containing doctrine "agreeable to the Word of God".'[70] The signing of the oath was generally done prior to the rite, but in a number of contemporary ordination rites of the Anglican Communion, the ordinand must sign the declaration, now greatly minimalised, in public, immediately after the oral declaration has been made.[71] In many cultures the public signing of oaths is not a common practice, and the action makes an impact beyond its intended meaning. When separated from the primary gesture of the imposition of hands and prayer of consecration, it remains one of a sequence of symbolic actions capable of powerful impact, but when it is bunched together with all the other symbolic actions and things and texts it can overshadow the primary action unless that is done with particular grace, time for silence, and solemnity of movement. Perhaps the wisdom of the sequence of the order of ordinations, with some dispersal of ritual symbolic actions through a series of liturgies or rites, would allow the power of the symbols to speak without competing with each other for primacy.

Conclusions

Like any symbol, any liturgy, any sacramental act, ordination means many different things. There is the spectrum of official meaning, the spectrum of public meanings, and the plethora of

---

69. *OR* XXXIX, 1.

70. Marion J. Hatchett, *Commentary on the American Prayer Book* (San Francisco, 1995) 518.

71. 'The Ordinand then signs the above Declaration in the sight of all present.' The same rubric is present in the USA *BCP* 1979 as in the Canadian *BAS* 1985, as well as others.

private meanings.[72] The key theological concepts underlying the IALC document on ordination (see the introduction above) and the accepted ritual shape of election, ordination through prayer and imposition of hands, and the assumption of the new ministry are the foundations of the official meanings. The newest ordination rites from throughout the Anglican Communion reveal both a faithfulness to the longer tradition of 'making' Christian leaders and a yearning toward adopting and adapting symbolic actions and things which express and create a multiplicity of meanings, all contributing to the goal that God's 'people may be strengthened and [God's] Name glorified in all the world.'

72. See Lawrence Hoffman, *The Art of Public Prayer: Not for Clergy Only* (Washington, DC, 1988).

Is there a place for anointing in Anglican ordination rites?

David R. Holeton

It took a long time for Christians to begin anointing with oil at the time of ordination. Today, there is scholarly consensus that the practice was unknown in the ancient churches of both East and West. While anointing is among the most ancient of rites associated with baptism[1] and ministry to the sick,[2] it does not begin to appear at ordinations until centuries later – first in Gaul and then, some centuries later, at Rome. In the Byzantine and Oriental churches, anointing at ordination either remains unknown[3] or, where it exists, was adopted from the Latin use during the time of the crusades.[4] Anointing at ordinations was also unknown in any version of the *Book of Common Prayer* and in any

---

1. It is difficult to say precisely when baptismal anointing first began. There is no clear evidence to confirm that the *sphragis* or seal spoken of in the epistles (2 Corinthians 1:21-22; Ephesians 1:13-14; 4:30) and Revelation (7:2ff; 9:4: 14:1; 22:3ff.) reflect a physical anointing during the first century. Certainly by the second century, however, the texts were understood as referring to an anointing with oil and the ritual practice was firmly (and universally) established.

2. This is, perhaps, the most ancient ritual use of oil by Christians who continued the traditional Jewish use in anointing the sick.

3. The Byzantine rite has no anointings at ordinations (see: *La Prière des églises de rite byzantin*, Feuillen Mercenier and François Paris eds, 2vv. [Chevtogne, 1947²] 1: 373-89) nor do the Alexandrian or East and West Syrian rites.

4. In the Armenian rite, the new presbyter is anointed on the forehead, hands and palms (Henricus Denzinger ed., *Ritus Orientalium*, 2vv. [Würzburg, 1863, Graz, 1963 reprint in 1 v., 2: 314) and bishops are anointed on the head and on both thumbs (ibid 2: 362) – practices adopted from the West. See: Gabriele Winkler, 'Armenia and the Gradual Decline of its Traditional Liturgical Practices as a Result of the Expanding Influence of the Holy See from the 11th to the 14th Century,' in *Liturgie de l'église particulière et liturgie de l'église universelle* (Rome, 1976) 329-368, particularly 339, and Claudio Gugerotti, *La liturgia armena delle ordinazioni e l'epoca ciliciana. Esiti rituali di una teologia di comunione tra Chiese* (Rome, 2001). In the Maronite rite, the hands of the new presbyter are anointed (Denzinger, ibid 2: 155-6) and the new bishop is anointed on his head and hands (ibid 2: 200-1).

Provincial alternative Anglican liturgical text until the waning years of the twentieth century since when provision for anointing at the ordination of presbyters and bishops has begun to appear in several Anglican ordinals.[5] Given the novelty of the practice for Anglicans, a brief review of the history and theology of the practice is important as various Anglican provinces have recently introduced or entertain the possibility of introducing this practice as they continue to renew their ordination rites.

In the older literature on the question, there was a diversity of opinion as to whether the Celtic or Gallican church was first to begin the practice of anointing at ordination.[6] While traces of that debate can still be found, there is broad agreement among scholars that the earliest known witness is found in two prayers for the anointing of the new priest's hands in the *Missale Francorum* – a manuscript now generally dated to the second half of the eighth-century, probably from Poitiers.[7] No anointing was provided at the ordination of a bishop – this first appeared in the *Gellone*, a Gelasian Sacramentary of the eighth century,[8]

---

5. The publication of *An Anglican Prayer Book* of the Church of the Province of Southern Africa in 1989 included provision for an optional anointing of the hands of the newly ordained presbyter (London, 1989, 592). The Anglican Church in Kenya made for a similar provision in its *Our Modern Services: Anglican Church of Kenya 2002* (Nairobi, 2002) 113. The Ordinal which accompanies *Common Worship* in the Church of England allows for the anointing of both presbyters and bishops. *Ordination Services* [GS 1535B] (London, 2005) 43, 70.

6. Beginning in the nineteenth century, some English scholars claimed that the practice originated in the mid-sixth-century Celtic church, and cited a passage from the *De Excidio et Conquestu Britanniae* of Gildas the Wise (c. 545) as proof. These claims passed into some widely circulated liturgical manuals such as Mgr Louis Duchesne's *Origines du Culte Chrétienne* thereby gaining a certain standing. In his *Ordination Anointings in the Western Church before 1000 A.D.* (Cambridge MA, 1933), Gerald Ellard demonstrated convincingly (ibid 9-13) that the text 'furnishes no secure evidence for an ordination sacring in the sixth-century Celtic church' (ibid 13) since when the claims for the Celtic origins of the rite have generally been abandoned by liturgists but not necessarily by the present 'Celtic industry'.

7. *Missale Francorum* (Cod. Vat. Reg. Lat. 257) Leo Cunibert Mohlberg ed, (Rome, 1957) 10 nos. 33-4.

8. Ellard (*Ordination Anointings*, 31) notes the political importance of this innovation, its appearance (both in space and time) being contemporary with the use of an anointing at the coronation of Pepin the Short.

but took some time to appear in other liturgical texts copied for use in Gaul. The reforms of the Carolingian church under Charlemagne attempted to sweep these anointings away when the Gregorian sacramentary was imported from Rome and was ordered to supplant the earlier local liturgical books. As Charlemagne's heirs did not pursue this policy of Romanisation rigorously (and in some ways subverted it) there followed a period when some Gallican ordination rites prescribed anointings (more often of presbyters than bishops) and others did not. Often forgotten in discussions of anointing at ordinations is the question of the anointing of the hands of the deacon, a practice which appears to be well established in parts of Gaul when Archbishop Rudolf of Bourges wrote to Pope Nicholas I in 864. This practice appears to have continued in England and Northern France until at least the twelfth century.[9]

In addition to these liturgical texts, there were other theological works which addressed themselves to the question of anointing at ordination. Theodulf of Orleans (c. 789) suggested to his clergy that, in recalling that they were ordained to the dignity of presbyter, their most important memory should be that their hands had been anointed.[10] Amalar of Metz, some forty years later, writes as if the anointing of the hands of new presbyters is a common practice[11] and effectively makes the anointing of the bishop's head (he makes no mention of the hands) fundamental to the rite.[12] While the historical veracity of these assertions has been challenged,[13] they may well reflect a wider Frankish opinion on a developing liturgical practice.

The place of anointing at ordination (particularly that of a

---

9. Ellard, *Ordination Anointings*, 80-84. He notes that the liturgical witness to the prayers accompanying this anointing ask that whatever the deacon may bless be blessed and whatever he may sanctify be sanctified (ibid 80-1). Such a rite would naturally disappear as the church's understanding of the 'power' to bless and sanctify came to be restricted to those who shared in the 'priesthood' either as presbyters or bishops.
10. Theodulf of Orleans, *Capitulare ad presbyteros parochiae suae* I in PL 105, 192-3.
11. *Liber officialis*, l. II, c. 13,1 *Amalarii episcopi opera liturgica omnia*, Jean Michel Hanssens ed. [Studi e Testi 138-140] (Vatican, 1948,1950) II:226-7.
12. Ibid. l. II, c. 14, 5-8 (Hanssens II:234-5).
13. Ellard, (*Ordination Anointings* 43-4), invoking both H. A. Wilson and Edmund Bishop, suggests that these assertions are what Amalar would like to have happen rather than what was taking place at the time.

bishop) gained untold strength through the incorporation of a number of either forged or heavily edited documents into the *False Decretals* whence they were widely disseminated into the liturgico-canonical literature.[14]

When news of the practice of anointing deacons and presbyters at their ordinations was first heard of by Pope Nicholas I, he replied by saying that not only are there no such anointings at ordinations in Rome but that he had never heard of such a practice taking place in any church and that it would be preferable to follow 'Roman and apostolic' practice and anoint neither deacons nor presbyters.[15] Initial Roman resistance on the matter was swept aside (as it was on other questions[16]) with the imposition of the Romano-Germanic Pontificals, and anointing at ordinations became a part of Roman use in the early decades of the tenth century.

What lies behind the innovation of anointing at ordinations when the churches of both East and West had lived without them for centuries? The question has been answered in various ways. Paul Bradshaw suggests that it is the result of what might be called the 'literalist Gallican mind'. When the Roman rite was imported into Gaul, prayers that had once been understood 'mystically and metaphorically' and which were not accompanied by any ritual sign-act were often associated with newly-created ritual acts and interpreted in a literal fashion unknown in their original context. James F. Puglisi suggests that: 'The auxiliary rites [anointings, investiture and *traditio instrumentorum* among others] multiply, like a theatrical production, to explain the meaning of the prayers which had become inaccessible to the faithful due to the language problem.'[17] While this process

---

14. The issue here seems to have been highly political. Faced with the mistreatment and expulsion of Frankish-appointed bishops by a newly restored Breton king, the anointing of bishops would give them a special (protected) status in the light of the text 'Do not touch my anointed ones.' (Ps 105:15; 1 Chron 16:22 NRSV).

15. Nicholas I, *Epistula* 19, 3 to Rudolf of Bourges (864) in *Sacrorum conciliorum nova, et amplissima collectio*, ed. Giovan Domenica Mansi (Venice 1759-1798) 15:390.

16. It is at this time, for example, Roman resistance to the recitation of the Creed at the Eucharist was also overcome.

17. James F. Puglisi, *The Process of admissioin to Ordained Ministry: A comparative study*, Vol. I: *Epistemological Principles and Roman Catholic Rites* (Collegeville, 1996) 154-5.

might simply be seen as an organic development of the liturgical rites, it is potentially a dangerous one when words, which are not generally understood, have ritual acts imposed on them. The visible, ritual acts quickly came to be understood as being more important than the unintelligible prayers they were intended to exegete. Soon, these new sign-acts became central to the liturgical action and came to assume a meaning independent of (and sometimes antithetical to) the texts they were originally intended to illuminate.

Thus, the metaphysical reference to 'the dew of heavenly unction' in the Roman ordination prayer[18] was understood in Gaul to refer to a physical anointing and came to be ritualised as such – first for presbyters, later for bishops.[19] If the anointing had served only to explicate the meaning of the act of ordination as presented in the historic texts[20] so that the 'dew of heavenly unction' had become one of a number of sign-acts in the rite as a whole, all may have been well. But the innovation took place in a context in which the theological understanding of ordination had evolved from the ancient one, in which the candidate was understood to be ordered for a particular ministry of service in the church, to one in which ordination was understood to bestow a particular sacerdotal character on the candidate and, with it, a certain power over the church. The anointing of the hands of the presbyter became one of the liturgical sign-acts of this new theology of ordination in which there was a bestowal of personal power. Whether the original intention behind the introduction of the anointings was the result of Gallican 'literalism' or an attempt to interpret words that were no longer under-

18. The text is first found in the so-called Leonine Sacramentary. *Sacramentarium Veronese*, Leo Cunibert Mohlberg ed, [*Rerum Ecclesiasticarum Documenta. Series Maior. Fontes* I] (Rome, 1966) 119 no 947; Bradshaw 1990, 215-6.

19. Paul F. Bradshaw: Bradshaw 1990, 18; 'A Brief History of Ordination Rites,' in Church of England Liturgical Commission, *Common Worship: Ordinal* [GS 1535] (London, n.d.) 34; 'What History can tell us about Ordination,' herein pp 59-70. It should be noted, however, that this is not uniquely a Gallican failing. Earlier generations of liturgists often gave a literal meaning to language that was being used spiritually and metaphorically and, from that, claimed anointing to be a patristic practice in both East and West.

20. As from the patristic period the post-baptismal ceremonies had helped to exegete the richness of the baptismal act.

stood, the innovation served to undermine the ancient theology of ordination as transmission of authority to preside over the liturgical assembly (which was ritualised in the imposition of hands and an invocation of the Holy Spirit) and, instead, reinforced a newer understanding of ordination which had come to be seen as the bestowal of a personal character where the anointings were understood as one of the marks which set those who were ordained apart from those who were not. For it was at this time that the 'clergy' emerged as a separate caste within the church, distinct from the *laos*, whose ordination bestowed on them a special character which made them ontologically distinct from the unordained.

As a ritual act, it is easy to see how the anointing at the ordination of presbyters could be seen as analogous to the anointing at baptism as each was a 'seal' understood to signify the imparting an indelible change of character. With this understanding of the clergy as separate and distinct from the *laos*, the anointing at ordination was also susceptible to being interpreted as making the recipients not only distinct but also better than those who had 'just' received the baptismal anointing.[21] Baptism, as the moment of 'ordination' to the royal priesthood, became subsidiary to ordination into the ministerial priesthood. The ecclesiological consequences were to last down to our own age.

Episcopal Ordination or Coronation?

Gerald Ellard[22] and Antonio Santantoni[23] both note the close relationship of the symbiotic relationship between the anointing of hands in the Gallican rites for the coronation of a king and the ordination of a bishop. Ellard writes:

> The appearance at the same time and in the same small area of both kingly and episcopal anointing can scarcely have been without mutual relationships. Which was the older? Did a novelty in the inauguration of a bishop, based ulti-

---

21. I have heard a number of sermons at the baptisms where the bishop explained the anointings he had received at baptism, confirmation and ordination in which it was clear that the latter was the most important of the three.

22. Ellard, *Ordination Anointings*, 31.

23. Antonio Santantoni, *L'ordinatione episcopale. Storia e teologia dei riti dell'ordinazione nelle antiche liturgie dell'occidente* [Analecta Liturgica 2 / Studia Anselmiana 69] (Rome,1976) 166.

mately on Old Testament analogies, recall that Israel's kings, too, had shared the blessings of the horn of oil? Or was it that the anointing of the monarch, howsoever suggested, showed the bishops that a desirable element was lacking in their own ordination?[24]

While, from the sources available, it is still not clear which anointing is of greater antiquity, it is clear that, as the rite for the ordination of a bishop evolved, the preponderance of the images and rites were drawn from those based on power and privilege (similar to those of a king) rather than on those traditionally associated with *episcopé*. Thus, the anointings and other innovations which were perhaps innocent in their inception, served to introduce and reinforce a theology of ordination that was alien to that of the ancient church.

The uncertainty that developed in the sacramental theology of the later middle ages as to what actually was essential for ordination was to complicate matters even more. The importance of the laying on of hands and prayer was so overshadowed by the more recently introduced sign-acts that some theologians held that it was the anointing that was essential and it was that act that conferred the power to consecrate (thus defining the presbyterate in terms of eucharistic ministry alone). Others held that it was the *porrectio instrumentorum* (the handing over of the instruments, e.g. the chalice and paten).[25] While Cranmer's Ordinal made the laying on of hands and prayer central, this question was not resolved for Roman Catholics until the publication of the Apostolic Constitution *Sacramentum ordinis* by Pius XII on 30 November 1947.

This brief review of the history of anointing at ordinations might be sufficient to place Anglicans on their guard, inviting them to question the purpose they might serve in the church today and to ask whether or not they detract from the centrality of the imposition of hands and prayer. If the practice is neither particularly ancient nor a practice found in any historic version of the *Book of Common Prayer*, how are we to understand and account for its recent introduction and spread through Anglicanism?

24. Ellard, *Ordination Anointings*, loc. cit.
25. See Bradshaw 1971, 6-7.

Ordination Anointings in Anglicanism

While anointing at ordination is a novelty in the 'official' liturgies of Anglicanism, the practice has been incorporated into the
use of some Anglo-Catholic dioceses since the early part of the
last century. This was part of the tendency among some Anglo-
Catholics to import as many 'catholic' ceremonies as possible
into Anglican liturgical practice so as to assert the catholicity of
Anglicanism itself. While many Anglicans today would grant
that this ritual borrowing greatly enriched Anglican worship, it
must be admitted that the process of ritual importation was
often not particularly discerning and there was frequently little
critical evaluation of either the antiquity of a practice or of its
associated theology. Gold and dross were imported without distinction. Thus, there appears to be little evidence that questions
were asked either of the antiquity of the practice of anointing at
ordination or of its possible theological implications. No doubt
Leo XIII's publication of *Apostolicae Curae*, with its declaration
that Anglican orders were null and void, pushed some Anglicans
to respond by incorporating into their use of the Ordinal as
many of the ceremonies in the Roman Pontifical as possible – including both the *porrectio instrumentorum* and the anointing of
presbyters and bishops without the slightest concern that both
these ceremonies are of rather late Gallican provenance and sit
ill with the theology of the historic Anglican Ordinal.[26]

Today, the motivation for introducing new ceremonies into
the renewed Anglican rites is much more complex than it was
during the height of the Catholic revival. While there are undoubtedly some Anglicans who would continue to favour the
importation of Roman Catholic or mediaeval customs as a
means of demonstrating the catholicity or historicity of Anglican
practice, their numbers probably would be small. Far more
would be convinced of the merits of a particular rite or ceremony
if it could be demonstrated that the practice was that of the
ancient (patristic) church and that it was an effective means of

---

26. Given the place that the anointing of the deacon's hands had in
mediaeval English tradition, the failure to interpolate the practice into
local uses of the Anglican Ordinal along with the anointing of presbyters and bishops would indicate that the motivation for ritual change
was more driven by a desire to amend what Roman Catholics were calling deficiencies in the Anglican Ordinal rather than by a careful reflection on the liturgical tradition and its theological foundations.

communicating a theology that could be claimed to be consistent with the historic faith of the church as understood within the
Anglican tradition. This raises a number of questions which
need to be posed before the practice of anointing at ordinations
can be endorsed without reserve.

Unresolved questions concerning anointing at ordinations:

1. In the New Testament, the anointing *par excellence* is that of
   Jesus at the time of his baptism in the Jordan. Christians
   share in that anointing at the time of their own baptism. Does
   anointing at the time of ordination detract from the unique
   character of that anointing – particularly when many new
   Anglican baptismal rites provide for an anointing with oil at
   baptism – either as a sign-act itself or in its interpretation
   alongside other anointings?[27]

2. As has been demonstrated, anointing at ordinations is a practice unknown in the patristic church and its subsequent introduction in the medieval west has a very complex history
   related to a significant change in the church's theology of
   ordination. While many liturgical rites have been either mis-
   used in the past or have had theologies imputed to them
   which we would not accept today, the rites themselves have
   been rehabilitated and have become a valued part of contemporary Anglican practice. Is anointing at ordinations a rite
   that is capable of such a rehabilitation or is the clericalism
   which it served to reinforce still so endemic in Anglicanism
   that it risks communicating the message that those who are
   anointed at the time of ordination are in some way set apart
   from the *laos* as a whole?[28]

3. In the history of anointing at ordinations, there was a time
   when deacons as well as presbyters and bishops were anointed.
   If the practice of anointing at ordination is to be restored, is

---

27. This question also needs to be posed of those Anglicans who would
anoint at confirmation.

28. The liturgical texts used for the anointing of presbyters came to be
associated with the priest as the one who had the power to bless and,
particularly, to consecrate the eucharist. Do we wish to narrow the
broad ministry of the presbyterate to blessing and consecrating? The
prayers used in the South African and Kenyan books are (variant)
translations of the modern Roman rite in which the petition asks that
the ordinand might be preserved '... to sanctify [God's] people and to
offer sacrifices of praise and thanksgiving.'

there any reason why deacons should not also be anointed?[29] If the response is that deacons do not 'consecrate' the eucharist, or that they do not have the 'power' to bless, do we not need to ask if our understanding of ordination is consonant with that articulated in the Berkeley Statement *To Equip the Saints* and other contemporary statements found in Anglican ecumenical agreements on ordination?

4. While practice has varied over which orders are to be anointed so that there have been times when only one, sometimes two, and sometimes all three orders were anointed, how (or where) that anointing has taken place has also varied over the ages. The oldest practice appears to have been the anointing of the hands of the newly ordained deacon or presbyter. Bishops were anointed on the head and, some centuries later, on their hands – presumably for those bishops who had never been ordained to the presbyterate and who could, thus, not 'consecrate' the host. A fundamental Old Testament image of the anointing of priests was the pouring of oil on the head.[30] In the rites of those two Oriental Orthodox Churches (Armenian, Maronite) where anointing at ordination takes place, the place of anointing also varies and can include the head, the forehead, the hands, the palms and the thumb. As Provinces consider the permissive use of anointing at ordinations, can a case be made for the anointing of each order to be the same? Are there grounds to suggest that different orders should receive different anointings? If the anointing is to represent a pouring out of the Holy Spirit on the candidate, would an anointing on the head express that best regardless of the order to which a person was being ordained?

5. The prayer used at the time of anointing has also varied over time. In the West, the prayers for presbyters came to focus on the power to bless and consecrate while, for bishops, images drew heavily on those of power and privilege similar to

---

29. In his article in this collection, Bishop George Connor notes that one bishop in New Zealand anoints new deacons on the forehead ('The implications of The Berkeley Statement … in the Anglican Church in Aotearoa New Zealand and Polynesia,' p 164 below).

30. Hence, *To Equip the Saints* (Part II: B: Anointing) suggests: When presbyters are anointed, it might be considered whether the anointing of the head would be a more appropriate symbol of their consecration to service. But this is also a primary reason for the anointing of the head of every Christian at baptism and, this risks a confusion of symbols.

those found in the anointing of a king at his coronation. Neither of these sit well with the theology of the historic Anglican Ordinal nor with modern Anglican ordination rites. What do we wish to say should we anoint at ordinations? Can we find a formula for the anointing of presbyters that does not elevate their eucharistic ministry above the others (preaching, teaching, pastoral care, leadership in the local community)? Finding texts that express something unique to ordination and which do not risk confusing this anointing with the baptismal anointing is a very difficult task, indeed.[31]

As has been outlined in this short study, anointing at the time of ordination has had a very complex history: unknown in the patristic church, unknown to this day in the Byzantine church and in most churches of the East, unknown in the Hispanic church, its appearance in the West was what some would call a product of the 'literalist Gallican mind' which was rejected when first heard of in Rome, and, finally, a newcomer to Anglicanism. Over the centuries the practice has been asked to bear a variety of theologies – some of which are incompatible with the theological understanding of ordination presented in *To Equip the Saints* and other contemporary statements found in Anglican ecumenical agreements on ordination. As are all symbolic acts, anointing is capable of expressing a variety of realities – both positive and negative. History has shown that the act of anointing has been subject to (and, perhaps, demands) frequent re-interpretation. Can we trust that the 'popular' understanding (more that of the clergy than of the laity who will remain, on the whole, unaware of its existence) will not perpetuate a clericalism antithetical to a contemporary Anglican understanding of ordination?

---

31. One might ask if the Church of England texts have not confused the issue by making each anointing rememorative of the baptismal anointing, risking a confusion between the ministry of all who are baptised and ordered ministry of presbyters and bishops. For priests: May God, who anointed Christ with the Holy Spirit at his baptism, anoint and empower you to reconcile and bless his people. (*Ordination Services*, 43) For bishops: May God, who anointed the Christ with the Holy Spirit at his baptism, anoint and empower you to bring good news to the poor, to proclaim release to the captives, to set free those who are oppressed and to proclaim the acceptable year of the Lord. (*Ordination Services*, 70).

Before anointing at ordinations becomes a general practice
within Anglicanism, there appear to be a number of issues to be
resolved: what is the act intended to express theologically?
Given that, until just over fifty years ago, it was held by some
that the anointing was the essential act of ordination (and not
the laying on of hands and prayer), what is the theological significance of anointing intended to be? Will we view clergy who
have been anointed differently than those who have not?[32]
Which orders ought to be ordained? All three? If not, what is the
theological rationale for ordaining some and not others? Where
ought candidates to be anointed? If on the head, how do we distinguish this sign-act from the anointing at baptism? If on the
hands, do we risk affirming a theology of ordination for the purposes of 'consecration' rather than service? All of this is clearly a
matter that invites considerable ongoing reflection and consultation so that Anglican ordination practices that are already
somewhat confused do not become even more muddled still.

---

32. I recall that at the time of my own ordination to the presbyterate, the
diocesan bishop would not anoint – much to the disappointment of
some. Several months later, at the ordination of a priest who was of
Armenian descent (and was to exercise an occasional pastoral ministry
to the Armenian community in the diocese as there was no Armenian
priest), he did anoint on the grounds that 'without the anointing, the
priest's ministry would not be accepted by the Armenians'.

The Presentation of Candidates

Ronald Dowling

Many years ago, as a young priest, I went to our local cathedral (the seat of the provincial archbishop) for the consecration of one of the provincial bishops. The bishop-elect was escorted into the service by two other bishops, and at the designated point in the liturgy was presented by them to the archbishop for the examination and then ordination with the laying of hands. Three other bishops read the scriptural readings, a fourth preached, and then at the climactic laying-on of hands about twenty bishops encircled the candidate, completely obscuring him from view as they did whatever it was that they did – for it was impossible to see. Clearly the bishops had enrolled another member of their 'club'. Only bishops took any active role in this particular ordination liturgy. I was tempted to wonder why the rest of us were there.

This was, of course, in the days in Australia when the *Book of Common Prayer* 1662 was the usage. The ordinal contained in that book required bishops to present candidates for the order of bishop, and the archdeacon to present candidates for ordination as priests or deacons. The entire process was a clergy affair – clergy making new clergy.

The renewals of the second half of the twentieth century brought not only new liturgical texts, but renewed understandings of the nature of the church (the two go together). A renewed and wider understanding of the church as the community of all the baptised, with some of these ordained as well, has led a wider understanding of the role of all the People of God in the ordaining of new clergy. It is now widely accepted that ordination involves all members of the diocese/province, not just the clergy. Paul Bradshaw asserts, and the Berkeley Statement certainly supports, that ordination is 'God's action through the church'.[1] This basic principle should therefore be discerned in every aspect of the ordination liturgy. For this to be abundantly clear, the various liturgical roles need to be exercised by various

---

1. Paul Bradshaw, 'Ordination as God's action through the Church,' *Järvenpää*, 16-28.

representatives of the ordained and lay members of the body of Christ in that particular diocese and/or province.

When it comes to the Presentation of the Candidates there are a couple of issues that might well be considered to show forth that a particular ordination liturgy is an expression of 'God's action through the church'. The first issue is the placing of the Presentation of the Candidate(s). There are two views about this. The first is based on the principle that what happens at the Gathering rite determines or colours the entire liturgical celebration. Therefore the ordination candidate(s) should be presented within the Gathering rite. This makes it very clear that the purpose of this particular assembly is to ordain persons as deacons, priests or bishops.

A second view suggests that the Presentation should be a response to the preached Word, and perhaps the renewal of baptismal faith/promises by the whole gathering. The Presentation would then lead directly to the Examination of the Candidates. If the process of ordination involves selection and examination and the laying on of hands with prayer, then this latter has something to say for itself in keeping all the major elements together. Both places have merit and those planning the ordination liturgy should give consideration to both.

The issue of who actually does the presenting is also a very important one. While some dioceses simply use one or two examining chaplains or the like to do this, there is a good deal to be said for having those who have played a part in the process of the candidate coming to ordination: family members if appropriate, representatives of the person's home parish (lay and clergy), theological teachers, field committee members, examining chaplains or the like, friends and others. The group might also include persons from the candidate's new place of ministry who will receive this new ministry. Presenters should represent a wide spectrum of the church, not just a few personal choices of the candidate. This would then be an icon of the church. To make this very clear the group needs to contain clergy and laity, provincial/diocesan as well as local. Many revised prayer books make this clear in their rubrics which now provide for clergy and laity together to present the candidates. However, some recently revised prayer books still take a minimalist approach in this area.

I am much impressed by the story of the Torres Strait

Islander bishop in northern Australia. The entire home village (where he had been parish priest) physically accompanied him to the cathedral for his episcopal ordination. Along with the two presenting bishops the entire group also presented him to the archbishop.

The Berkeley Statement goes on:

The particular process through which candidates have come to ordination ought to determine who will present them ... during the Presentation the presenters should affirm the candidate's call and readiness for this new and particular ordained ministry. A question concerning calling should follow and be answered by each candidate individually.[2]

Even when a number of candidates are being ordained at the same liturgy, it is important that each candidate answer the question about calling for themselves. It is also preferable that the question be addressed to each candidate in turn.

The Statement goes further:

Sometimes candidates – or others on their behalf – may tell their story, providing informal personal testimony about their experience of vocation but in some cultures it is usually easier for personal information to be conveyed in other ways (for example, printed out or spoken about at the end or after the service).[3]

Again in an ordination liturgy with a number of candidates this may take too much time. An ordination is a lengthy and many-facetted liturgy and each unit or part of the liturgy should be kept in proportion with the others. The centrality of the laying-on of hands needs to be guarded. Extensive, personality-based presentations could easily overshadow this.

For far too many years, ordinations have focused on the ordinand(s) and the ordaining bishop. It is time that the People of God played a full and visible part in the rite.

---

2. *To Equip the Saints*, Part II: The Presentation of the Candidates.
3. Loc. cit.

Music as Theological Expression of Anglican Ordination Rites

Carol Doran

One does not often find the first subject for discussion at an ordination planning meeting to be the ways everyone *other than the ordinand* might participate in the rite. The word 'ordain' itself, meaning 'to invest with ministerial or priestly authority; confer holy orders on,' seems to focus attention on the one or ones receiving that ordination. In fact, 'ordain' is a transitive verb. It describes an action to be taken. In our time, the ones who are taking that action are understood to have an important place in this rite. The liturgical participation of those who have encouraged and supported the formation of the ordinands, who have affirmed their call to ordination and who will gather to witness their ritual entrance into a new ministerial order, follows naturally from their participation in the process leading to ordination.

> Ordination is an acknowledgment by the church of the gifts of the Spirit in the one ordained, and a commitment by both the church and the ordinand to the new relationship. By receiving the new minister in the act of ordination, the congregation acknowledges the minister's gifts and commits itself to be open to these gifts.[1]

A turning away, in recent liturgical revisions, from ordinal patterns which cherished a medieval understanding of ordination has encouraged clear and emphatic discouragement of the expression of clericalist attitudes in ordination liturgies. Louis Weil has written, '… ordination rites must be crafted so that no diminution of the baptismal identity is implied.'[2]

Those who are about to be ordained may not be thinking about the implications of this change when they begin to plan music for the liturgy. The experience of qualifying to receive Holy Orders might seem to earn privilege for the ordinand's choice of music to be sung and played in the liturgy. But a reclaiming of the strong baptismal ecclesiology that has shaped

---

1. *BEM*, Ministry 44.
2. *Järvenpää*.

our understanding of ordination as 'the liturgical expression of the church's appointment of its ministers'[3] also appropriately shapes the planning of music for that ordination liturgy.

The ordinand's favourite music can be blended with music that best expresses the community's voice. And with care, an appropriate balance between word and symbol (which includes body-language, movement, posture, arts, dance as well as music[4]) can be planned. Music and other arts can be 'extremely important in shaping the whole continuum of liturgical action. [They] are carriers of cultural meaning in themselves.'[5]

Willingness to work with such a model of worship planning expresses significant confidence in both the viability of the community's voice and the community's counsel. It also leaves behind the assumption that there is a single 'correct' Anglican way to prepare the musical feast of ordination music. David Holeton cites the Lambeth Conference 1978 as the Conference which '… shifted the weight of appeal from the *Book of Common Prayer* to the *spirit* of the *Book of Common Prayer*, thereby giving a certain approbation to some of the creative forms of liturgical expression which were beginning to emerge in various Provinces.'[6]

This observation is able to be stated in relatively few words, but the implications of appropriating this 'shift' into one's individual life and the life of one's community have shaken the foundations of our practices of corporate prayer in many and dramatic ways. For some, there is discomfort in having the congregation's song accompanied by drums, piano or harp, instead of the more familiar pipe organ. The recent resurgence of the ancient ministry of the cantor, which encourages the people's periodic sung response, may seem to violate a frequently held belief that the liturgical use of a solo voice inappropriately draws attention to the singer. For many people, questions of unity and authority seem just as troubling when expressed in the diversity of the church's song as they do when new liturgical texts are introduced.

This is important because the music in the ordination rite is most effective when it is the music of the community as well as

---

3. *To Equip the Saints*, Part I: The Act of Ordination.
4. *Järvenpää*, 58.
5. Mary E. McGann, *Exploring Music as Worship and Theology: Research in Liturgical Practice.* (Collegeville, Minn, 2002) 20.
6. *Down to Earth Worship*, 6.

the ordinand's music. Those choices which express the intellectual and cultural understandings of the people will be the music they sing with the greatest conviction. The authenticity of such choices are critical because the way in which people take their part in making music in church is a strong indicator of the extent to which the liturgy is genuinely their prayer.

Unlike new texts, which arrive in carefully planned publications, however, new musical practices often develop gradually in the life of a community; e.g. the use of one refrain from the Taizé Community and, later, by many other refrains. Often they may not become the subject of intentional community discussion. Whereas texts are able to be closely examined and evaluated for their theological and poetic values, musical innovations often are embraced or discarded on the basis of how well the community, by their enthusiasm or lack of it, indicates its opinion of the new music or musical practice.

Some people might express themselves verbally, but it is likely to be a comment such as 'I liked that,' or 'I didn't like that,' rather than an analysis of the musical or ritual aspects of the composition. Few of our parishioners are prepared to offer comments such as, 'That chord progression at the end cancels the momentum that had been building up all through the piece,' or 'that hymn is too lively to be sung when we are kneeling.' But whether or not people are prepared to discuss specific choices of congregational music in terms of music theory, it is probably fair to say that most people are well aware of the hymns and songs on which their congregation 'grooves,' or when they are 'all in sync'.[7]

The planning of music appropriate for an ordination might best begin with an agreement by the group to set aside a certain portion of the larger planning meeting for a specific discussion about music. A careful study of the rite (as well as its rubrics) to be used will indicate the places where music is appropriate. Some rubrics are specific: '... the congregation sings a hymn.' Some use the word 'may' when describing, for example, music to be offered before the liturgy begins: 'a hymn, psalm, or anthem may be sung.' Some prayer books state clearly what is

---

7. A recent book by Robert Wuthnow (Berkeley, 2003) was given its title, *All in Sync*, because these words were used by a churchgoer being interviewed by the author to describe the people's experience of strong congregational singing.

assumed by many, that 'Where rubrics indicate that a part of a service is to be "said," it must be understood to include "or sung" and *vice versa*.'[8]

It will be easy to identify, from that list of opportunities for the use of music within the ordination rite, which are appropriately sung by all the people together, by the bishop, by cantors, or by the newly ordained (e.g. the Dismissal, in the case of a deacon). Instrumental music may also be part of the liturgy.

The one text mentioned by name in the ordination rite, frequently identified as 'sung' and, in some sources, printed in the prayer book itself, is the hymn *Veni Creator Spiritus*.[9] Neither its origin nor its date of composition is certain, although it is assumed it was written in the ninth century; it was included (in English translation) in the English Ordinal of 1550.[10] Rubrics often use the words 'is sung' when naming the *Veni Creator Spiritus*. The singing usually takes place during the moments preceding the Prayer of Consecration, when the ordinand kneels before the bishop.[11]

This is a moment of great drama in the rite. Planning for the use of this classic text offers an opportunity to draw upon music's nature to support and enhance liturgical action. Prayer books do not recommend musical settings for the *Veni Creator Spiritus* text. It will be the work of dedicated and prayerful liturgical planners to consider questions which could lead to a decision about an appropriate tune and musical accompaniment for it.

Among the questions to be considered might be: Will the call-and-response model be more likely to encourage the Spirit in this community? Who will be the best leader of this song? Is the bishop an experienced and confident singer, or would the

8. *Book of Common Prayer* USA 1979, 14.

9. Sometimes *Veni Sancte Spiritus* is also given as a choice; *A New Zealand Prayer Book* [1989] says 'A hymn invoking the Holy Spirit may be sung.'

10. Raymond Glover, (ed), *The Hymnal 1982 Companion*, Volume Three B, (New York, 1994) #503.

11. Several of the contemporary prayer books consulted (*The Book of Common Prayer* of the Church of Ireland [2004], *Our Modern Services*, the Anglican Church of Kenya [2002], *A New Zealand Prayer Book* [1989], and *The Alternative Service Book* of the Church of England [1980]) specify the use of the *Veni Creator Spiritus* in ordinations of bishops and presbyters, but not deacons.

bishop be pleased to have a cantor take the leader's role in singing this text responsively? Would it be better for the people to sing a version for their voices alone? Would the choir's singing of *Veni Creator Spiritus* be best because it would leave everyone else to pray silently? Will instrumental accompaniment enhance the singing, or should this be a moment of unaccompanied singing? Is there a similar text which the congregation knows and sings well that would be a better choice for this liturgical moment? Each of these choices will result in a specific outcome. Taking time at the liturgical planning stage to consider each one carefully will yield valuable benefits and minimise disappointment at the ordination itself.

Many factors will shape the decisions to be made by the planners. The size of the space and the relative number of those gathered for the occasion matters a great deal. The kinds of worship and musical experience that have become customary practice within the host congregation will be an indicator of the musical settings in which they will be most comfortable singing and leading their guests' participation. Availability of particular gifts of musical leadership, both vocal and instrumental, should strongly influence the choices of musical settings for the occasion. And the congregation's attitude toward and experience of music itself will determine its role in the ordination rite.

The fact that many who will be present and participate in the ordination may not be members of the host congregation and, in fact, may not have had experience of Christian community and worship should be an important consideration for those planning music. Under these circumstances, it is inhospitable to assume that 'everybody knows' a particular musical selection. It is important to have available, either in hymnal copies available for everyone, or a printed order of worship, both words and music of every selection of congregational music to be sung in the liturgy.

It may even be advisable to take a brief time just before the liturgy begins (not more than five minutes) to welcome the people and introduce music that probably will not be familiar to those assembled. Marion Hatchett reminds us that the need for musical leadership is great because this particular assembly probably has not prayed together before.[12]

---

12. Marion Hatchett, *A Guide to the Practice of Church Music* (New York, 1989) 93.

Consider the reality of this situation when choosing music for the ordination. Enthusiasm simply cannot survive too much unfamiliar music. The guest can be overwhelmed and even discouraged by encounters with an overabundance of new ways, no matter how well-meaning may be the host congregation's intention to welcome their visitors into music with which the *hosts* are entirely comfortable.

The rich and sometimes bewildering culture that emerges in the life of the church can both sustain and stifle the vitality of the church, as well as affect the way in which the church is perceived by those outside. This, in itself, needs to be reflected on in the consideration of order and the celebration of ordination.[13]

The planning committee will be well advised to take time to examine carefully the overall design of the ordination liturgy they are planning. It is likely that there may not be an appropriate place for *all* the musical selections suggested for inclusion in it. Louis Weil writes about a tendency to 'overload and clutter our rites.'[14] '… [F]or the sake of a spiritually sound understanding of what these rites signify, it is crucial that secondary elements be clearly distinguished from what is primary.'[15] Recognition by the church of God's call of the candidate, together with prayer with the laying on of hands are seen as the central focus of all three (deacon, presbyter and bishop) ordinations.[16]

Music's compelling beauty, its potential to express gentleness and, at other times, grandeur, can be useful in clarifying this difference. Unyielding vigilance is necessary to avoid use of either 'decorative frills' or 'Centre-stage Performance,' music simply because someone on the planning committee 'likes' a particular selection.

The Sixth International Anglican Consultation on Liturgy, meeting in Berkeley, California in the summer of 2001 identified these nine elements of the Ordination Rite:[17]

1. *The Gathering of God's People*
   This first act is of critical importance in expressing the church's welcome to all who have come to participate in this

---

13. *Järvenpää*, 54
14. *Järvenpää*, 49.
15. Ibid.
16. *To Equip the Saints*, Part II: A. General Principles 5.
17. *To Equip the Saints*, Part II: B. Elements of the Rite.

ordination. Some communities will choose music that is qui-
etly reverent, using either instrumental or choral music, or
both. The music from the community at Taizé, especially the
Veni, Sancte Spiritu, has been particularly useful here.

Others will want to create a warm and lively welcome by
inviting the participation of all in singing a series of congregational songs and hymns. Themes of these selections may
differ according to the order of ministry. The bishop's calling
to guard the faith, unity and discipline of the church suggests
a body of hymnody different from the deacon's ministry as
'sign and animator of the Christ-like service of the whole
people of God in the world.'[18]

The Gathering may also include the ritual entrance of the
liturgical ministers and honoured guests. Choosing entrance
music which uses a sung congregational refrain will invite
the people's musical participation while, at the same time,
recognising the likelihood that they will be looking at the
procession as it is passing their pew rather than at the hymnal.

2. *The Presentation of the Candidates*

When the Litany for Ordinations is included, an uncomplic-
ated musical setting will encourage all to participate in this
prayer. The one leading the Litany could be a musically gifted
member of the congregation.

3. *Proclaiming and Receiving the Word of God*

The Gradual Psalm offers an appropriate musical offering
during this section of the liturgy. The responsorial pattern,
with cantor and brief congregational refrain, is particularly
welcoming to ordination guests who might be unfamiliar
with the practice of chant.

4. *Re-affirmation of Baptismal Faith*

The Creed might be sung on a monotone. Unless the host
congregation normally sings the Creed, however, an occasion such as an ordination attended by many guests from
outside the congregation would not be an appropriate time
to introduce the practice.

5. *Exhortation and Questions*

This exchange between the bishop and the one(s) to be ordained normally is not sung.

6. *Prayer with the Laying on of Hands*

With the candidate(s) kneeling before the bishop, a hymn in-

---

18. *Järvenpää*, 9.

voking the Holy Spirit (usually Veni Creator Spiritus) is
sung.
7. *The Welcome*
   The people's acclamation might include spontaneous (or
   planned) singing and drumming.
8. *Celebrating at the Lord's Table*
   The musical settings of the Eucharistic Prayer as well as the
   Holy, Holy, Holy Lord, the Great Amen, the Lord's Prayer
   and Fraction Anthem should probably be the ones the host
   congregation sings best so that their strong voices might give
   comfort and leadership to those who may be singing them
   for the first time. These brief congregational responses
   should be printed (with permission to copy sought and received) in the worship programme with the assumption that
   newcomers are not likely to be able to find them in the hymnal rapidly enough to enable their singing with the group.
9. *Going out as God's People*
   The sung blessing and dismissal, with joyful Alleluias, is a
   fitting conclusion to this rite.

Music's ability to express the theology of Anglican ordination rites will be moderated by the abilities and experience of
the ordaining community in welcoming its participation. The
two persons who will make music's functioning effective will
be, as always, the congregation's ordained leader and its musician. The ordained leader has oversight of all that is carried out
liturgically in the congregation and the musician is called to assist the people to draw on their musical gifts to help build up the
Body of Christ, the congregation.

The occasion of an ordination provides a particular framework for this work, which, in fact, is carried out on a daily basis,
but will be formed according to a specific design for the purpose
of this particular liturgy. The ordinand's conviction about
music's potential to participate in the community's prayer will
also be a vital force in planning the liturgy. In the best of all possible situations, the memory of the full-bodied singing of all who
will surround and join in prayer for the ordinand's new ministry
can inspire that ministry for a lifetime.

The Church of England

Paul Bradshaw

Although the 1662 ordination services still remain a legal option in the Church of England, the rites used at virtually all ordinations up to the end of 2005 were those of the *Alternative Service Book 1980*. The other rites in that book ceased to be legal at the end of the year 2000, when they were replaced by those in the new *Common Worship* series (hereafter *CW*), but as no provision had then been made for ordination services in this collection, the life of the *Alternative Service Book* ordination services was extended to the end of 2005 in order to allow time for new rites to be drawn up and approved by the General Synod of the Church of England. There are a number of ways in which these new rites, authorised for use from September 2005, incorporate elements that were listed as desirable in the 2001 Berkeley statement and had not been part of earlier English ordinals. The most significant of these are as follows:

The IALC statement proposed that the gathering rite should 'convey the sense that the whole church is coming together to order its life for ministry' and suggested that one possibility was for there to be a brief dialogue between bishop and people, 'setting the context by celebrating the ministerial gifts of the whole church'. The *CW* ordination rites all begin with such a dialogue:

There is one body and one spirit.
There is one hope to which we were called;
one Lord, one faith, one baptism,
one God and Father of all.

This is then followed in each case by a statement by the president about the church and about the baptismal calling of all God's people, before it speaks of the particular ministry about to be conferred.

The IALC statement also proposed that the candidates should be seated at the beginning of the service with those with whom they were closely linked rather than with the rest of the clergy. The *CW* rites in a note permit this as an option, and suggest that the ordinands sit with those who are to present them.

The IALC statement suggested that the choice of those to present the candidates should be determined by the particular process by which they had come to ordination. While the *CW* rites do not specify who should be involved in the presenting the candidates, they do suggest who might be the appropriate persons to answer the questions that are then put about their call and preparation. In the case of deacons it could be 'the Director of Ordinands or someone who has been involved in the ordinands' formation and training'; and in the case of priests, 'the training incumbent or someone who has been involved in with each ordinand's formation and training'. The archdeacon, who was traditionally responsible for presenting the candidates and answering the questions for both deacons and priests, is given responsibility for testifying that the necessary oaths have been taken and declarations made. In the case of a diocesan bishop, the rite suggests that the presentation may be made and the questions answered by representatives of the diocese of which he is to be bishop, including a lay person, and in the case of a suffragan bishop by his diocesan bishop (who will have nominated him for the office).

The IALC statement encouraged the use of the readings of the day. While the *CW* rites continue to provide appropriate readings for ordinations to each order, they do permit the use of the readings of the day, 'especially on a Principal Feast or a Festival'. The IALC statement also asserted that 'the questions put to the candidates should focus on the specific qualities and duties required of the particular order', and that after this was 'the appropriate point' … 'for the bishop to ask the people if it is their will that the candidates be ordained.' The *CW* rites have followed this pattern.

The IALC statement said that the ordination prayer might be punctuated by 'appropriate congregational responses'. Provision has been made for this as an option in the *CW* rites. The words 'Lord, send your Spirit' or any other suitable invocation of the Holy Spirit may be used as a response at the end of each paragraph of the ordination prayer; and it may be introduced by an appropriate phrase. The IALC statement also insisted that 'the way in which bishop, ordinands, and others move to and from the hand-laying should not by fussiness detract from the central act, nor should it destroy the unity of the presidential prayer.' This is echoed in the note in the *CW* rites that states that 'it is important that any movement during the Ordination Prayer does not detract from the unity of the prayer as a whole.'

The location of the giving of the Bible gave rise to a certain amount of dissension at Berkeley, some wishing to keep the traditional Anglican custom of doing it immediately after the ordination prayer, whereas others thought it more appropriate for it to be transferred to the final part of the service, because it fitted naturally into the sending out of the newly-ordained; and both points of view are reflected in the IALC statement. A similar division of opinion existed in the English Liturgical Commission and in the General Synod itself, and so the CW rites also allow for either position to be adopted.

The IALC statement argued for a restoration of the ancient custom of a ceremony of welcome by the church after the ordination prayer, and this has been done in the CW rites. It is initiated by a member of the same order to which the newly ordained have just been admitted and continued by the whole congregation, drawing on scriptural verses appropriate to each of the orders.

At the ordination of a deacon, a deacon says to the newly ordained:

We preach not ourselves but Christ Jesus as Lord,
and ourselves as your servants for Jesus' sake.
We welcome you as fellow servants in the gospel:
may Christ dwell in your hearts through faith,
that you may be rooted and grounded in love.

At the ordination of a priest, the dean, an archdeacon or another senior priest says,

God was in Christ, reconciling the world to himself,
and has given us the ministry of reconciliation.
We welcome you as ambassadors for Christ:
Let the word of Christ dwell in you richly.

In the case of a bishop, one of the bishops present says,

Guard the truth that has been entrusted to you
by the Holy Spirit who lives in us.
We welcome you as a shepherd of Christ's flock.
Build up the Church in unity and love,
that the world may believe.

The exchange of the Peace in the eucharistic rite then follows. The IALC statement proposed that at the end of the service

there should be a 'handing over' by the bishop of the newly ordained to representatives of those among whom they will serve.
This has been included as an option in all the *CW* ordination
rites.

Finally, the IALC statement raised the possibility of the use
of anointing in ordinations. The *CW* rites allow for priests to be
anointed on the palms of their hands, and for bishops to have
their heads anointed before the ceremony of welcome. A formula,
differently worded for each order, is provided to accompany
this optional action.

The Church of Ireland

Brian Mayne

The Church of Ireland was represented at Kottayam and Berkeley by Bishop Harold Miller, chair of the Irish Liturgical Committee, and by Brian Mayne, who also took part in the interim conference at Jarvenpää in 1997. As our province was in the middle of a thoroughgoing revision of the Irish *Book of Common Prayer*, the relevance of the Berkeley Statement to our work was immediate. Our province would be probably the first to have ordination services re-shaped under its influence. Just as previous IALC Statements from Toronto and Dublin influenced the modern initiation and eucharistic rites already agreed for the new edition of the Prayer Book so the Berkeley Statement was carefully considered. That a representative consultation of the whole Anglican Communion had drawn up a statement and made recommendations to provinces revising rites meant that, although it was just over ten years since the Church of Ireland had moved from the 1662 ordination services, General Synod was prepared to accept changes to what had already become well-accepted services.

As soon as the Statement was available, all members of the Liturgical Advisory Committee (LAC) were circulated with it and Bishop Harold and I answered questions about it at a meeting. Bishop Harold passed copies to the other bishops and warned them that the forthcoming draft ordination rites would reflect the thinking that lay behind it.

We consulted Paul Bradshaw before proposing a first draft to the LAC. Bishop Harold and I presented this to the Committee over two sessions. Harold vacated the chair for these meetings to facilitate those who had contrary views or serious doubts. With one exception the idea of an underlying baptismal ecclesiology was accepted. That one voice came from one who has a very low view of baptism and who has successfully prevented any progress on the admission of children to communion before confirmation.

In the opening Gathering of God's People a dialogue between the bishop and congregation sets ordination within the whole ministry of the baptised people of God. Sponsors present the ordinand (even when a bishop is to be ordained). The Collect is the same for each order and is a prayer for all God's people in their vocation and ministry and for those now to be ordained. The Creed is introduced by the words: 'Mindful of our baptism we proclaim the faith of the universal church ...' The first draft offered the Apostles' Creed but that proved a step too far for those used to ordination taking place after the Nicene Creed, so although the Nicene Creed is only the creed of baptism in the Eastern Church that is the creed ordered in these services.

The charges in all three rites have been shortened from the 1991 rite that was almost identical to that in the *Alternative Service Book* of the Church of England. Parts of each charge have been relocated into the prayer with the laying on of hands and into final exhortations at the end of the service. The committee, to restore the 'chill' factor in the charge for priests, added two paragraphs to the draft: this emphasises the heavy responsibility of ministry. Unfortunately, as with such amendments, the paragraphs stand out as being in a different style! After the ordinands have responded to the bishop's questions the congregation is asked if it is their will that the candidates should be ordained. This was not in the Irish 1991 rite.

The ordination prayers reflect the character of the different orders and are to be prayed with all standing – the bishop no longer sits monarch-like. The laying on of hands occurs within the prayer. There are two forms of this: in one congregational responses are interpolated at the end of each paragraph, 'Glory to you, Lord' to the thanksgiving paragraphs before the laying on of hands, and 'Pour our your Spirit, Lord' to the petitions of the bishop after the laying on of hands.

Vesting in the 'customary manner' may take place after the ordination prayer 'if this has not already been done' and in the notes to the ordinal it is suggested that the ordinand be vested in the vesture of the order before the service begins. This option was taken in several ordinations in 2004 and certainly assisted the 'flow' of the service. In the draft the giving of the Bible was moved to a position at the end of the service as suggested in the Berkeley Statement, but after the bishops saw the draft they insisted on the giving of the Bible being restored to its traditional position. There is no tradition in the Church of Ireland of other 'gifts' being handed over at the ordination of priests. The pastoral staff is to be presented to a new bishop after the blessing who, carrying the staff and the Bible received earlier, leads diocesan representatives out of the church.

The ordination services were presented to General Synod for first reading in 2002 and received final approval in 2003. The only change to the draft was a restoration of the Bible references for the readings so the Berkeley preference for the readings of the day was placed in a secondary position. This reflected existing practice rather than because it was well thought out. Bishops and clergy are so used to special 'ministry' readings at cathedral ordinations that they cannot see the significance of the eucharist of the day as the setting for ordination. An attempt was also made to remove the alternative ordination prayer with its congregational participation but the committee successfully argued for the more obvious participation of all the baptised in the prayer.

Summer ordinations in 2004 were the first at which the new ordination rites were used throughout the Church of Ireland. Experience is that they worked smoothly. Lay and clerical sponsors presented those to be ordained deacon and priest and parish representatives accompanied each new deacon and priest as they left the worship area at the end of the service. Ideas, which had crystallised over three important meetings of IALC, were taking shape before our eyes.

The Episcopal Church in the Philippines

Tomas S. Maddela

Introduction

Until the early 1970s, ordination services in the Episcopal Church in the Philippines (ECP) were celebrated using the form in the 1928 *Book of Common Prayer* of the Episcopal Church in the United States of America (ECUSA). Subsequently, the form of Ordination for Trial Use became the normative rite. When the ECUSA 1979 *BCP* was ratified, the forms of Ordaining Bishops, Priests and Deacons contained in that Prayer Book became the normative rites.

In the early 1980s, as plans for the eventual autonomy of the ECP from ECUSA were being laid down, the work of drafting the various rites which would go eventually into the ECP's *Book of Common Prayer* also began. The first rites to be drafted, reviewed and approved for Trial Use were The Holy Mass, Holy Baptism, The Celebration and Blessing of Marriage, and The Divine Offices of Morning and Evening Prayer. It was not until 1988 that the first draft of the 'Rites of Ordination of a Bishop, a Priest, and a Deacon' were initially reviewed by the National Commission for Liturgy and Christian Education. This first draft represents materials almost entirely drawn from the 1979 *BCP* of ECUSA with a few and minor amendments. The draft underwent review five times more over the course of eight years. In 1996, ECP Synod approved its trial use. The rite for Trial Use practically followed the 1979 *BCP* of ECUSA in its entirety and it was in this form when it was incorporated with the rest of the *BCP* materials eventually ratified during the 1999 Synod, in time for the celebration of the ECP's Centenary.

One can take comfort, however, from the fact that the actual use of the rite has seen numerous revisions in the different dioceses, especially as translations in the local dialects came into vogue. These, however, may be seen as cases of liturgical accommodation rather than serious attempts at inculturation. In general, however, one can discern certain principles at work in the celebration of ordination:

1. Ordination rites in the ECP are grounded in a baptismal ecclesiology which *not only sets ordination to particular ministries
   firmly within the context of the ministry of the whole people of God,
   but also demonstrating the principle that 'in, through and with
   Christ, the assembly is the celebrant…'*
2. The ECP also accepts the principle that an ordination service
   is an ecclesial event in which the church's life and ministry is
   ordered. It is thus normative to celebrate it in the context of
   the principal eucharist on a feast day.

   It is customary for ordinations in the ECP to take place on a
   major feast that falls on a weekday, rather than on a Sunday,
   but always in the context of a Solemn Eucharist. This enables
   as many clergy and laity as possible to be present at the celebration. Consideration is especially given to those coming
   from the remotest parts of the diocese especially in view of
   the fact that it has become obligatory for all clergy of that diocese where the ordinand(s) is (are) canonically resident to be
   present on the occasion.
3. Contrary to the principle that each ordination service should
   be for only one order to make clear the distinct character of
   diaconal, presbyteral, and episcopal ministries, in the ECP
   this holds true only in the case of ordination to the episcopate. It is common to hold ordinations to the presbyterate
   and diaconate at the same time. There has never been a case
   though, where an ordination service also became an occasion
   for the Licensing of lay ministers.

   It is now also an accepted practice in the ECP for an ordinand
   to be wedded on the same occasion as his/her ordination.
   The reason for this is largely economic. In Filipino culture,
   great occasions call for exuberant festivities with extravagant
   feasts. Although unwritten, there are community expectations concerning the nature of the feast that must accompany
   an important occasion and they can be economically burden-
   some for the host.

General Features of the Rites of Ordination

Preparation for Ordination
Although not an integral part of the ordination service itself but
one that flows into it, it has become normative in the ECP to
require the candidate for ordination to go on a spiritual retreat
from two to three days prior to the service of ordination itself. In

the case of a candidate to the episcopate, a bishop normally conducts such retreat. In the case of ordinands to the priesthood and diaconate, a bishop or any clergy from the diocese, nominated by the candidate, may conduct it. On the eve of the ordination, while the retreat is ongoing, a Vigil of an Ordination Service may be held, during which time, the liturgical vestments with which the candidate will be vested at the time of ordination may be blessed. In the meantime, for the duration of the retreat, the candidate is in clausura, neither being allowed to be seen or spoken to by anyone except the retreat master until after the formal presentation of the ordinands during the service itself.

The Entrance Rites
At the appointed time of ordination, if the place where the retreat is being held is not far from the church where the ordination will take place, the solemn procession at the start of the ordination service may begin from there. In such a case, many of the clergy and laity may join in the procession.

Otherwise, it starts from another suitable place outside of the church. Prior to the start of the procession, the chief ordaining bishop or consecrator inquires from the retreat master if each candidate is ready to proceed. If the retreat master responds affirmatively, the procession commences. If the retreat master, however, feels that there is reasonable cause to believe that the candidate has yet doubts or scruples that need to be resolved, s/he may advise the bishop to call off the ordination or postpone it.

It is customary to begin the ordination service with a solemn procession of the candidate with the presentors (comprising of representatives of the clergy and laity of the diocese), the assisting ministers (acolytes, chaplains to the bishop, master of ceremonies), the retreat master, the ordaining minister and co-presiders. Candidates for ordination to any order wear only albs with their hoods entirely covering the head.

The procession may be accompanied by traditional instrumental music or hymn singing by the whole congregation while church bells joyfully ring.

As soon as the procession enters the church, the candidates are immediately seated apart from, rather than with, those with whom they are closely linked as regards their ministry.

After the customary salutations and Collect for Purity, the

Preface to the Ordination Rites is read. There have been objections in the past from individual theologians against the inclusion of the reading of the *Preface* since the whole service has a strong didactic character enabling the people to understand the distinctiveness of each of the ordered ministries. Despite these objections, however, the practice continues to persist.

The Presentation

Following the reading of the *Preface to the Ordination Rites*, the candidate is presented. When there are two or more candidates, they are presented individually. When the service involves conferral of two different orders, the candidates for the priesthood are presented first.

While lay people are included among those who present the candidates, my personal observation is that, with a few exceptions, included also are those who have no participation at all in the discerning and nurturing of the candidate's call to ordained ministry. They are customarily nominated by the candidate and approved by the ordaining bishop.

In the case of the consecration of a bishop, immediately after the presentation, the chief consecrator requires that the *Testimonials* be read. Appointed readers then read in turn the Evidence of Election, the Evidence of Ordinations, the Consent of the various Standing Committees of the dioceses of the Province, and the Consent of the Bishops of the Province.

In the case of ordination to the priesthood and diaconate, the service proceeds immediately with the Promise of Conformity which the candidate recites with his/her right hand raised. It has become common practice also to require the candidate to sign a written form of the Promise of Conformity which is then attested to by the presenters who also sign the document in the sight of all present.

Litany for Ministry

The assent of all people is then obtained. If no objection is made, the service proceeds with the singing of the Litany for Ministry which is led by appointed cantors. All kneel while the candidate(s) prostrate(s). The text of the Litany is uniform for all orders and serves as the form of intercession. It thus includes prayers for the world, the church and its mission, all sorts and conditions of people, as well as special petitions for the ordinand(s) and his/her household.

The ordaining bishop or chief consecrator concludes the litany with the collect for the church or mission and the Collect of the Day.

The Liturgy of the Word
The proclamation of the word has always been an integral feature of the ordination service. On principal feasts or major feast days, the readings are taken from the proper of the day. Otherwise, they may be taken from a list of recommended readings for ordination. On this solemn occasion, it is also customary to chant the gospel using traditional style. It has become a common practice for the homily to be in two parts: The first part is normally an exposition of the appointed scriptural readings and the second part is a 'Charge' to the candidate(s).

In the consecration of a bishop, the Examination follows immediately after the homily and the bishop-elect leads in the recitation of the Nicene Creed after the Examination and before the Prayer of Consecration. At the ordination of a priest and/or deacon, the recitation of the Nicene Creed precedes the Examination.

The Examination
The Examination is conducted by the ordaining bishop or chief consecrator seated at the centre of the chancel while the candidate stands before him. The first part of the Examination is the charge to the candidate and defines the nature of, and the responsibilities pertaining to the office to which s/he will be ordained and followed by a series of questions ascertaining that the candidate freely and willingly submits him/herself to fulfilling the tasks being entrusted to him/her. When there are other bishops present, it is customary to assign to each bishop a part of the Examination.

The Prayer of Consecration
The Prayer of Consecration begins with the responsive singing of the *Veni Creator Spiritus* or *Veni Sancte Spiritus*, with the ordaining bishop singing the first part of each versicle and all others responding by singing the second part. This is always followed by a period of silence, during which time, all pray in their hearts for the sending of the Holy Spirit. Then the ordaining bishop begins the Prayer of Consecration and at the moment of

Epiclesis, all bishops present lay their hands on the bishop-elect; the bishop and all priests present lay their hands on the candidate to the priesthood, and the bishop alone on the candidate for the diaconate.

The Vesting of the Newly Ordained

Immediately after the Prayer of Consecration, the ordaining bishop takes off the hood of the newly-ordained and sponsors (donors of the vestments) are called upon to vest him/her with their proper eucharistic vestments in the sight of all present.

At the consecration of a bishop, the new bishop is also presented with the pectoral cross, mitre, ring, pastoral staff and a Bible. At the ordination of a priest, the newly ordained is presented with a Bible and a chalice and paten. At the ordination of a deacon, the newly ordained is presented only with a Bible. The giving of these symbols of office are all accompanied by euchological formulae explaining the significance of each.

Presentation of the Newly Ordained

After having been vested, the ordaining bishop formally presents the newly ordained to the community. It is customary also to ask immediate family members and relatives of the newly ordained to come forward and join in the presentation. People normally greet the newly ordained with either applause or fanfare. It is common also to ring the bells joyfully during this time.

The Eucharist

It is customary for the newly ordained bishop to preside at the Liturgy of the Eucharist and give the pontifical blessing at the end. The newly ordained priest co-presides with the bishop and may give the blessing. The newly ordained deacon takes his/her place at the eucharistic table and exercises his/her diaconal liturgical ministry then.

Post-Eucharistic Blessing

When a bishop is ordained, immediately after the dismissal and prior to the recessional, it is customary to request the new bishop to be seated on a chair at the centre of the chancel and for all the bishops and clergy present to kneel individually before him/her to receive a blessing. Lay people may also come forward to greet the new bishop and receive the blessing. Gifts may also be presented at this time.

When a priest is ordained, the same honour is bestowed upon the newly ordained or this may be done after the priest's First Sung Mass (*Missa Cantata*) on the Sunday following the ordination. This, too, is customarily celebrated with much fanfare and festivity.

At the ordination of a deacon, the newly ordained stands by the door of the church after the service to receive the greetings of the people as they come out. Gifts may also be presented to him/her at that time.

Conclusions

From the foregoing description of the key features of the rites of ordination in the ECP, it is easy to see that the work of the IALC on ordination has had barely an impact. While maintaining the core of the ordination rite, which is the laying of hands and the invocation of the Holy Spirit, the rites easily yield to the pressures of what may be considered as the genius of the Filipino culture – preference for the ceremonial, exuberant and festive elements. It is not hard to see how secondary elements can easily be magnified and assigned values which they do not deserve although care is always exercised that this is not done at the expense of the essential elements.

This, however, lends the celebration a good balance. While its language is too legalistic and so theologically cerebral, it is, at the same time, garbed with elements that touch the emotions and aesthetic sense of worshippers. The celebration can, in fact, be regarded as a cultural event to which tribal Filipinos can easily relate.

It must also be insisted that the rites have very strong didactic qualities. What the written language fails to achieve – lead the people to a clear understanding of the nature and meaning of ordination and ministry – the ritual accompaniments are able to supply.

It is part of the agenda of the ECP to review all existing vernacular translations of the rites and make them more expressive of the thought-patterns of the Filipinos (e.g. through use of dynamic equivalence) and at the same time imbue the rites with more cultural values, e.g. recognition of and reverence for leadership, hospitality, and openness and adaptability to changes.

Aotearoa, New Zealand and Polynesia

George Connor

Introduction

The Ordinal used in the Anglican Church in Aotearoa New Zealand and Polynesia is the one printed in *A New Zealand Prayer Book – He Karakia Mihinare o Aotearoa* 1989. This generally follows the pattern set by The Ordinal 1980 which in turn was influenced by ECUSA's 'Prayer Book Studies 20 - The Ordination of Bishops, Priests, and Deacons' published in 1970 as part of that church's preparation for their *Book of Common Prayer* 1979.

The introductory note to the 1989 Ordinal states:

The provision of an ordained ministry, to serve the local congregation in the name of Christ and the universal church, is one of the responsibilities of the apostolic church. These services provide for the ordination of such ministry.

The Ordination Liturgies follow a common pattern and are based on a common understanding of ministry. In each service of ordination the words used at the introduction to the presentation of the candidates acknowledge that all Christians have a ministry by virtue of their baptism, and that some members of the baptised community are also called and empowered to fulfil an ordained ministry, and to enable the total mission of the church.

Within the ordained ministry there are three orders: deacons, priests (also called presbyters) and bishops. Each order is equally important; yet those in the various orders differ in the tasks they do on behalf of the whole church. The description of these tasks is set out at *The Presentation* and *The Commitment*.

The assent of the people that the candidate should be ordained is an integral part of the service.

The set readings highlight the biblical understanding of ministry, and in the sermon the preacher proclaims the enabling power of the Holy Spirit to provide the appropriate gifts of ministry.

In *The Commitment*, the candidates affirm their standard

of faith and their willingness to minister within the discipline and authority of the church. They express their spiritual lifestyle and their dependence on God for their gifts of ministry.

The Invocation is followed by *The Ordination*.

The whole ordination is set within a *Liturgy of the Eucharist*, using any of the authorised forms.

These services, allowing for an appropriate definition of the role of each order in ordained ministry, affirm the understanding of the church that all ministry has its source in Christ's ministry, and is part of the response to the command of Christ to the church to fulfil its apostolic mission. [ANZPB-HKMOA page 887]

Most of these principles are echoed or further spelled out in The Berkeley Statement. This is true not only of the various sections of chapter one, 'The Ordered Nature of the Church', but also of the details referred to in chapter two, 'The Liturgy of Ordination'.

Changes in ordination liturgies since A New Zealand Prayer Book –
He Karakia Mihinare o Aotearoa
The only legislative changes made to the Ordinal in our Prayer Book since its initial authorisation relate to the instructions on what to do 'when it is necessary to ordain deacons and priests in one service' [see *Additional Directions* – ANZPB-HKMOA page 922].

The original instruction provided for the following sequence: The Presentation of deacon candidates, The Presentation of priest candidates, and later after the Proclamation and Affirmation of Faith, for the full deacons' sequence of Commitment, Invocation, Ordination, giving of the New Testament, before the full priests' sequence of Commitment, Invocation, Ordination, and giving of the Bible.

This was found to be cumbersome, and the General Synod agreed to, in 1998 and confirmed in 2000, a new direction allowing the deacons' and priests' presentations to be in a combined form, i.e. with all the common elements said only once, for the Commitment to be amalgamated, the Invocation said only once, and then the Ordination of a Deacon to be followed by the Ordination of a Priest and then the giving of the New Testament and the Bible, and the vesting and giving of symbols of ministry after the Ordination of the priest(s).

No changes to the Ordinal but changes to the way of ordering the service as a result of the growth of Local Shared Ministry parishes and Ministry Support Teams

The Common Liturgical Commission (this is a three Tikanga commission; for an explanation of 'Tikanga' see below) was asked to consider a separate ordinal for use in Local Shared Ministry / Mutual Ministry parishes where there was a Ministry Support Team of which those ordained were a part. This was not agreed to but the Commission, after discussion with the bishops, supported a way of ordering the service by way of informal additions which preserved the integrity of the ordination liturgy but showed the mutual ministry principles more clearly.

Despite the clear statements about the nature of the ministry of all the baptised in the Presentation it was thought helpful to include further direct reference to baptismal ministry in the Gathering of the Community and to balance the sense of overemphasis on the ordained by introducing a new section for *The Renewal of Baptismal Vows* before the Presentation. This provided for an introductory paragraph, the responsive questions about reaffirmation and faith commitment with prayer from the confirmation service. After the Presentation and before the people's acclamation for the candidates for ordination a new section allows the ministry of the Ministry Support Team, including those to be ordained, to be acknowledged. After the Invocation and before the ordination the Ministry Support Team is *re-commissioned* with prayer, then the ordination proceeds. The Prayers of the People, which were omitted in the 1989 Ordinal, may follow vesting and greetings.

There are no changes to the actual formularies of the ordination liturgy.

Direct Ordination

In 2002 the General Synod/te Hīnota Whānui received the Berkeley Statement *To Equip the Saints* and commended it to bishops and episcopal units.

In the episcopal units interest arose from two aspects of the matter. For some there was interest in clarifying the difference between vocational deacons and transitional deacons. In Local Shared Ministry situations where some were being called to be deacons and others being called to be priests the view was expressed that it was inconsistent for the bishop to ask the deacon candidate 'Do you feel called to the office of a deacon?' when they had been called to be a priest and not a deacon, though the church says they must become a deacon first.

Because of this interest expressed by some dioceses and the feeling that the matter ought to be examined more carefully, the Standing Committee of General Synod appointed a Commission on Doctrine and Theological Questions to consider doctrinal implications and report to the 2004 General Synod/te Hïnota Whänui.

'The Doctrine Commission noted:

- Theological arguments and historical precedents have been advanced to support both sequential and direct ordinations.
- There are not sufficient grounds on the basis of the church's history to regard any direct ordination as invalid.
- That it does not know of any doctrinal objections to Direct Ordination.
  There is theological support for the orders of Bishop, Priest and Deacon, which are the components of the sequence of ordination.

The Doctrine Commission agreed:

- That further theological conversations may result in indigenous theologies emerging from any of the three Tikanga and which may be adopted by all Tikanga.
- There may be practical, contextual and cultural reasons why either pattern of ordination is preferred. Whichever pattern is followed, in whatever context, it should be theologically grounded.'

'Tikanga' is a word used to describe each of the three cultural streams or components of the Anglican Church in Aotearoa New Zealand and Polynesia, and indicates respectively the Mäori, Päkehä (of European culture), and Pasefika cultures. The term is defined as social organisation, language, laws, principles, and procedure [Preamble 12]. The Constitution/te Pouhere when it was revised in 1990 gave considerable freedom to each Tikanga to develop its ministry and mission according to each Tikanga's cultural norms. Authorisation of Forms of Worship not inconsistent with the Constitution/te Pouhere and the Formularies of the Church can be developed within a Tikanga.

Other matters raised by the Berkeley Statement

Laying on of hands
Some consideration has been given by our Common Life Liturgical Commission to alternatives to what some liken to an unseemly rugby-scrum with priests around the candidate during the laying on of hands. The Roman custom of bishops at an episcopal ordination and priests associated with the bishop in presbyteral ordinations laying hands in silence one after another has attractions for some. It avoids the moment-of-consecration rhetoric and allows the prayer to be said for all the candidates together rather than being repeated. However, we did not find general enthusiasm for change.

Cultural expression
The different cultures that make up our part of the church all add their style to an ordination occasion but none seem to want to alter the ordination liturgy itself. The cultural aspects enhance the occasion or embellish the day by creating the context, the before and after events and the music.

Anointing
This is not a common feature of ordinations in this part of the church. One bishop anoints the hands of new priests, another the foreheads of new deacons. The rubric that nothing should interfere with the essentials of the rite seem to predominate.

Who can be recognised and who must be 're-ordained'?
A new situation for us resulting from the mobility of people around the world and between cultures brings new questions. One of our Canons, which is also a formulary, expands and explains the Preface to the Ordinal in the 1662 *Book of Common Prayer*. One section talks of the 'Admission of Clergy of Churches in Communion with this Church' and 'recognises as being in full communion with itself (a relationship of unrestricted *communio in sacris* including the mutual recognition of ministries) these churches, namely: The Church of England and all other churches of the Anglican Communion, and such other churches as shall be recognised by General Synod from time to time as being in the same full communion.' In this category we have Standing Resolutions mentioning also the Old Catholic Church, the Philippine Independent Church, and the Mar

Thoma Church. There is another clause of the Canon that speaks of 'Admission of ministers ordained by Bishops not in Communion with this Church.' This states that 'when a priest or deacon ordained by a Bishop of the Roman Catholic Church or other church in communion with the See of Rome or other such church as shall be recognised by General Synod for the purpose of this Canon shall apply to a Bishop of this church to hold office ...' certain documentation needs to be sighted. Recently we added the Lutheran Churches in Scandinavia and North America who have entered full communion relationships with other parts of the Anglican Communion but not yet with us to this category. But what of those who have been ordained in the breakaway Anglican/Episcopal churches? Their orders may be 'valid but irregular' but we have not yet found a way to recognise them and a bishop may be required to 're-ordain' such persons if they are to serve in this part of the Anglican world.

Conclusion
The implications of the Berkeley Statement *To Equip the Saints* lie behind any future work our part of the Anglican Communion does on the Ordinal. We are pleased that those who prepared *A New Zealand Prayer Book – He Karakia Mihinare o Aotearoa* 1989 were sufficiently aware of the issues involved to anticipate most of the Berkeley Statement's provisions.

Ecumenical Orders:
The Reconciliation of Ministry between Anglicans and Lutherans in North America

William H. Petersen

This chapter considers elements of late-twentieth century liturgical renewal and theological restatement that have combined ecumenically at the beginning of a new millennium to produce a reconciliation of ordained ministries among two Anglican and two Lutheran churches of North America.[1]

> In order to advance toward the recognition of ordained ministries, deliberate efforts are required. All churches need to examine the forms of ordained ministry and the degree to which the churches are faithful to its original intentions. *Churches must be prepared to renew their understanding and their practices of ordained ministry.*[2]

This is, of course, a key passage in the 1982 Lima statement (*BEM*) that reformulated the paradigm and, indeed, altered the trajectory of the ecumenical movement since its publication.[3]

---

1. The four churches are: the Episcopal Church in the United States (ECUSA), the Anglican Church of Canada (ACC), the Evangelical Lutheran Church in America (ELCA) and the Evangelical Lutheran Church in Canada. Prior to the constitutional formation of ELCA and ELCIC in 1988 the American Lutheran Church and the Lutheran Church in America were transnational ecclesiastical realities. Though the scope of this chapter is perforce limited to North America, a review of the ecumenical literature will demonstrate the deep cross-reference that occurred among those working toward full communion between Lutherans and Anglicans in the British and Irish churches and those of the Nordic and Baltic countries (see *Together in Mission and Ministry: The Porvoo Statement*), on the one hand, and, on the other hand, those documents produced by LED (*Implications of the Gospel, Concordat of Agreement*, and its successor *Called to Common Mission*) in the USA and CLAD (*Report and Recommendations, Interim Sharing of the Eucharist*, and *The Waterloo Declaration*) in Canada. Both contexts have constant reference to the 1987 *Niagara Report* of the Anglican-Lutheran International Commission's consultation on *episcopé*.
2. *BEM* VI, Ministry 51. Emphasis added.
3. This claim demands a longer explanation than can be here indulged. It must suffice to say the Lima Statement marks a shift from what I have

The ecumenical significance of the Lima proposal to the churches goes beyond the aegis of the World Council of Churches since that gathering of theologians included not only member churches (Eastern and Oriental Orthodox, Anglican, Lutheran, Methodist, Reformed) but also representatives of the Roman Catholic Church and of the Baptist, Adventist, and Pentecostal traditions.

The process of receiving *BEM* in the traditions party to its formulation has varied along a spectrum from simple commentary to official incorporation of its principles into the ecumenical vision and platform of particular churches. In the present period at the beginning of the twenty-first century when the ecumenical bark appears becalmed, the successful declaration of full communion between Anglicans and Lutherans appears, then, as an encouraging breath of fresh air.

The citation is relevant to the present chapter precisely because its last sentence is a commission that the International Anglican Liturgical Consultation seeks to accept and address for its own communion in *Anglican Ordination Rites: The Berkeley Statement: To Equip the Saints*.[4] Since 1997 the IALC has been reflecting on all the elements within and surrounding liturgical renewal of ordination liturgies in the Anglican Communion. In view of this the present chapter seeks to show how the ecumenical context can be helpful to that task as well as to issue a caveat about the process of liturgical renewal in the area of ordination.

It is a commonplace of our time that Christians everywhere live in an age of liturgical renewal, theological restatement, and ecumenical rapprochement. This truism is more or less realised among churches depending upon factors at play in their particular history, culture, and geography, by each other. Within this situation ecumenical conversations have been enabled to move with some success toward fundamental agreement in the first two areas of *BEM*. This is remarkable in itself given the conflicts over baptism and eucharist in the sixteenth century and the en-

---

elsewhere called 'blender' ecumenism to a 'partnership' paradigm that is more critically appreciative of particular developments within traditions. The resultant trajectories, while not abandoning the multi-lateral approach, nonetheless gave impetus to a multitude of bi-lateral ecumenical dialogues with goals variously ranging from mutual understanding, to resolution of historical condemnations, to full communion.
4. The ecumenical context of a baptismal ecclesiology and of the reform of any and all Anglican ordination rites is emphatically recognised at the outset (n 6) of the IALC Berkeley Statement: *To Equip the Saints*.

shrinement of the battle cries or scars in the ecclesial formulae or practices of the various traditions. All traditions have, of course, discovered in the face of the contemporary world that the old dividing questions have long lost their currency. Hence, theological restatement and liturgical renewal, in a reciprocal or mutually influential manner, have been ecumenically fruitful. Yet when it comes to polity, and particularly the reconciliation of ordained ministry, progress has been conspicuously slow or simply absent.

The reconciliation of ordained ministries that has occurred and continues to progress among Lutherans and Anglicans in North America is a case in point. While it has, to be sure, issued in a reconciliation of ministries that is still in the process of reception, it did, nevertheless, come near to shipwreck not only along the way but after the inauguration of full communion.[5]

On one hand, the opening sections of *Called to Common Mission* and *The Waterloo Declaration* recount the long history of fundamental doctrinal and liturgical agreement between Anglicans and Lutherans that was recognised in the national dialogues from their inception. And, in addition to agreement in the gospel and in the right administration of the sacraments, Anglicans and Lutherans enjoyed a history not only free from official condemnations,[6] but exhibiting of points of positive contact and mutual appreciation at least until developments of the nineteenth century and sometimes beyond. The issues, rather, lay precisely in the area of polity and had two aspects in regard to the reconciliation of ordained ministry.

The Anglican tradition had through the challenges of the sixteenth and seventeenth centuries retained episcopacy and, indeed, in the nineteenth-century articulation of its Chicago-Lambeth Quadrilateral ecumenical platform, insisted upon an

---

5. Due to the fact that both traditions were able to endorse an ecclesiology that holds church as prior to orders, full communion was initiated on the basis of a reconciled presbyterate (that is, one that could be interchangeable between the traditions) and a plan to effect over time the reconciliation of episcopates through mutual participation in the ordination (consecration/installation) of each other's bishops.

6. This, of course, discounts Henry VIII's counterblast *Assertio septem sacramentorum* against Luther. The Articles of Religion witness better to the claim as does the fact that from 1714 the Church of England's 'defender of the faith' was Lutheran in the person of the Hanoverian monarch.

historic episcopate as essential to unity. Anglicanism had, as well, retained the three-fold ordained ministry by continuing the orders of deacon, presbyter, and bishop. For its part, the Lutheran tradition in facing some of the same challenges insisted upon a single ordained ministry and emerged various in its application of episcopé, some regions transferring ecclesial oversight to the 'godly prince' and others retaining an historic episcopate.[7]

In ecumenical dialogue toward the object of reconciled ministry, the problem reduced itself ultimately to the following: (1) can both traditions be satisfied to understand a single ordained ministry (that is a ministry of divine intention and institution) for the church that may be three-fold in its expression; and (2) if Anglicans do not insist on historic episcopate as a pre-condition of unity, might not Lutherans freely accept it as a sign and agent (among other signs and agents) of unity?

It is important to note that the problem was *reduced* to this. The years of dialogue had produced significant agreement in the gospel and revealed a process by which Anglicans and Lutherans were able to move toward an understanding of apostolicity and tests of its ecclesial presence beyond their respective historical tendencies to locate it exclusively in continuity of right order (Anglican) or continuity of right doctrine (Lutheran). The key was discovered in their mutual appreciation for continuity of right praise as the third element and the one which keeps the other two together with itself in consideration of apostolicity.[8] In

---

7. This former arrangement ended, of course, with the end of the German monarchy in 1918 and was replaced by clerical oversight that was in some cases given the name 'bishop', a development that had, in any case, been emerging for some time during the previous century. The North American situation in regard to Lutheranism and historic episcopate involves developments complicated by ethnic as well as polity considerations. This came on the basis of a common statement (1) on *Implications of the Gospel* (wherein the church appears as the prime implication of the gospel in human history, thus intimately relating church and gospel) and (2) on historic episcopate as part of but not exhausting the concept of apostolicity, see: *Towards Full Communion* 27 ff.
8. The conjoint daily worship (alternating the liturgical materials and practices of the two traditions) which characterised the North American dialogues (LED and CLAD) allowed the representatives to be led by experience into reception and articulation of this insight and, indeed, provided the basis for that relationship of 'interim eucharistic fellowship'

this, then, proponents of liturgical renewal within and among traditions may rejoice in an important recognition.

The remaining problem itself, however, was not easily resolved. As a Lutheran ecumenical theologian observed late in the course of the process, 'If Lutherans and Anglicans cannot solve this problem [reconciliation of ministries], then there really is no hope for the ecumenical movement.'[9] In the event, of course, the question of the historic episcopate as between Lutherans and Anglicans in North America has been in principle resolved and by the process indicated. This development has occurred on the basis of the ecumenical trajectories envisioned by BEM and carried forward through painstaking dialogue and ecclesial reception. Even the fact that Lutherans 'install' bishops where Anglicans 'consecrate' them (which might have provided a cause for continued separation) was, in the end, overcome by an aspect of liturgical renewal that emphasises the centrality of action and intention: both rites involve prayer with the laying-on-of-hands by bishops with the intention of making bishops for the church.[10]

By contrast, at the same time that these developments were taking place in the arena of ecumenical rapprochement, a very different approach characterised the appearance of renewed ordination rites in the two traditions, and especially this was so for North American Anglicans.[11] A renowned Anglican liturgist and veteran member of ECUSA's Standing Liturgical Commission of

---

which, in turn, provided the context wherein proposals for the actual reconciliation of ordained ministry between the traditions could be reached.

9. Comment from William Rusch at a meeting of the North American Academy of Ecumenists, Toronto, Ontario, September 1998.

10. This is most clearly stated in *The Waterloo Declaration*, Introduction, § 9: 'By recognizing the installation of a bishop as ordination,' the ELCIC has clearly expressed its commitment to the office of bishop as the personal expression of *episcopé*.

11. After a period of trial usage (from 1967), the Episcopal Church adopted the *Book of Common Prayer* 1979 which included a much changed 'Ordinal'. Likewise, the Anglican Church of Canada after a similar period of trial usage (from 1971) authorised *The Book of Alternative Services 1985*. The 'Ordinal' in the latter is similar to the BCP 1979 in shape and content. By 1978 North American Lutherans of the ALC and LCA had a new Lutheran *Book of Worship*. The Ordinal for those and the successor churches ELCA and ELCIC have a common ordinal in a separate book *Occasional Services* authorised in 1982.

the General Convention noted that the new ordination rites sought in their order of appearance as well as in their shape and content to emphasise that the three orders of bishop, priest, and deacon were distinct and that the liturgies for ordination in each case must reflect that order's integrity.[12] Thus the trajectory of liturgical renewal.

In congruence with such an understanding, the IALC's Berkeley Statement explicates its understanding of the episcopal, presbyteral, and diaconal orders in a similar fashion. This latter document also continues an emphasis present from the inception of liturgical renewal in ordination rites, namely, an ecclesiology that sets the ordained within the *laos tou theou*, the people of God. An even finer point is put upon this by the Berkeley Statement's insistence upon a baptismal ecclesiology that locates the font of all ministry precisely there – at the font![13]

That similar developments through liturgical renewal and theological restatement were occurring among Lutherans in North America is to be discerned by a comparison of the rites which appeared almost simultaneously in the two traditions. The comparison must, of course, be presented in the presbyteral context because of the already indicated differences between Anglicans and Lutherans in regard not to the fact but to the expression of *episcopé*, and *diakonía*. It needs to be emphasised here that the differences in question are not regarded, whether by the *Waterloo Declaration* or *Called to Common Mission*, as church-dividing.

It will be noted in the chart below that the Anglican side must comprehend the Episcopal Church's 1979 *Book of Common Prayer (BCP)* and the Anglican Church of Canada's 1985 *Alternative Services Book (ASB)*. In the case of the two Lutheran churches involved, the 1978 *Lutheran Book of Worship (LBW)*, common to both churches, provides the eucharistic context of the rites which are actually found in their *Occasional Services* companion to the *LBW*. North American Anglicans may find it odd that the Lutheran ordinal appears separately, but should re-

---

12. H. Boone Porter, 'The Theology of Ordination and the New Rites,' *Anglican Theological Review*, 59,2 (1972) 69-81. The article is a seminal one and though the trial rites upon which he was commenting were somewhat altered in the event, the basic theological and liturgical substance of his essay stands. This is nowhere so evident as in the IALC proposals of the Berkeley Statement some three decades after Porter's article.
13. See *To Equip the Saints*, especially Part I: Baptism and Ministry.

member that their own tradition has always considered the
Ordinal a separate book. Though it has been customary to pub-
lish them together in the North American context, this was not
always the case in the Church of England. Finally, it is interesting to note that of the four churches involved, the Episcopal
Church appears to have been the most conservative in its revision by keeping the presentation of ordinands and litany for ordinations where it was placed in all previous Anglican ordinals,
namely, at the outset of the liturgy.

Comparison of Presbyteral Ordination Rites

BCP 1979 / BAS 1985		LBW 1978+ Occasional Services 1982
Opening Hymn		Opening Hymn
Acclamation		x
Presentation of Ordinand	*BCP* here	x
Litany for Ordinations	*BCP* here	x
Collect for Ordinations		Collect for Ordinations
OT, Psalm, NT, Gospel		OT, Psalm, NT, Gospel
Sermon		Sermon
Nicene Creed		Nicene Creed
		('may be said' here)
Presentation of Ordinand	*BAS* here	Litany for Ordinations
Address & Examination		Address & Examination
Litany for Ordinations	*BAS* here	Litany for Ordinations
Veni Creator Spiritus (sung)		*Veni Creator Spiritus* (sung)
Consecration of the Priest		Thanksgiving & Laying on of Hands
The Peace		Charge and Acclamation by the People
The Great Thanksgiving		The Peace
Postcommunion Prayer (thanks plus prayer for ministry of newly ordained)		The Great Thanksgiving
Blessing & Dismissal		Postcommunion Prayer
		Blessing & Dismissal

NB: Texts of Presentation, Examination, and Consecration of Priest are identical except for oaths of conformity in regard to the particular national church.	NB: The pattern of prayer at the ordination is the same in the Lutheran & Anglican rites: thanksgiving, laying on of hands, prayer for the ordinand's ministry.

Comparison of these rites and their rubrics or other liturgical directions (not shown here) underscores the setting of ordination within the context of the Eucharistic Assembly with lay and clerical participants fulfilling various ministries in the liturgy. Also, it is mandated that the traditional hymn invoking the Spirit just prior to the ordination (whether in litany or unison form) be sung by the entire assembly. Finally, after the ordination of the candidate in the Lutheran and Anglican rites there is an investiture with insignia of order.[14]

All of this is well and good liturgically speaking, but it still does not address that half of the ecumenical problem between Lutherans and Anglicans concerning whether we are talking about one ordained ministry, which may be conceived as triplex or, indeed, three ordained ministries. In the event, the dialogues leading to *Called to Common Mission* and the *Waterloo Declaration* were able to proceed toward acceptance and a process of reception in their respective churches by emphasising the former rather than the latter alternative.

This leads me, finally, to the articulation of a *caveat* envisioned at the outset. It is observable that theological restatement, liturgical renewal, and ecumenical rapprochement can be mutually beneficial when they go forward hand-in-hand. When, however, our several traditions undertake these necessary aspects of ecclesial life and mission without constant reference to each other and always with reference to ecumenical perspective and consultation, results can provide new causes of misunderstanding or difficulty.[15]

---

14. Here is a place in both rites where a reform according to the proposed IALC guidelines in *To Equip the Saints* might well be effected among Lutherans and Anglicans, namely, either vesting the ordinand before the liturgy or making sure that the vesting is done inconspicuously after the ordination and welcome, removing it from immediate proximity to the ordination (*To Equip the Saints*, Part 2: C. Vesting.)

15. This will be particularly important in consideration of the diaconate. As the Berkeley Statement notes, there continues to be confusion among Anglicans about its place and importance. Some of the same issues obtain among Lutherans. As a result, the diaconate has most unfortunately appeared ecumenically as a kind of dangling participle. Anglicans and Lutherans will do well, then, in the revision and/or renewal of ordination rites to revisit ALIC's *The Diaconate as Ecumenical Opportunity* as they live further into full communion.

Thus, as Anglicans undertake the renewal or even reformation of their ordinals, it will be important that they do so with the results of ecumenical rapprochement clearly in mind. From the present case in point, it will be important in this regard for Anglicans to talk about and present ordained ministries in such a way as to emphasise their unity for the service of the church. For Lutherans, on the other hand, it will be important to talk about and present ordained ministry for the service of the church in such a way as to reflect the integrity of the orders involved. Constant vigilance about these matters, then, is required of all parties in every respect to the end that all may be edified in the Body of Christ.

Works Consulted or Cited not otherwise included in the list of Abbreviations at the beginning of this book.

Implications of the Gospel: Lutheran-Episcopal Dialogue, Series III (Cincinnati, 1988).
Lutheran Book of Worship (Minneapolis, 1978).
Lutheran-Episcopal Dialogue: Report and Recommendations (Cincinnati, 1981).
Occasional Services: A Companion to the Lutheran Book of Worship (Minneapolis, 1982).
Toward Full Communion and A Concordat of Agreement: Lutheran Episcopal Dialogue, Series III (Minneapolis, 1991).

Ministry and Local Covenants in the Church of England

Phillip Tovey

On an international scale the Church of England has two sets of full communion agreements: firstly, with the Old Catholic Churches of the Union of Utrecht, the Mar Thoma Syrian Church, and the Philippine Independent Catholic Church, under the approach of the Bonn Agreement and, secondly, with some northern European Lutheran Churches under the Porvoo agreement. In these there is full recognition of orders. However, similar agreements have been more difficult in England itself. In 1972 the Church of England rejected union with the Methodist Church and in 1982 rejected Covenanting for Union with the Methodist, United Reformed (URC), and Moravian Churches. The Church of England has since signed covenants with the Moravian Church and the Methodist Church, but as yet these do not allow full interchange of ministry.[1]

In light of the failure at the national level people began to respond locally. The first negotiations with the Methodist Church had begun in 1963 and some parishes began to work locally anticipating the success of the scheme. When it failed, they continued to work together, sharing buildings and ministry as locally appropriate. This was further encouraged after the failure of the national covenant and thus in 1987 the General Synod of the Church of England approved two Ecumenical Canons B43 and B44.[2]

Canon B43 sets out how far local ecumenism can go within the present rules.[3] Canon B44 opens up the possibility of the bishop entering into agreement with other churches to form a Local Ecumenical Partnership in which there might be sharing

---

1. See also Phillip Tovey, 'Liturgy and Ecumenism: Three Models of Development,' in Paul Bradshaw and Bryan Spinks eds, *Liturgy in Dialogue* (London, 1993) 73-79.
2. See Colin O. Buchanan, *Anglicans and Worship in Local Ecumenical Projects* [Grove Worship Series no. 101] (Bramcote, Notts.,1987).
3. See General Synod of the Church of England, *Ecumenical Relations Canons B43 and B 44: Code of Practice* (London, 1989).

of buildings, sharing of congregations, and sharing of ministry.[4] The Code of Practice discusses and regulates the possibility of ministerial interchange in presiding at the eucharist (which is allowed), joint confirmations, and ministerial interchange in participation at ordinations (which is not allowed). I have been involved in three different LEPs, each time setting them up, and I want to use them as case studies to illustrate the different models of sharing of ministry under the Ecumenical Canons.

St Francis', Banbury

St Francis', Banbury, was a new church on a new housing estate on the edge of Banbury in the diocese of Oxford. Land had been allocated for a Roman Catholic Church but they could not find the money to put up a permanent structure that was required by the local council. Thus five denominations, a local Brethren church, the Church of England, Methodist Church, Roman Catholic Church, and the United Reformed Church, contributed money and time to construct a shared building. This was regulated under an Act of Parliament, The Sharing of Church Buildings Act 1969, which gave a legal framework to share property. The operation of each of the congregations was agreed in a Local Covenant, which specified relationships between the denominations and was signed by all parties at a public ceremony.

The Roman Catholic Church at St Francis kept their own congregation, but there was shared worship, e.g. carol services, the Week of Prayer for Christian Unity, Stations of the Cross, and a Passover meal. There was much local co-operation but no ministerial exchange.

The Shared Congregation contained members of the Church of England, Methodist, and United Reformed Churches. This was both a shared congregation and shared ministry. A shared congregation meant that there was a shared roll of members. This was complicated because the denominations, for financial contribution reasons, requested that people be identified as linked to one denomination. However, we began from the first to have joint confirmations, in which candidates would have the simultaneous laying-on-of-hands from the bishop, a Methodist minister and a URC minister. These were then administratively labelled as one third to each denomination for the purpose of de-

4. See: E. Welch, and F. Winfield, *Travelling Together. A Handbook for Local Ecumenical Partnerships*, (London, 1995).

nominational funding. The joint confirmation took place each year and followed a rite produced by the ecumenical Joint Liturgical Group.[5]

When the church started, there was one full time Anglican priest, and one part time URC non-stipendiary minister for the shared congregation. Methodist input was through a regular slot in the Circuit plan in which Methodist ministers came to St Francis and St Francis' ministers led services on the Circuit. B44 allows ministers of other churches to preside at Church of England rites and Anglican priests to preside at rites of participating denominations. We planned to have two eucharists a month for the main service, one Church of England and one Free Church. However, these eucharists were not necessarily led by the minister of that particular tradition. There were also early morning eucharists which also used a variety of traditions. This was quite demanding on the presider as they had to learn to be able to lead in a variety of styles. Issues of the elements of the eucharist and methods of distribution were agreed from the outset, as it was not economic to use all the approaches of the participating denominations. This, plus the liturgies of the churches all being influenced by the liturgical movement, made producing a broadly similar framework with space for denominational variation fairly easy.

For baptism we composed our own rite, later approved by a county ecumenical body. Non-sacramental rites were of a mixture of traditions and led by laity as well as clergy.

I was succeeded by another Anglican priest. The URC minister then retired, and the Anglican priest was later succeeded by a full time URC minister. Meanwhile, three of the laity have been authorised as Methodist Lay preachers. So the mix of ministry keeps changing, but the shared congregation shows vitality. This is one model of local ecumenism including shared ministry and a shared congregation.

Churches Together in Wheatley

Moving from a town to a rural setting I found that one of the villages, Holton, was a part of a Fellowship of Churches in the neighbouring and much larger village. They had a covenant that they would work together, which entailed co-operating in a

5. Joint Liturgical Group, *Confirmation and Re-affirmation of Baptismal Faith* (Norwich, 1992).

variety of activities including some shared non-sacramental worship. The Anglicans and URC wished to work even closer together and have shared ministry, so within a local covenant the URC and Anglicans agreed to become an LEP. This included two Anglican churches and one URC church. There was no plan to join the congregations together or have joint confirmation. We did however have shared services and interchange of ministries.

The inauguration service to this new arrangement happened in Holton. Holton was a village where Cromwell located his army to attack Oxford, the latter being royalist in the civil war. The Wheatley URC congregation had its roots in those who left the church with the introduction of the 1662 *Book of Common Prayer* at the restoration of an episcopal Church of England. Thus, to invite the URC minister to preach and preside at a 1662 service was to heal some local tares in the fabric of the local churches.

The interchange of ministry in this model was more on an occasional basis. This changed when the part-time URC minister retired. At that point the Anglican priest of Wheatley also became the minister of the URC church. This continued for a few years until his retirement. There is now a full time Anglican priest in Wheatley, a part time URC minister, and a house-for-duty priest in Holton. The partnership also benefited from a local preacher who is licensed both as a URC local preacher and an Anglican reader. It was possible to have mutual recognition of this lay ministry.

University Chaplaincy

Yet another model of shared ministry is in chaplaincy. Hospitals, the armed forces, and colleges all have chaplaincies, many of which are ecumenical (and some inter-faith). As vicar of Holton I was also a part of the chaplaincy team for Oxford Brookes University. This had been ecumenical for a long while on an informal basis. However, there was no signed covenant and it was not clear who was in this team. In practice it relied on the choice of the full-time chaplain. Chaplaincy was a part of Student Services, where it was acknowledged that the university had a responsibility to provide for students' spiritual needs. There are groups of most major religions within the university, but the ecumenical chaplain was the only one with a salary from the university.

Covenanting here was to commit local churches to work together in a team with such shared ministry as was possible. The
team included a great breadth of ecclesial communities from the
Russian Orthodox to a house church, twelve denominations in
all. This was a very wide remit. There was some shared worship
but much more shared planning of events. The ecumenical
chaplain was also expected to liaise with leaders of other faiths
and have information in the chaplaincy centre for all beliefs or
none. Covenanting together was part of a common Christian
witness to the university community.

Learning from these three models
What can be learned from the Church of England experience? A
number of points can be raised.

First, it is possible to have local agreement well in advance of
the wider national denominational agreement. The ecumenical
canons do show one way to enable bishops to set up such places.
However, LEPs are left with the problems that have not been
solved at the national level, e.g. what does membership mean?[6]
National churches might also be moving at different speeds on
liturgical issues, e.g. baptised children and communion, or on
questions of orders, e.g. ordained local ministry. This can leave a
lot of tension in the LEP.

Second, there are many examples of good relationships.
However, there are also examples where things have gone
wrong and LEPs have fallen a part. This can particularly happen
with the change of ministers, or key lay leaders.

Third, while LEPs might pioneer, they are in danger of becoming isolated and not leavening the whole lump. One of the
problems in England has been that the system is bureaucratic
and this leads to many meetings. Trying to minister with a deanery, and a circuit, and a district means three sets of meetings and
three different sets of administration. This consumes ministerial
time, which can detract from the mission of the local church.
England needs to reform its legislation to simplify the bureau-
cracy of setting up and running such partnerships.

Fourth, with regard to shared ministry there is an uneven
playing field between the denominations. While it was possible
with the bishop's permission for an Anglican priest to be 'recog-

6. See: Phillip Tovey and J. Waller, *Worship in Local Ecumenical Partnerships*, [Grove Worship Series no 147] (Cambridge, 1998).

nised and regarded' as a Methodist minister, and while working in an LEP to be seen as a URC minister, there is no such equivalent hospitality for Free Church ministers working in parishes of the Church of England. This will be so until the questions of acceptance of orders are resolved at a national level.

Each church has a culture around ministry, ordination, and presidency. An LEP was a wonderful place to experience some of this. It requires quite a lot of flexibility to operate in a rather fluid context where the cultures intermix. However, in reality each parish community develops its own ethos and in that sense the life of an LEP is not that different from any other congregation. What they do show is the potential for ecumenical shared ministry teams, but there is still a lot more work to be done on the theology and practice of ordination.

The Mutual Acceptance of Ordained Ministries in South Africa

Ian Darby

In 1995 the ground breaking decision was made by members of the Church Unity Commission to accept mutually the ordained ministries of each other. Their governing bodies resolved to:

1. reaffirm [their] commitment to seek that unity for which Christ prayed and to which we are led by the Holy Spirit;
2. accept that the ordained ministers of Word and Sacrament in the member churches of the Church Unity Commission have been called and ordained by God in Christ and exercise a sacramental, preaching, teaching and pastoral ministry in the Church of God and not simply in the particular church to which they belong;
3. permit such ordained ministers to serve in each others' churches, while remaining ministers of their churches, and to exercise such ministry within the other churches when duly authorised or appointed so to do.[1]

This resolution is a culmination of thirty years of endeavour. It falls short of full reconciliation and interchangeability, but there is now no need for further ordination when appointments are made in churches other than the minister's own.

The principle of mutual acceptance has been the basis of ecumenical progress since 1968 when the Church Unity Commission was formed in South Africa to engage in the search for union. At a time when ecumenical enthusiasm was at its height, all mainline denominations were invited to gather for this purpose. The six that accepted were three Presbyterian bodies, as well as the Methodist, Congregational and Anglican churches. Apart from one Presbyterian which was founded by the Swiss Reformed Mission, the other denominations had their missionary and settler origins in the British Isles.[2]

---

1. *CUC Newsletter* (1996, 1).
2. Since the formation of the CUC the member churches have changed their names and two have united. These are the present members: The Anglican Church of Southern Africa, The Evangelical Presbyterian Church in South Africa, The Methodist Church of Southern Africa, The United Congregational Church of Southern Africa, and The Uniting

The relationships between the six members commenced on the basis of the mutual acceptance of their faith and mission. In 1970 the Commission proposed a Declaration of Intention to Seek Union, and this was adopted by each member and celebrated around the country on 24 November 1974.

The Declaration took the following form:
To seek the union of the Church of the Province of South Africa, the United Congregational Church of Southern Africa, the Methodist Church of South Africa, the Presbyterian Church of Southern Africa, the Bantu Presbyterian Church and the Tsonga Presbyterian Church.
We believe that God redeems this work through Jesus Christ and that he calls his church to share in this mission. In humble penitence we recognise that our divisions impair our witness to Christ in the world today.
We believe that it is God's will that his church should be a visible one, and that the Holy Spirit is moving us to seek this union.
We recognise the Holy Scriptures as the supreme rule of faith and life, we share the apostolic faith confessed in the ancient Creeds of the church, and we observe Baptism and Holy Communion as Sacraments of God's redeeming love in Jesus Christ.
We acknowledge that ministry of each communion is a real and effective ministry of the Word and Sacraments.
Therefore we now pledge ourselves to seek together the visible unity which we believe to be God's will for his church

We undertake:
1. to seek agreement on a common form of ministry of Word and Sacraments, with due regard to those patterns of ministry and oversight to which God has already led us;
2. to admit to the Lord's Table communicant members of all our Churches as an immediate and visible sign of our common quest;
3. to work for increasing co-operation in all areas of church life;
4 to signify our solemn acceptance of this pledge by partici-

---

Presbyterian Church in Southern Africa.

pating, throughout our churches, in services of commitment to the search for union.[3]

In its time, the Declaration was far more far reaching than the resolution of 1995, twenty-one years later. In one statement we have agreement on the faith of the church as well as on the scriptures and the sacraments. While there is to be a seeking for an agreement on the ministry of word and sacrament, it is accepted that each member church has a real and effective ministry.

At this same time the Church of Scotland and the Scottish Episcopalians were taking part in their reunion discussions. Both churches had reached the position where they were ready to explore the possibility of entering into a relationship which would involve acceptance of each other's ministries, and the welcoming of each other's communicants, within the context of a binding agreement to unite, the essentials of both churches being assured.[4]

One must be reminded that the mutual acceptance of membership and ministries had never been a problem for those of the Reformed and Methodist traditions. Anglicans, nevertheless, had recently received encouragement from their bishops at Lambeth. In 1968 the Conference resolved that 'under the direction of the bishop, Christians duly baptised in the name of the Holy Trinity and qualified to receive Holy Communion in their own churches may be welcomed at the Lord's Table in the Anglican Communion.'[5]

In South Africa the response to the Declaration was rapid. In the following year the Anglican Synod of Bishops agreed that parish church councils could invite any Church Unity Commission ordained minister to preside at the eucharist in an Anglican church, bringing his or her congregation with its liturgy and customary usage. As a bonus for the host congregation, this invitation could be made when its own priest was at synod or playing golf.[6]

A further consequence of the 1974 Declaration was that women clergy were presiding at Anglican altars long before they were canonically accepted in 1992. The Anglican news-

---

3. *CPSA Canons and Constitution*, 2002, Resolution of Permanent Force, 1.

4. *Anglican-Presbyterian Conversations*, (1966) 35.

5. *Lambeth Conference Report*, 1968, Resolution 45 (London, 1968) 42.

6. *Bishop's Newsletter*, Diocese of Natal, October 1975.

paper, *Seek*, displayed a picture of the Reverend Margaret Constable, chairperson of the United Congregational Assembly, presiding at her installation eucharist in St Cyprian's Cathedral, Kimberley.[7]

What did not succeed was the plan for structural uniformity. Support for this form of reunion had begun to wane, as had been happening in Nigeria, Sri Lanka and in England. Also what failed to be passed was a section of a proposed Covenant, whereby there would be the laying-on-of-hands in mutual recognition of members and ministers. The Anglican Provincial Synod of 1982 rejected all clauses that required the mutual laying on of hands. All member denominations, however, agreed to the following clauses of the Covenant which committed them

1. to work together for the spread of the gospel, for justice, peace and freedom and for the spiritual and material well-being of all people;

2. to seek to become a fellowship in Christ that is not divided by tradition, nation, culture, class and colour;

3. to pursue means whereby, under the guidance of the Holy Spirit, the Covenanting churches in each place may act together in worship, witness and service.[8]

So committed, the churches were now ready for a very special challenge.

South Africa was already deeply involved in the struggle against the injustices of apartheid. If schemes for reunion appeared to be set on one side, the churches' voice against oppression was more united than it had ever been before. Religious piety is far more evident in Africa than elsewhere in the world, and in South Africa during the 1980s not a protest meeting, nor trade union congress, nor political funeral could be held without speeches and prayers from leaders of the full Christian spectrum. There was already a unity of the faith, combined with a typically African mutual respect for different traditions.

A definitive step was taken in 1989 when the Anglican Provincial Synod agreed to recognise

as communicant members, without requiring any further sacramental rite, those desiring admission who have been baptised by water in the name of the Father, and of the Son

---

7. *Seek* (August, 1982).
8. *CPSA Acts and Resolutions*, Provincial Synod 1982, Resolution 1.

and of the Holy Spirit, and who have made a profession of faith and have been recognised as communicant members by any of the Covenanting Churches.[9]

Episcopal confirmation could no longer be insisted on for those wishing to become Anglicans. Yet the distinctiveness of this concession to admissions from Covenanting churches was blurred by the Anglicans encouraging their own members in the 1990s to admit to holy communion those who were baptised but not yet confirmed. There has also developed the unofficial Anglican relaxation of the requirement of episcopal confirmation for those being admitted from other Protestant bodies such as Lutherans and Dutch Reformed.

United congregations and non-denominational church schools were soon asking for an order of confirmation which could be used as an act of unity. Orders of service had been provided since 1974 for occasions of unity, and there was also an order for a Sunday service. There was as yet no liturgy of initiation. A service was produced whereby the laying on of hands would be provided by representatives of the participating denominations. A service of the induction of a minister was also included using the same principle of representation by participating denominations. The minister's own denomination would provide the president of the service.[10]

United congregations have continued to increase in number, mostly in the wealthier English-speaking suburbs. Some recent schemes have emerged in country districts, where they might co-exist with denominational congregations of another language group, suggesting that the united assembly is avoiding having to mix with them. There are instances of tensions between these congregations and their parent denominations over financial quotas, or simply over loyalty. Most of these united churches, nevertheless, are an encouraging witness to the quest for Christian unity.

This brings us to the year 1995 when the mutual acceptance of ordained ministries was achieved. It was not all plain sailing. The proposed wording was to include 'mutual recognition', and only in the last few months before their Provincial Synod, the Anglicans indicated that they would be unable to agree to the

---

9. Ibid., 1989, Resolution 25.
10. *Unity in Worship* (Johannesburg, 1997).

word 'recognition'. The word 'acceptance' was the substitute, much to the disappointment of the Presbyterians who discerned that re-ordination would still be required by Anglicans for a complete transfer of ministry.

One consequence of this resolution was the call for preparing an ordination service for use in united congregations. Congregationalists and Presbyterians ordain ministers in the local church. Anglicans increasingly are doing the same. Such an ordinal has been drafted, with the principle again of representatives of the churches participating in the laying on of hands.

A further consequence has been that at any ordination, ministers of the Covenanting churches could be invited to take part. This statement would be made at the beginning of the service:

> Ministers of other Church Unity Commission member churches are taking part in this ordination service. Their participation affirms that our churches accept one another's ordained ministers as called and ordained by God in Christ through his church and permit them to exercise that ministry within any of our churches when authorised so to do. It does not make the person being ordained a minister of any other denomination than the one concerned.[11]

Lay presidency at the eucharist is an issue to which, it seems, a blind eye has been turned. With the exception of the Anglicans, this practice has been an accepted principle of the member churches, the authority for it usually being given to probationers for the ministry. Anglicans find more volatile issues over which to argue, so it is quite feasible that a Methodist probationer might be found presiding at an Anglican altar, as long as she or he remains faithful to Methodist customary usage.

Each of the Covenanting denominations possesses a diaconate. So far there has been no desire to bring about uniformity to what are differing systems. Since 1995, however, there have been several consultations which have reached a consensus on the understanding of the ministry of oversight. It has been agreed that oversight is expressed in three forms, communal, collegial and personal, and that such a ministry may be found in all our member churches. Of personal oversight, nevertheless, there is no agreement on the permanence of the office or on whether or not it constitutes a separate order.

---

11. *CUC Newsletter*, loc. cit.

Methodists introduced bishops in 1988, initially as a replace-
ment of the district chairperson. Since then such appurtenances
as pectoral crosses, stoles, rings and crooks have been collected,
all with a growing background of purple, and titles not always
being discarded upon termination of office. Congregationalists
have introduced a regional moderator with the function of *pastor
pastorum*. This entails having direct pastoral responsibility for
ministers and their training and presiding at ordinations. For
Presbyterians, the ministry of personal oversight is limited to
the parish minister. It remains for the Church Unity Commission to assist the churches to accept and to recognise the possession of *episcopé* by its members.

Acceptance and recognition have been the principles which
have guided ecumenical progress since the 1960s. This has been
a slow but steady journey, and what has been achieved in mutual
understanding and acceptance has freed the churches to give
time to the more pressing demands of mission and ministry in
South Africa.

'Flying Bishops': Extended Episcopal Care in the Church of England

Colin Buchanan

Problems set by the Ordination of Women

The Church of England (and this is a uniquely English story) considered the ordination of women as presbyters in various stages, and through various reports and debates from 1966 to 1992. When its Synod finally gave the necessary two-thirds majorities in each of three Houses in November 1992, it completed a process which, in this particular case, had begun in a diocesan motion in November 1984. The intervening eight years had enabled profound thought to be exercised about not only the principle of such ordinations, but also the provision to be made for those who in conscience could not accept the propriety and/or the validity of such ordinations. Concern that a Christian church should make the right reconciling, or at least alleviating, moves towards this minority led to some complications in the proposed legislation. Nor was the motivation solely charitable – there was a lurking fear both that parliament, which in the established Church of England, has final say over ecclesiastical legislation, might itself veto any proposal which too greatly disadvantaged any opponents of the change, and also that fair-minded members of Synod might themselves be dissuaded from supporting the change if the upshot were likely to be too disruptive. Concessions were going to be in order, not simply out of Christian care for another's conscience, but also, quite opportunistically, to gather the largest number of votes. This factor in turn meant that any synodical or parliamentary acceptance of women's ordination would actually be a qualified 'yes', not simply what has been called a 'one-liner' (i.e. legislation without qualifications).

For these purposes, most of the opposition has to be seen as anglo-catholic, even as determinedly anglo-catholic. There were opponents of women's ordination among evangelicals, but the concern of these was: (a) lest women come to hold undue authority in the church; (b) almost entirely divorced from any questions about sacraments; (c) totally unrelated to issues about the view of women's ordination taken by the papacy; and (d) not greatly bothered about relations with any episcopate. The voting figures were affected by evangelical opponents, no doubt, but the actual provisions made had little relationship to them. The question was the meeting of anglo-catholic consciences.

These latter consciences took two or three different forms:

(a) The argument through the 1980s was largely concentrated on the matter of substance – could a woman be ordained presbyter, or, even more precisely, could a woman preside at communion? The arguments developed with issues about the eucharistic president as an *alter Christus* or at least an *imago Christi* – and the maleness of Christ's incarnation settled the matter for the dissentients. The argument was, of course, further bolstered by the maleness of the twelve apostles, and the unbroken witness of two millennia of episcopal churches since.

(b) An argument intended to bring even supporters of women's ordination into opposition was that such ordinations were certain to split the Church of England. While every supporter at, say, a diocesan synod who was swayed into voting against, then assisted the statistics of apparent division for the General Synod later to ponder, yet this tactic might in turn mean that, once a change was authorised, much of the apparent opposition prior to the vote would melt away after it and have no problem in going along with it.[1]

(c) The argument that was not much deployed in the 1980s was that the Church of England General Synod had no 'right' or 'power' to alter the inherited threefold orders, and would be acting *ultra vires* if it tried. If there were to be a change to admitting women, then it would have to come from an Ecumenical Council or, in the post-1870 world, from the pope. This argument has been much heard since the ordination of women actually began, but it was much more muted in the 1980s. I think there were two reasons for this:

(i) There was first a decision to be taken about women as deacons, and anglo-catholics were generally much more sympathetic to this move than to their ordination as presbyters. It did not involve eucharistic presidency. But it did involve

---

1. Proponents of women's ordination were, of course, simultaneously insisting that *not* to go ahead would be highly divisive also – possibly, it was hinted, even to the point of unauthorised ordinations, and/or non-presbyteral eucharistic presidency by non-compliant women. But hints were as far as proponents could properly go.

creating a precedent unilaterally in the admissibility of women to an historic order – and in the 1980s many were prepared to let that precedent go by unchallenged, and not use any argument about taking liberties with an historic order being *ultra vires* in the way they so vehemently did later.

(ii) A genuine belief that to take certain action would be *ultra vires* for our Synod, if carried through with integrity, would have entailed: first challenging each occasion on which it came on the agenda, then moving a procedural motion to proceed to 'next business', and finally leaving the chamber in protest if the Synod rejected the procedural motion. This, though high-minded, would have been a recipe for defeat, and the opponents knew it. In the 1980s opponents could muster a blocking third in the House of Clergy, but that would have evaporated if even a small number of them had declined to take part. They thus had to debate and vote on the stages of legislation, even though they thereby conferred a legitimacy upon the process which they later tended to deny.

A great advantage of such a position was that, if Rome ever did change its ways, Anglicans could smoothly move into line, as the decision was now being made by real authority! A disadvantage, people like me would say, was that no decision we could now take would ever have the same enormity to it that Elizabeth's defiance of the Pope's excommunication had had, and that Elizabeth and her counsellors were defying the whole tradition of the whole church being in communion with itself, and the Church of England would thereafter inevitably, by virtue of this self-chartering, be making far-reaching unilateral decisions, including those about the threefold orders of ministry.

So how was the Church of England to 'meet' this opposition? The answer was threefold:

Provisions of the Measure and the Act of Synod

First, there was separate legislation by 'Measure' to provide financial relief to stipendiary clergy who considered the change in the Church of England's orders such as to force them out of their calling, and thus out of their houses and stipends.

Secondly, there was provision within the main Measure for

parishes to decline the ministry of women, either to preside at communion ('Resolution A') or to be incumbent ('Resolution B').

Thirdly, over and above these legislative provisions, there was an issue about episcopal ministry. It became clear that a proportion of parishes wished to distance themselves from the sacramental ministry of their own diocesan bishops. The rationale for this distancing was not so much the (cartoon) jibe of 'tainted hands' (i.e. those which had ordained a woman), but that, by ordaining women, bishops would have so muddled the presbyterate that it would be prudent to abstain from their own presbyteral ministry – i.e. holy communion. The opponents' own proposal was 'AEO' ('alternative episcopal oversight') which, if taken seriously, would have created something like archipelago dioceses led by 'alternative' bishops. The House of Bishops responded with 'extended episcopal care'. Parishes would have to vote for a petition to their own diocesan (and this was called 'Resolution C'). They would request from him the ministrations of a bishop whom he would name to give them the episcopal care and sacramental ministrations he might previously have exercised himself. But this would be granted by the diocesan bishop, and would only be exercised on the basis of the bishop so ministering doing so *as an assistant bishop in that diocese* and under the authority of the diocesan bishop.

When the two Measures, having secured their majorities in Synod, were on their way to being debated in Parliament in 1993, the House of Bishops produced for General Synod a draft 'Episcopal Ministry Act of Synod' to give substance to 'extended episcopal care.' This set out in order of priority three ways in which parishes which sought such episcopal care might receive it. They would by definition be parishes in dioceses where the diocesan bishop favoured women's ordination – in the seven or so dioceses where the diocesan would not ordain women, all parishes were expected to be content. A reverse kind of arrangement was then needed whereby a neighbouring bishop would ordain women for the diocese.[2]

The first of the three ways of 'extending episcopal care' antic-

2. The original Measure did permit any diocesan in office at the time the Measure came into force to declare his whole diocese a 'no-go' area for all women presbyters, but it became clear, as the date for it to come into force drew near, that no diocesan bishop was going to act on this swingeing provision.

ipated was 'diocesan arrangements to be made by the diocesan bishop'. This was the obvious way to meet the minority in a diocese where the suffragan bishop or some assistant bishop was opposed to the ordination of women. At the time of writing arrangements of this sort obtain in Newcastle, Wakefield and York.

The second way was 'regional arrangements to be made by the diocesan bishops of each region'. This kind of arrangement I experienced in both Rochester and Southwark dioceses, where the bishop of Fulham, a suffragan of London, was specially commissioned to be an assistant bishop in these two neighbouring dioceses. We also found that, having the 'care' of twenty-three or so parishes in Southwark diocese (out of nearly 400 in total) he came to our diocesan staff meetings, and joined in formal and informal bishops' meetings in Southwark, so that, despite his prime calling by the church to extend episcopal care in this way, he made it clear he was not a single issue person.

The third way was 'provincial arrangements to be made by the archbishops of the province'. Steps were to be taken to create two new suffragan sees for Canterbury diocese and one for York, and these three suffragans, entitled 'provincial episcopal visitors' (PEVs), were then to be made available for any diocesan bishop in the respective provinces who had been unable to make arrangements in one of the two ways outlined above. So in early 1994 there were consecrated men to be Bishops of Ebbsfleet and Richborough in Canterbury diocese and of Beverley in York diocese, and to take up the role of 'PEV'.[3] It is these bishops who

---

3. In case there is any uncertainty, the constituency concerned did not doubt the episcopal role (and, so to speak, potency) of the archbishops and other bishops who consecrated them. They did, however, have to receive communion from them, at the very point where they were taking office to minister communion to those who would not receive from their archbishop or diocesan bishop. There was a flurry in the press when a second PEV was being consecrated in the late 1990s, as the two bishops presenting him declined to receive communion from George Carey. But I think there was no case where the newly consecrated bishop himself so declined – and Archbishops of Canterbury have at intervals told the House of Bishops that all the bishops were at least in communion with each other (though that has to be open to enquiry, as most of us have not often asked 'who is not here?' or 'which of us is not receiving communion?'). So the clinical and highly sterilised separation has retained the occasional risky contact.

have become known as the 'flying bishops', a term halfway between familiarity and contempt. It has some cogency, in that
they are covering areas up 200 miles or so in length, and doing
so in order to minister in a relatively small number of scattered
parishes. In the diocese of Bradford, in which I am an honorary
assistant bishop, there are 143 parishes, and only two have
passed 'resolution C' and asked for the ministrations of the
northern PEV.

It is obvious that Parochial Church Councils have to have
passed both A and B (as under the official Measure) before they
can address resolution C. A diocesan bishop is not legally bound
to 'extend' his episcopal care in one of the three ways above, if a
parish does pass resolution C; but the episcopate has bound itself by a 'Code of Practice' and is treating the Act of Synod and
the Code as morally binding. It will be seen that 'flying bishops'
are but one category of the episcopal ministry which is provided
for such parishes, and that it is partly a matter of historic chance
in which dioceses their services are needed, and in which not.
The only difference is that, being suffragans of the archbishops,
they have a further role identified in the Act of Synod which
would exist irrespective of how many or how few dioceses
found a need for their services:

> Each provincial episcopal visitor shall act as spokesman and
> adviser to those who are opposed and shall assist the arch-
> bishops in monitoring the operation of the Act of Synod.

This gives the three PEVs an institutionalised role which
goes beyond the count of the actual parishes seeking their services. The three are invited to attend the House of Bishops (in
fact one has been elected to represent other suffragans as a full
member of the House), and are expected to have eyes and ears
open to 'their' parishes and to be able to report on them to the
various diocesans.

Assessing the Act of Synod

What are the pros and cons of the whole arrangement? I begin
with the pros.

Firstly, the territorial and administrative unity of each diocese is still intact. Appointments to parishes continue with the
same diocesan involvement as before; deanery and diocesan
synods and committees function as before; finance functions as
before; representation on General Synod functions as before.

The diocesan bishop is still the diocesan bishop, and bishop of his whole diocese.

Secondly, the 'resolution C' parishes have a fairly strong cordon around them, and, though they may be on good terms with their diocesan bishop (and other bishops in the diocese) only the bishop allocated to them under one of the three ways above will come for confirmations or other sacramental occasions requiring a bishop. If a deacon or presbyter is to be ordained for that parish, then the allocated bishop will come to officiate at it.[4] Diocesan clergy, bishops or presbyters, may come and preach by invitation, and may even do formal 'Visitations'; but they will not preside at communion. As to neighbouring clergy (e.g. supplying during holidays) the clergy of 'resolution C' parishes have to decide who are 'kosher' and who not – in broad terms clergy from 'A and B' parishes may well be acceptable, others less probably so.

Thirdly, there is the case of the women clergy. In some ways they have gained from these provisions, though in ways not immediately obvious. I sketch out some features of it:

(a) It is, as suggested above, unlikely that an unqualified decision to ordain women would have been passed in General Synod, so that the provisions which qualify it are also the supports which got it through.

(b) Unless a parish has passed any of the resolutions, it is deemed to be open to the ministrations of women as much as men. No parish can otherwise say 'we would rather not have a woman' when it comes to making appointments – and, if it does pass resolutions, it may well seriously reduce the number of men who would be interested in serving there. The resolutions have cut away at mere prejudice and brought folk up against the alternative of theological objections – or none.

(c) The women are actually there. Even bishops who do not think women can be ordained are having to engage in making appointments of women presbyters, doing appraisals of them, writing references for them, and generally mixing among ordained women. Living with simultaneous affirmations and

---

4. It has to be acknowledged that ordinations are very few and far between for them. The general air of middle-term pessimism induced in the constituency by the decision to ordain women has undoubtedly had an effect – few but masochists will offer for ordination in contexts where the future is portrayed as bleak.

denials of women's orders is bound to work on behalf of the women in the longer run.

(d) The future lies with the women, and they can afford to take the longer view – and it has been to their advantage that there was not a large march-out or internal rebellion from the 'traditionalists'. While around 400 clergy (mostly, I think, over fifty years of age) have accepted financial relief and left, there have been no martyrs or victims of their own consciences. Between departure with compensation, and remaining in ministry with resolutions A, B and C, or resolutions A and B, most have 'found their own level' and have been both contained and affirmed – so that the ordination of women has not been as wounding as envisaged, and thus any backlash about it has also been limited.

The cons

(a) There is a sense of a church living with an enormous internal contradiction, and even, to its own disadvantage, of sustaining and keeping within its borders those who wish to eliminate the ordination of women.

(b) There has been, for better but probably for worse, a particular division among Anglican 'catholics' – those opposed to the ordination of women, largely associated with Forward in Faith, grouping in a last-ditch kind of way, and severing connection with Affirming Catholicism (and other similar groups), whom it accuses of being spineless and unprincipled. The division has run right through theological colleges, religious communities, the shrine at Walsingham, friendships and families. The journal of Forward in Faith (*New Directions*) is fairly unsparing of the others.[5]

(c) The Act of Synod has given rise to its own opponents – GRAS (Group for the Rescinding of the Act of Synod). They have simply said that a decision is a decision is a decision and the church ought to live by it and not hedge and trim it. I have joined with FiF supporters in diocesan synods to resist the efforts of GRAS, as firstly I was a signatory of the Act, and believe it not yet to have run its time; secondly, the opponents are disregarding the qualifying factors initially built in

---

5. For good measure the 'FiF' folk tend to be purist about sexual *mores*, and reckon that it is 'Aff Cath' which has lapsed readily into homosexual practices.

(though, to be fair, they usually acknowledge the legal resolutions A and B and say it is only C they oppose); and, thirdly, as Geoffrey Kirk, the leader of FiF (and one of 'my' clergy when I was Bishop of Woolwich), says, 'But we will still be here' – and I suspect individual bishops would be driven back to local arrangements not unlike what we have got, if the Act of Synod were rescinded.

(d) But many will simply see the provisions as the death-knell of the traditional diocese. It has become conventional among Anglicans to describe the diocese as the unit of the visible church on earth and such a disunited unit sounds to many like a contradiction in terms. It is perhaps possible to set against this judgment three major qualifiers:

Firstly, there is surely some element of the local unit in the eucharistic assembly (which is certainly how the vast number of worshippers conceive of church – and perhaps with good biblical justification).

Secondly, it is virtually how the Church of England was organised in much of its history – the local clergyman and his church had a virtual autonomy and only very rare visitations by bishops or archdeacons.

Thirdly, even the anglo-catholic constituency of the Church of England, deriving from the Tractarians, has often, despite its theoretical dependence upon the episcopate, sustained its life in stoutly affirmed and no less stoutly practised parochial independence – and even disobedience.

These considerations perhaps make provision for individual parishes not quite so alien a concept ecclesiologically as good middle-of-the-way Anglican thinkers might conclude.

I freely acknowledge it is odd to the point of being bizarre to have a system where not all the clergy and not all the parishes will receive communion from their own bishop. But very tough consciences are at stake – and the tidier alternatives during this transition are either not available or carry a higher cost. What is clear is that those who believe the president of the eucharist must be ordained in the historic succession, and doubt whether women can be so ordained, are not going to change their minds or practices through majority votes in a synod. What is equally clear is that draconian legislation, which probably could never get passed anyway, would be counter-productive – driving clergy and perhaps whole parishes out into a wilderness, for the sake of having a tidy and uniform church left when they have gone, that is to provide an illiberal ecclesiology. If the unity of the church is to be preserved by a process of cutting out dissentients, then we have come upon a very curious feature of Anglican history; and these dissentients only claim to believe what they and we all believed the day before yesterday, and can properly ask how that became penal.

...the end of the plank?
In one sense, while 'flying bishops' get observers (and GRAS supporters) hot under the collar, in the light of history it will all prove peanuts. As I write, a new General Synod of the Church of England has just been elected and it has five years to bring about the ordination of women to the episcopate – or not. Already the Church of England does not know what to make of presbyters ordained elsewhere by women bishops.[6] It is now wrestling with the double issue (as in 1992 about the ordination of women as presbyters), both how to bring about the desired end, and also how to cater for the uncompliant minority who not only oppose the legislation, but believe that, if it comes to pass, women bishops will be incapable (or, at best, doubtfully capable) of conferring true orders. The answer of the opponents is that they must be granted a 'Third Province' (sometimes called a 'Free Province'), and their own report, from the group which shadowed the official Rochester Commission, offers as an appendix a well considered plan for the territorial division of the country to provide this archipelago province, including provision for parishes to transfer reasonably easily from one province to another in either direction.[7]

However, it is morally certain that the House of Bishops (if no-one else) would not accept this division, and yet the Synod will again be unwilling to provide a one-line legislation. Does any solution lie between these two wings? At the time of writing it appears that a plan for Transferred Episcopal Arrangements (TEA) will gather support. This, as I understand it, would entail parishes which passed the equivalent of resolution C being

6. See chapter 12 of my forthcoming book, *Minding Synod's Business* (Church House Publishing, 2006).
7. See their major report, *Consecrated Women? A Contribution to the Women Bishops Debate* (Canterbury Press, 2004).

transferred from their diocese directly to the care of their metropolitan. The Archbishops of Canterbury and York would have
to remain male (if that is not a solecism), and then, working no
doubt through suffragans, even flying suffragans, would have
direct (rather than extended) care of the parishes which so bid.
At the time of writing FiF have sounded as though they would
reject this, on the grounds that they are only interested in a third
province. Yet, if they give a clear message that they will not live
with TEA, then it is morally certain that Synod will see no point
in legislating for it, and they will be landed with the clean but
punitive 'one-line' Measure. So they will need to accommodate
themselves, and make faintly positive noises, I suspect. And it is
happening as I write: the General Synod during 2006 is making
fundamental decisions about what kind of solution it is pursu-
ing. As a caustic poem once had it: 'Good God,' said God. 'I've
got my work cut out.'

Ten Years On: An Anniversary Sermon*

Elizabeth Smith

We have just heard from our friend the apostle Paul, who put most of his stuff about sex into 1 Corinthians, and most of his stuff about money into 2 Corinthians. Today, though, we're in chapter three of 2 Corinthians, where Paul has been putting up yet another defence of his apostolic authority. Paul is obviously feeling embattled and undermined, and his cranky Corinthians have been giving him serious grief. At the end of chapter two he has announced indignantly that 'we're not peddlers of God's word' – it's the royal or apostolic 'we' here, Paul means that he himself is not a dodgy travelling spiritual salesman – but 'a person of sincerity, a person sent from God and standing in God's presence.'

And then came the bit that was read for us earlier. 'Am I inflating my apostolic CV?' asks Paul. 'No, never! I've already got all the credentials, all the referees I need,' he says – and then he launches into a wonderful if slightly mixed metaphor. 'You are my letter of recommendation,' says Paul. 'I wrote you! I wrote you on my very heart!' The implication here is that if the Corinthians are having a go at demolishing or belittling Paul, they will be shooting themselves in the foot – they are going to demolish and belittle themselves, since their destiny is so tightly bound up with Paul's own.

Then he says it again slightly differently – this time, 'you Corinthians are a letter of Christ' – now that's upping the ante – 'prepared by us' – by him – Paul's going to hang onto his own role if not as the author now, at least as the scribe. This letter of Christ is 'written not with ink but with the Spirit of the living God, not on tablets of stone but on tablets of human hearts.' The implication here is that if the Corinthians look credible, if they're

---

* This sermon was preached at the Eucharist at St John's Bentleigh, Melbourne, Australia on 14 June 2003 celebrating the tenth anniversary of Elizabeth Smith's ordination to the priesthood. The congregation included members of her present parish community, clergy colleagues, and members of various parishes and organisations who had been part of her journey towards ordination from the early 1980s onward. The texts were: 2 Corinthians 3:1-11, 17-18; Psalm 29; John 14:15-21.

authentic, if they're sincere – then Paul looks all the better for his part in their story.

Now, despite all the grief that Paul's writings have given to me and many other women over the years, I can relate to this dilemma of his about the somewhat uncomfortable relationship he has with these people who both recognise him as their leader, and who also want to avoid going where he's trying to lead them. I can also relate to Paul's wanting to get the Corinthians to take more responsibility for their own witness to the world, get over their leadership issues, and get on with their mission.

Church leadership has clearly been a difficult business since the very earliest times, as well as in our lifetimes. Ten years ago and for the ten years before that, the Anglican Church was full of leadership hopes and fears, and sometimes the hopes were the same as the fears, it depended on whom you were talking to.

For example, some of us hoped that ordaining women to the priesthood would change the church forever – and some of us were afraid that ordaining women to the priesthood would change the church forever. Some of us hoped that God would be seen in a wider range of images, and that the church would not look so stuck in the sexist mud. And some of us were afraid that, with women in the priesthood, our good old God would become completely unrecognisable, and ecumenically we'd have burnt all our bridges. Some of us hoped that once we ordained women to the priesthood we could relax, get over our internal Anglican squabbles, and settle back into business as usual. Others of us were afraid it would soon be back to Anglican business as usual.

Ten years on, I suspect that on a scale of one to ten, the score would be as follows:

changing the church: four;
re-imagining of God: three;
rehabilitation of the church's public image: five;
ecumenical progress: four;
business as usual: eight and a half or nine.

The trouble is, middle-Anglican business-as-usual is, if any-thing, less exciting now than it was a decade ago, and some of us, when we are not in denial, can see a real possibility of the middle ground of Anglicanism going out of business altogether.

For example, back then, we were ashamed of our reputation for treating women as second-class Christians. Now, we are ashamed of our reputation for poor responses and even cover-ups of sexual misconduct in the church, and we are miserably aware of how some of the leaders we saw as our best and our brightest have feet of very crumbly clay.

Back then, we were tied in knots over how to interpret the large chunks of the Bible that had for so long been used to keep women out of spiritual leadership. Now, we are tied in knots over how to interpret the tiny handful of biblical texts that seem to refer to homosexual people, and which some would use to rule gay and lesbian Christians out of equal spiritual partnership (and if that kind of interpretation wins the day, we can expect a big backlash against women again, given that there's so much more anti-women material in the Bible than there is anti-gay.)

Back then, we worried that our liturgy and our theology were weary and dated, and we hoped that someone would put a new spin on faith both for us and for the non-church-goers. Now, we are still worried that our liturgy and theology are still weary and dated, but there are even fewer of us to make the transition to something fresher. And that transition often has to be made in the face of real opposition from those of our fellow Anglicans who are hoping to go on as usual, and to let the non-church-goers look after themselves.

If you were part of the Anglican scene ten years ago, I wonder what difference you thought ordaining Elizabeth Smith would make? To you personally, to your church, to me, to God? Now there's an interesting question to revisit. I've been pondering what I was hoping for about my own ordination as a priest.

Firstly, I thought it would get me out of the diaconate where I had spent six and a bit years – so that the real deacons could get on with defining their diaconal ministry without tripping over wannabe priests everywhere – keep up the good work, Cheryl and Bevil and Cinti and the rest of you!

I also hoped it would let me be a liturgical leader in a eucharistic community, to preside as a priest at the community's celebrations, which seemed like the right way for my particular set of talents to be used in Anglican parish life.

And I hoped that having dealt with the big anxiety of 'will we, won't we, should we, could we have E. Smith as a priest?' I could get on with doing my share of the next stage of changing the church and re-imagining God and re-speaking the Good News.

I guess two out of three's not too bad … But what in fact happened? Well, after I spent eighteen months finishing my doctoral studies – that thesis with both the 'f' word and the 'h' word in it – that's 'feminist' and 'hermeneutics' – I bundled up my calling to the priesthood and I went in for what you might call a specialist branch of the discipline. I went in for vicaring. There is a smattering of vicars out there in the congregation today, and if you ask any of them I'll bet they'll tell you that vicaring with all its joys and troubles can really put you off being a priest … though I guess being a parishioner can quite easily put some of you off being a Christian, so the honours are probably about even!

For this particular priest, then, vicaring in the middle of the suburbs is a bunch of paradoxes.

Vicaring is about keeping the show on the road, *and* keeping on reminding people that the road is supposed to go somewhere, like, possibly, heaven, rather than the 1950s or even the 1970s.

Vicaring is about burying a generation of faithful parishioners who know exactly how they liked to be Anglican, *and* recruiting a new generation of parishioners who are only just finding out what it means to be Christian, let alone Anglican, and who will need a rather different diet if they're going to grow to spiritual maturity in the twenty-first century.

And above all, vicaring is about keeping on and on and on about God, since only God has the ghost of a chance of making the changes, *and* at the same time keeping on and on and on about the church. It's about bringing to consciousness all the customs and conventions that middle Anglicanism has taken for granted for so long we tend to call them not customs but 'traditions' – and which will swamp and suffocate us if we don't face them, sort them, recycle some, and thoroughly compost the others.

So what has kept my spirits up this past decade, in the midst of the paradoxes? Well, you have – the combination of little kids who've never known a church without women priests, and 80-somethings who've gone into a late-life spiritual growth spurt, and the people, including my clergy colleagues, in every age group in between who do show a keen interest in God as God, ruler of the universe, not just he who must be obeyed, but also she who must be enjoyed. What keeps me going is your prayers, your stretching, your risk-taking, your grappling with the new, your willingness to go below the surface of the familiar to find the radical roots of the tradition, well fertilised by all that compost of recycled custom, ready to put out new shoots and bear fresh fruit for a new century.

Now to go back to Paul and his cranky Corinthians. What this passage gives me today, for my next decade in the ordained ministry as a priest, is a glimpse of how we just might get to those longed-for changes in the church, how we are going not just to rehabilitate our shabby public image as Anglicans, but to genuinely shine.

Paul's metaphor starts off being about the Corinthians' relationship with him. By the end of the chapter, though, it's about their relationship with God and with the world around them, and the relationship is positively glorious. The glory of God shines on the leader and on the people, on the Corinthians and on Paul – it's no longer the royal 'we' Paul is using here, it's 'all of us,' he says, who shine with reflected glory. That glory transforms 'all of us,' and by a process of reflecting and transforming, that glory shines out from 'all of us' so that what Jesus Christ is up to, everyone can see.

I am absolutely convinced of two things: one, that only a glorious God can possibly be the remedy for a church that's suffering from blandness, lethargy, disillusionment and denial; and two, that the more the merrier: the more Christians who take responsibility for reflecting Jesus Christ in the world, the merrier our mission will be.

On the 'glorious God' front, the Trinity gets my vote every time – just the kind of unity in diversity, just the kind of mystery and mastery, just the kind of compassionate community that can nudge the current spirituality revival away from crystals and candles and reincarnation, and on towards the Word made flesh and the Spirit of freedom and the resurrection of the body.

On the 'merry mission' front, you get my vote. We have got to get beyond this assumption that better clergy will fix our image and solve our problems! We have got to get to the point where each and every person who's been baptised is willing to shine a bit gloriously in the world, reflecting glory from the face of Jesus Christ, flowing with freedom from the Spirit. Those letters of Christ that are written in Holy Spirit ink on human hearts – we had better get lots of them circulating pronto.

As a priest in the church, I get to read lots of those letters. Some of what is written on our hearts is a trifle dull and repetitive, some of it's full of scribbled-out bits and some of the fine print probably needs to be gone through by the Plain English police – all of us could do with a bit of canny editing! But the same Spirit who did the writing in the first place can be trusted with the editing. And for me, it is a privilege of priesthood to read the beautiful things that God is writing on your lives – and often, as one of your community storytellers, I get to read them back to you.

Meanwhile, what I long for is to see more Christians taking more pleasure in reading each other's lives as letters of Christ. I long to see more Christians shining with glorious reflected Trinity-Godness, sparkling with the Spirit's freedom. I long to see middle-suburban Christians excited, rather than terrified, by the prospect of their lives – our lives – being read by total strangers as letters of Christ. I long to see people who have never yet been formally introduced to Jesus of Nazareth keen, after reading these letters, keen to become much more closely acquainted with the Christ whose glory shimmers and scintillates in lives full of love, and forgiveness, and freedom.

As long as you're willing to be those letters of Christ, I'm willing to be with you as a scribe, as a reader, and as one who in my turn is being written by the Spirit. I know that whatever it is that the Holy Spirit is writing on my heart, it has all your names on it.

Lay presidency – can it be tolerated?

Charles Sherlock

In my younger days I spent a dozen summer holidays on beach mission teams. One daily activity was holding a service on the beach, on top of a large, brightly decorated pile of sand known as 'the pulpit'. Two cardinal rules applied to anyone leading a service. The first was, never wear sunglasses, no matter how glaring the sun. The point was not to cause sight problems, but to let children see your eyes, and so encounter you without barriers, as a person. The second was easier on the eyes, but harder to keep: never leave the pulpit empty. A child's attention span is short enough, and loss of continuity means a loss of focus on what was going on.

These two lessons burnt their way into my psyche, as highly relevant to presiding in liturgy. Sometimes a service feels like a rabble. You don't really have a sense of where things are headed, and there is little 'flow'. A series of people appear up the front, in varying styles of dress, some speaking formally, others chatting on – you become irritated and disjointed. What is wrong? Possibly a number of things: but it is likely that (in beach mission terms) 'the pulpit was left empty'. The presiding was sloppy, non-existent, or itself had no sense of the flow and shape of what was going on. The presiding person had abdicated responsibility, and the gathering had descended to become just another (ineffective) meeting.

Another service may be beautifully ordered – every step, movement, verbal and symbolic nuance carefully planned – but lifeless, mechanical, rigid. Here it is likely that 'the sunglasses were left on': the personhood of those presiding was so hidden or reserved, perhaps out of respect for the objectivity of faith, that Christ was imaged more like a moving statue than 'truly human'.

Presiding – embodying God's initiative

Presiding means far more than merely 'leading' (a term unknown in the New Testament). It enacts in a personal way the primacy of the divine initiative – we love God only because God first loved us. Without the personal, purposeful love of God coming to enable us, our worship is mere activity. And without God's Word being spoken to us face to face, in a connected manner, our hearing, singing, speaking degenerate into a mere succession of theological terms or spiritual jargon. Presiding thus embodies God's initiative to gather Christ's people, and proclaim the gospel words of forgiveness, thanksgiving and blessing.

Most Sunday services in contemporary Anglican prayer books open with a heading, 'Gathering'. An early draft of *A Prayer Book for Australia* had 'Gathering of the People', but it was quickly realised that this could be misinterpreted as if 'we, the people' did the gathering: it changed to 'Gathering in God's Name'. We do not gather because it is our idea: we are gathered by God, called into God's own presence, as those baptised into the divine Name. We are not a shapeless mass of individuals who have chosen to exercise our particular choice of religious franchise. 'We are the body of Christ' – and bodies have structures, sinews, a head and toes. Effective presiding combines these things into a coherent whole – the pulpit is not left empty, as it were. Such presiding effects the personal representation of Christ to us, and the enabling of response by us in a corporate way. It is more than organisational arrangements, or filling out a roster, as if 'anyone' could be that week's ears, eyes, prophets, revealers or singers (a distortion of 1 Corinthians 14). It reflects what it means to be part of God's people, led by Christ our head and brother, through the Spirit. And this is the underlying ethos of the Articles, Ordinal and *Book of Common Prayer* of the Anglican tradition, where the emphasis falls upon those who are 'clergy' – that is, 'called out ones' – to take up their responsibility to see that God's people are gathered, taught, fed and graced for ministry.

Presiding – a dialogue and responsibility
Such a vision of liturgical leadership points to a dialogue shape for presiding at a service – any service, not just the eucharist. On the one hand, personal presiding embodies God's initiative in gathering and addressing us. On the other hand, corporate presiding enables and focuses our response in prayer and offering. Traditionally, the first embodiment of presiding belongs to the ministry of the bishop (or presbyter / priest, as the bishop's delegate), who call God's people together, 'collects' our prayer,

speaks God's words of greeting, forgiveness, peace, and blessing, and presides over the ministries of scripture and supper.
The complementary embodiment of presiding is the ministry of
the deacon(s), welcoming us, enabling our confession and intercessions, gathering up the offertory, preparing the Lord's Table,
and sending us out in the dismissal to offer our worship in daily
life. (The deacon has other more pro-active ministries also – especially being an advocate for those in need, and reading the
gospel – but this is another story. I do not believe that deacons
should preside – but some would claim that every priest is also a
deacon.)

Such a view tries to avoid two extremes: the 'list of concert
items' style of service, and the 'master of ceremonies' approach
to leading. The first lacks shape, continuity, flow: 'the pulpit is
empty' because the organic character of the body of Christ has
been forgotten. It is a danger into which some more 'contemporary' services are falling. The second, 'MC', ethos can become
non- or even impersonal: 'the sunglasses are left on' – the communal nature of the people of God has been suppressed. It is the
danger of the hidebound conservative (whether ritualistic high
or stiff low).

Fundamental to effective liturgy is the need for those who
preside to accept the great responsibility they have been called
to carry – to represent God to us (as windows, not walls).
Conversely, those who assist need to do so gladly and skilfully,
enabling our response to God. Who better ought to undertake
such responsibilities than those 'called and sent to the same',
namely bishops, priests and deacons? To preside and enable the
priestly people (*laos*) of God is a great privilege, and a serious responsibility. When it is undertaken in the gentle power of the
Spirit of Christ, it helps the whole *laos*, ordained or not, to worship not only in our assemblies, but also in our lives.

Where an egalitarian ethos prevails, often linked with exag-
gerated sensitivity to Reformation concerns about sacerdotal
views of priesthood or the superstitious use of symbols, those
ordained to preside can take a minimalist approach to what they
'do' in the assembly. Presiding means much more than saying
one paragraph in an authorised Thanksgiving Prayer and leaving everything else to others – 'the pulpit is left empty'.
Sometimes fear of the symbolic leads to poor body-language or
stilted, impersonal actions with book, water, bread or wine – the

sunglasses need to be taken off. Closely related to this is the popular but false idea that 'minister' and 'to minister' in the New
Testament refer to any Christian: careful study of the scriptural
text shows that these terms do not refer to every Christian, but to
those commissioned for gospel ministry, who thus bear Christ's
authority to minister. The 'priesthood of all believers' (a scriptural notion, if not in these words) is not the 'priesthood of each
believer', an unscriptural notion on several fronts.

Can lay presidency be tolerated?
It is against this background that the question 'can lay presidency
be tolerated?' should be posed. The presiding described above is
'lay' in the sense of being 'untrained', and though it may be tolerated in terms of being 'legal', it is scarcely tolerable as regards
building up the people of God. But the chief issue lies elsewhere:
if 'lay' presiding, 'lay' administering or 'lay' enabling trans-
gresses the calling to be bishop, priest or deacon, something has
gone very wrong in our self-understanding of what it means to
be church, and what corporate worship in Christ entails. The
people of God are reduced to being an audience for clerical
sport, or for 'worship leaders' to entertain or work on us.

Before going further, two preliminary facts need to be noted.
First, the issue cannot be related to direct pastoral experience by
priests or bishops, because if present s/he should be presiding.
Secondly, the attitude of lay Anglicans towards being offered a
layperson to preside needs to be considered: in my opinion
many, including those of 'Protestant' leanings, would find
themselves in a difficult position (cf Dix, *The Question of Anglican
Orders*, albeit responding to a layperson of definite anglo-
catholic commitment). It should also be noted that 'experiment'
with lay presiding, apart from pressing pastoral circumstances,
would be quite irresponsible, unless an ultra-egalitarian or anti-
sacerdotal 'point' is trying to be made – which raises a host of
other issues.

So behind the question 'can lay presidency be tolerated?' lies
a series of questions about what it means to be – and to 'do' –
church (remembering that *ecclesia* in the New Testament works
more like a verbal noun than anything else: 'to go to church' is a
going 'to church'). Yet if a congregation is viewed as a collective
of individuals exercising a (usually homogenous) free-market
religious choice, then 'lay presidency' can not only be tolerated –

it is the only form of presidency which makes sense. If seen (by faith!) as a community of diverse people interacting together as the body of Christ, however, then 'lay presidency' makes little sense. It is important to state that I hear Anglican (but not, e.g. the Churches of Christ) proponents of 'lay presidency' as assuming the first model, though I find it hard to believe that this is seriously intended.

Similarly, if the (wider) church is understood as a mere linking of self-sufficient congregations for organisational purposes, then who is 'lay' is determined wholly at the local level. Once again, 'lay presidency' can here not only be tolerated – it is the only form of presidency which makes sense. The pulpit is indeed empty, and anyone may step up to fill it. Conversely, where the wider church is understood as the people of God who share in the communion of God across space and time (including eternity), the 'saints' of every age and place, then it is difficult to imagine why anyone might be interested in the question. Once more, it is important to state that I hear the Anglican proponents of 'lay presidency' as assuming the first model, with little sense of the wonderful mystery of being 'in Christ' together with others, the mystery represented in the bishop's calling to be a focus of unity. Presiding among the people of God entails far more than having 'leadership' (a modern, more than biblical, concept) in a particular congregation. It involves visible communion in authority, faith, morals and discipline across time and space.

Thirdly, if ordained ministries are seen merely as useful ways to identify certain individuals with particular training to do certain (paid) tasks, then it seems unjust not to encourage 'lay presidency'. On the other hand, if ministers are Christians called to be (diverse) signs of God's grace, whose 'life and doctrine' are to 'set forth God's lively Word' (as BCP puts it), then 'lay presidency' is a contradiction in terms. Again, I hear the Anglican proponents of lay presidency caught up in the functionalism of the former option, even though there is substantial common ground about the inseparability of 'being' (viz. justification by grace, through faith) and 'doing' (the necessary fruits, but not conditions, of this work of God).

Finally, if the Lord's Supper is perceived to involve a group of individuals doing at the same time what each can and does do separately, viz. 'remember' Christ's saving work, then presiding becomes an organisational question of whose turn it may be to lead. Where, on the other hand, this supper is understood as the celebration by an organic Christian community of what Christ has done for us – a 'perpetual memorial of his precious death and passion' – and so being drawn into the corporate move-ment, in Christ, through the Spirit, of offering ourselves in praise to the Father, then the sense of this action being a re-sponse to the divine initiative is central, and 'lay' presidency be-comes undesirable as well as unimaginable. This sense is classi-cally represented by ordination, which all Anglicans regard as intolerable to set aside. (I remain convinced that ARCIC and *BEM* have resolved differences over eucharistic theology suffi-ciently for these not to constitute a problem.)

Tolerated – by whom, and for what?
This paper has not sought to rely on 'legal' arguments based on canon law, rubrics or the like, but upon 'first principles' read against today's individualistic, post-Christendom context in western societies. That said, it is useful to note the wording of the Preface to the Ordinal (1662):

> No man shall be accounted or taken to be a lawful Bishop, Priest or Deacon in the Church of England, *or suffered to exe-cute any of the said Functions* (my emphasis) except he be called, tried, examined and admitted thereto, according to the Form hereafter following, or hath formerly had Episcopal Consecration, or Ordination.

Ministry is here grounded in a process of calling and examin-ation in the public realm. Further, it is not only recognition as a bishop, priest or deacon which is restricted, but also the exercis-ing of the functions associated with these offices. Emergency circumstances allow all sorts of variations, for example a non-ordained person being authorised to minister, including presid-ing (for say, a community isolated by flood, or a prisoner-of-war camp). Yet the Preface is directed towards regular church life, and it (within a Reformation ethos) restricts to the ordained not only their identity as such, but also the functions which they normally exercise.

The 'official' line, then, clearly does not tolerate lay presidency, and some historic English court cases have issued sanctions for its breach, albeit with politics being closely involved. The ques-tion today cannot be settled in this way – it merely encourages schism. What is needed is a response to the question from consideration of what gospel ministry, the ministry of word and sacraments, means for the post-Christendom western contexts in which 'lay presidency' is proposed. Given what I hear about these from most of its Anglican proponents (whether 'evangelical' or 'liberal catholic'), 'lay presidency' can indeed be tolerated, even seen as necessary. Yet what I hear is a lightweight, even irresponsible view of the Christian tradition, in which the divine initiative is replaced by that of the individual. It entails a surrender to the contemporary agenda of the western world, allowing its free-market / franchise and post-modern, pluralist 'anything goes' mentality to shape church life. Some Anglican evangelicals have moved outside their own inheritance on these issues, seen in the abandonment of liturgy, lectionary, distinctive dress, church year etc.

Yet I find it hard to believe that Anglicans can seriously hold such views. There is far more in common between mainstream evangelical, anglo-catholic, charismatic, 'broad' etc Anglicans on these matters than may at first sight appear. If so, it should be possible for us to affirm together a common understanding of

- the essential facets of what being church means, and how this is expressed in liturgy (including preaching), teaching and pastoral ministry, and mission;
- ordained ministries involving public responsibility for the gospel in its various dimensions, with corresponding responsibilities;
- liturgy as the corporate celebration of the wonder-full, empowering grace of God by the *laos* of God, in a particular place and time, enabled by the ministries given by Christ through the Spirit.

So, can lay presidency be tolerated? The answer depends on what is believed about the nature of the church and its ministry of word and sacraments, and whether some current notions about these can be tolerated. If the pulpit is empty, and/or we are wearing ministry sunglasses, it would seem not.

But 'toleration' (or not) has an unfortunate Anglican history, and one always has to ask – tolerated for what purpose? By whom? And with what sanction? The question ought not to be one of toleration, but of how we promote the mission and ministry of Christ in today's world – keeping the pulpit full, and removing every barrier to the full reception of God's truth, love and grace.

Ordination and Homosexuality: the Anglican Debate

Gillian Varcoe

Discussion of homosexuality in the Christian context is bedevilled at its outset by virtually irreconcilable starting points. To some Christians it is self-evident that the biblical prohibitions, as they read them, against homosexual behaviour are universally applicable. To others it is equally self-evident that the gospel demands an inclusive reading of scripture, especially where some readings of the text are used to justify discrimination against the marginalised or oppressed. The discussion is further hampered in the Anglican Communion by cultural positions that are not always understood or, where understood, tolerated.

Criteria for ordination

All kinds of groups have historically been excluded from ordination, such exclusions generally reflecting the particular prejudices of the societies in which the church has existed: the grounds for exclusion have thus ranged across race, gender, education, sexual orientation, marital status and physical disability.

In the Old Testament, priesthood belonged to a tribal group and within that group females and the handicapped were excluded. The New Testament barely addresses the issue, and where it does is unhelpful. For example, a prescriptive and literal use of 1 Timothy 3 would exclude the entire Roman Catholic priesthood on the grounds of their failure to marry, and all women on the grounds of their inability to marry one wife. Unruly or unfaithful children exclude many Protestants and Anglicans and 'above reproach' might be said to exclude the rest.

Of course, where a resort to the rules is found not to help, a dose of Pauline theology just might: the call of the Christian is to be loving, peaceful, joyful, patient, gentle, kind, generous, faithful and self-controlled. Ordaining people with the skills to do the task at hand and who are substantially on the path to such Spirit-governed wholeness would seem to be the right approach.

As Anglicans we subscribe to the criteria set out in our various ordinals, however these tend to combine all of the above: a mixture of gospel, law and cultural presupposition.

Cultural hermeneutics
The way we interpret the scriptures is culturally influenced (if not determined). Some subgroups of Christians in the world today still insist that women wear head coverings and grow their hair long (1 Corinthians 11), and forbid the wearing of trousers by women, but most adopt the dress codes, 'fashions', of the cultures in which they live. This is a missional imperative. The gospel cannot be preached unless it makes connections with the culture in which it is incarnate. The scriptures must always be interpreted anew in each place and generation.

When the societies in which Christianity has lived historically were comfortable with slavery, racism and the subordination of women, the biblical record was used to justify such things. Change came in response to social pressures against injustice, sometimes involving leadership from Christians, and always accompanied by a new exegesis of the scriptures.

In the case of homosexuality, the cultural issues are complex. No culture embraces homosexuality as a preferred norm; the debate goes on, not only between different parts of the world but also within diverse societies such as the United States; it is not a straightforward global North/South debate. Christians are being challenged to look anew at the biblical record in the midst of an unresolved cultural debate. Some, fearing for already failing social institutions such as marriage, or themselves uneasy about issues of sexuality, reiterate the conservative line. Others, aware of our history as followers rather than leaders where issues of justice and equality (not to mention sexuality) are involved, and seeking to find the mind of God in this time and this situation, believing that a resort to proof texts does not on its own show us God's mind and will. What does it mean to be created in the image of God? How are we to address modern scientific insights into the physiology and psychology of sexuality? How do we address the challenges to faithfulness in marriage and sexual freedoms before marriage?

A more contentious issue is the idea that the scriptures are also written (as well as needing to be interpreted) from a cultural perspective. However, all hermeneutics implicitly accepts this idea. Even literalists are highly selective in their application of scriptural norms, and are governed by cultural presupposition in their choices. Thus Robert Gagnon writes:

The Holiness Code is very much concerned with matters of purity and many of the requirements no longer have force today; for example, the forbidding of sex with a woman during her menstrual cycle (Leviticus 18:19; 20:18), the prohibition against breeding two different kinds of animals, sowing with two different kinds of seed, or wearing clothes made of two different materials (19:19), or the command not to round off the hair on one's temples or mar the edges of one's beard (19:27). Some of these commands may have arisen out of traditional taboos regarding the sacral quality of blood and semen, a concern not to mimic fertility practices of the Canaanites, a desire for consistency in maintaining clear social boundaries and the divinely ordained categories of creation, and/or the intent to symbolise Israel's 'set apart' status (that is, its separate and pure devotion to God).[1]

'The forbidding of sex with a woman during her menstrual cycle' is an enlightening exclusion. Gagnon does not discuss why it 'no longer has force today': he is apparently not shocked by it, therefore it is not 'abhorrent' (a favourite word of his applied to homosexual acts), therefore it does not apply. Exegetically he is on shaky ground. Acts 15 deals with the story of the early church's struggle with Levitical issues: Gentiles are free with regard to the law with some exceptions. They are 'to abstain from things polluted by idols and from fornication and from whatever has been strangled and from blood' (Acts 15:20). The blood taboo lies at the heart of Old Testament culture and law. It is explicitly included in the Acts exceptions. It vanishes without a trace, along with the strangled food taboo, as it ceases to be culturally relevant. 'Fornication', of course, does not.[2]

---

1. Robert A.J. Gagnon, *The Bible and Homosexual Practice: Text and Hermeneutics* (Nashville, 2001) 121.

2. It will not do, however, to assert that homosexual acts are by definition in this category and therefore forbidden. What constitutes *porneia* might also be a matter for new debate in each generation. Gagnon continues: 'Obviously, one cannot simply say: it is in the book of Leviticus so obey it. On the other hand, it would be a mistake to regard the statutes in the Holiness Code as consisting of largely irrelevant purity regulations. ... Christians do not have the option of simply dismissing an injunction because it belongs to the Holiness Code. The same God

Similarly, in an interview published by the Episcopal News Service (17 December 2003), George Carey, the former Archbishop of Canterbury, when asked the difference between ordaining women and ordaining gay and lesbian people says this:

> One has got to say it demeans women for an argument for the ordination of women to be an extrapolation for practising homosexuality. The ordination of women theologically stems from the gifts of the Spirit of Pentecost. Women are made in the image and likeness of God. Under the new covenant it is axiomatic that it should be exercised.

The implication that gays and lesbians are in some way *not* created in the image of God is extraordinary. Again, I would argue that the issue is cultural: it is difficult in modern western cultures to hold to the view that women be treated as they were in biblical times. Indeed, it is abhorrent to most that it should be so. It is however easy for people to hold such a view in relation to gays and lesbians because it is culturally supported and reinforced. Religion always tends to a powerful reinforcement of the *status quo*: one of its main functions is the strengthening of social organisation and control.

The gospel, justice and culture
An earlier draft of this chapter entertained the idea of it being culturally appropriate to ordain gays and lesbians in some places but not in others. Certainly such an approach is pragmatic and if accepted would maintain the unity of the communion in

---

who gave the laws of the Mosaic dispensation continues to regulate conduct through the Spirit in believers. A substantial case must be made for affirming conduct that was regarded with such revulsion.' However, given the exegetical mess, it seems difficult not to dismiss the Holiness Code, except as an historical document which informs us of the cultural climate in which it, and later documents, was written. Indeed, were it not for the current debate I doubt that we would ever refer to it at all. J. Neil Alexander, *This Far by Grace: A Bishop's Journey Through Questions of Homosexuality* (Cambridge, Mass, 2003) has this to say (p 37): 'It is interesting that we [Episcopalians, and probably Anglicans generally] are nearly unanimous in the dismissal of the holiness code as it applies to those of us who live on this side of the resurrection, except for two verses that appear to address the question of same-sex behaviour, Leviticus 18:22 and 20:13.'

spite of differing practice. Unity, however, is too often preferred
over justice. Nowhere in the world are gays and lesbians treated
uniformly with respect and acceptance, where the threat of
ridicule and violence are not present to a greater or lesser extent.
The church's position on the issue fosters these cultural prejudices and encourages violence.

One of the arguments against the ordination of 'practising
homosexuals' is also cultural: that this would create scandal. In
some places, however, the exclusion of gays and lesbians from
ordination creates the scandal. It certainly makes it virtually impossible for the church to provide pastoral care and fellowship
to gays and lesbians. The local church becomes simply another
dangerous place for them, another place of rejection and potential violence. What is scandalous is that such violence is seen as a
lesser offence than homosexuality and that Christian leaders
anywhere in the world would encourage such violence, either
actively or by their silence, in an effort to distance themselves
from the 'taint' of homosexuality.

Another ethical issue is that for centuries the church has preferred lies to truth. Gay priests have served the church well and
faithfully since its founding. Anecdotes abound of bishops being
appalled at candidates for ordination whom they have foolishly
asked if they were gay answering truthfully; 'If only you had
lied', they say.[3] The issue is being debated now because people
have ceased to lie.

The church must also be held accountable for its hypocrisy,

---

3. See Alexander, who quotes a speaker in the debate on the consecration of Gene Robinson: 'Towards the end of the debate, a bishop rose to
speak. He is a man for whom I have developed great love and respect.
He is counted among the most conservative bishops of our church. ...
He told the House of Bishops that ... Canon Robinson was a devoted
servant of Christ ... one of the most gifted and experienced priests that
this church has elected to the episcopate in a long time ... If he had
stopped right there, I might well have been convinced. But he didn't
stop. He went right on to say that he wished he did not know about
Canon Robinson's personal life. If Robinson's personal life were a secret,
there would have been no debate, no controversy, and there would
have been great rejoicing among everyone because Canon Robinson
was finally where he should be, in the House of Bishops. In that moment, it became crystal clear to me that I had a moral obligation to give
my consent to the election of the bishop-elect of New Hampshire. It was
time to *tell the truth.' This Far by Grace*, 60; (author's emphasis).

on the one hand attacking homosexual lifestyles as promiscu-
ous, on the other denying gays and lesbians support for and
modelling of committed long-term relationships. 'Celibacy or
marriage', we say, 'but marriage is only for heterosexuals.' If it is
accepted that the ordained (celibate of not) are called to model a
holy life, then ordained gays and lesbians (celibate or not) are
called to model holiness in their own relationships.

The exegetical dispute over the texts that reject homosexual
acts is not possible to resolve. The biblical text can, however, be
used to move us forward in our conversation. I have already referred to the Galatian fruits of the Spirit as the primary marker
of Christian holiness. Paul explicitly separates them from the demands of Torah ('against such there is no law'). What might this
mean in the context of this debate? The parable of the good
Samaritan gives us a clue. In one simple story Jesus profoundly
undermines our hardwired tendency to demonise the 'other'.
Christianity struggles with the paradox of the essential subver-
siveness of the gospel against religion's essential role of reinforc-
ing cultural mores. Jesus' challenge to the Pharisees is not about
Jewish religion, but about the general religious impulse: to be
right, to judge others, to adopt as law what reinforces our
prejudice.

Continuing the conversation
What are the issues and how much do they matter?

It seems to me that this is not primarily about gays and lesbians in the church or about their ordination. The majority of
gay and lesbian people in the world could not care less about an
internal Anglican squabble, although it is certainly important to
Anglican gays and lesbians who remain faithful to their faith in
spite of all. Nor is it about defending God's holiness. God is
quite capable of doing that without us, and even – eventually –
sorting out our mistakes.

Perhaps one area of agreement is that a major issue is mission: how are we helped and how hindered from proclaiming
the gospel in the particular cultural contexts in which we find
ourselves? How often do we find ourselves adopting the surrounding culture's values even when the gospel challenges
them? Throughout Christian history we have done so in the face
of appalling injustices such as slavery and the subordination of
women.

What are the issues around the authority of scripture and how we use it? As with the debate over the role of women in the church, it should be taken as a given that our disagreement is about interpretation, not about authority. We forget at our peril that the Word of God is not a book but a person.

The bishops at Lambeth clearly believed that unity was an issue. I speak, however, as a woman in a Province which is still arguing about women in the episcopate. What kind of value system makes unity more important than justice or standing with victims of discrimination and violence? If our debate about gays and lesbians serves to give comfort to their oppressors, then we become guilty of that oppression. In any case, unity does not arise from agreement; it arises from mutual respect and the desire for understanding. That can only be achieved by listening: to one another and to the Spirit and Word of God.

Further reading
For a thorough and conservative examination of the biblical material, see Robert A.J. Gagnon, *The Bible and Homosexual Practice: Text and Hermeneutics.* (Nashville, 2001). Still one of the best, although a little dated, liberal treatments is John Boswell, *Christianity, Social Tolerance, and Homosexuality* (Chicago, 1980).

An even-handed and thorough examination of issues of sexuality is provided in *Some issues in human sexuality: A guide to the debate. A discussion document from the House of Bishops' Group on Issues in Human Sexuality* (London, 2003). It does not attempt to dictate response.

Two articles, both by westerners, deal with homosexuality in some African contexts: Willis Jenkins, 'Ethnohomophobia?' *Anglican Theological Review*, 82,3 (2000) 551-64 and Kevin Ward, 'Same-sex relations in Africa and the debate on homosexuality in East African Anglicanism,' *Anglican Theological Review*, 84,1 (2002) 81-102. Both challenge ethnocentric approaches to cultures that are foreign to us, noting that ethnocentricism is not confined to the West. For South Africa, see Paul Germond and Steve de Gruchy, eds, *Aliens in the household of God: homosexuality and Christian faith in South Africa* (Cape Town and Johannesburg, 1997).

The Berkeley Statement:
To Equip the Saints

I
THE ORDERED NATURE OF THE CHURCH

The Calling of the People of God

The whole of creation is called into being through the abundant love of God, who in Christ participates in the world's life so that we may share in the triune life of love and joy. Through the Holy Spirit God baptises us into the life and ministry of Christ and forms us into the *laos*, the people of God, who as signs and agents of God's reign participate in God's mission of reconciling humanity and all creation to God. This is the *ecclesia*, the church, the new community called into being by God.

The foundation of the life and ministry of the church is therefore baptism.[1] As Jesus' ministry was inaugurated by baptism, so in our baptism into the life of Christ we are anointed by the Holy Spirit 'to bring good news to the poor ... to proclaim release to the captives and recovery of sight to the blind, to let the oppressed go free, to proclaim the year of the Lord's favour' (Luke 4:18-19). In baptism, the people of God are revealed to be a holy people (1 Peter 2:9-10), ministering to the world in the name and in the manner of Christ.

Baptism and Ministry

God bestows upon the church a variety of gifts to build up the body of Christ and to participate in God's mission in the world.[2] Within the Spirit-filled body, different charisms are given by God to every member, including prophecy, evangelism, teach-

---

1. Beginning our theology of ministry with the baptismal ministry of the whole people of God has significant implications for ecumenical dialogue. Provinces are urged to consider this baptismal perspective in their ecumenical discussions.

2. 'The complementary gifts bestowed by the Holy Spirit in the community are for the common good and for the building up of the church and for the service of the world to which the church is sent' (*Virginia Report* 3.20).

ing, healing, discernment, wisdom, administration and leadership (Romans 12:4-8, 1 Corinthians 12:4–12).

In order that the whole people of God may fulfill their calling to be a holy priesthood, serving the world by ministering Christ's reconciling love in the power of the Spirit, some are called to specific ministries of leadership by ordination. Although the New Testament refers to a number of different ministries of leadership (see Ephesians 4:11-12, 1 Timothy 3:1-13, 1 Peter 5:1-5), by the second century the ordering of bishops, presbyters, and deacons emerged within the wider context of the ministry of the whole church.

Over the course of Christian history, there have been various understandings of the relationship between the people of God (the *laos*) and ordained ministers. In some times and places, ordination was viewed as conferring a status elevating ordained ministers above the laity. However, understanding baptism as the foundation of the life and ministry of the church (that is, having a baptismal ecclesiology) leads us to see ordained ministers as integral members of the body of Christ, called by God and discerned by the body to be signs and animators of Christ's self-giving life and ministry to which all people are called by God and for which we are empowered by the Spirit.

Cultural Shaping of Ministry
The ways in which the church develops its theology, orders its life for mission, and takes up the threefold ordering of ministry interact with various aspects of our cultures. Cultures involve social styles, conceptual and material symbols, the technologies that sustain life, and languages, the arts, and other media of communication. They include the way people are present to themselves and to each other in community, as well as the ways in which leaders emerge, are acknowledged, and exercise their relationships and roles within communities.[3]

The gospel both affirms and challenges these cultural expressions of relationships and leadership. The historic threefold ordering of ministry will be embodied in different manners in various parts of the Anglican Communion, but ordained ministry must always be in service of the ministry of the whole people of God. The task of discerning which aspects of the culture offer

---

3. Structures of decision-making and styles of leadership in the church often reflect, at least to some extent, the parallel structures of society.

patterns of leadership and ritual celebration that enable ordained ministers to serve the people of God belongs to the people of that culture. This work of inculturation is always carried out in faithfulness to the baptismal call to participate in Christ's ministry.[4]

Bishops

God bestows upon the church the ministry of oversight (*episcopé*) which historically found its focus in the office of the bishop. As the one called by the baptised community for a ministry of oversight, the bishop is the sign of unity and of continuity with the apostolic tradition of faith and life. In the liturgical role, 'the bishop expresses the unity of the church by presiding at its liturgical rites. Whenever possible, the bishop presides at baptism, whether of adults or children, and eucharist, leading the people in offering the sacrifice of praise and thanksgiving.'[5] The role of the bishop is summed up in this way in the *Virginia Report* of the Inter-Anglican Theological and Doctrinal Commission:

> 'The calling of a bishop is to represent Christ and his church, particularly as apostle, chief priest, teacher and pastor of a diocese; to guard the faith, unity and discipline of the whole church; to proclaim the word of God; to act in Christ's name for the reconciliation of the world and the building up of the church; and to ordain others to continue Christ's ministry.'[6]

Pastoral oversight involves humble self-offering on behalf of others, rooted in the ministry of Christ, who as good shepherd lays down his life for his people. Thus episcopacy is exercised as a service to the community, a ministry that is intended to build up the whole people of God.

In reflecting on the role of the episcopate, it is important to consider the historical, cultural and social contexts in which the episcopal office has developed. In the pre-Nicene period, the church was seen as a sub-culture within the wider society. The bishop was teacher and pastor and the bond of communion both within the local church and between the various local and reg-

---

4. For further discussion, see *Anglican Orders and Ordinations* (JLS 39) pp 52ff.
5. *Walk in Newness of Life*, 3.39 (Grove Worship booklet W 118).
6. *The Virginia Report: The Report of the Inter-Anglican Theological and Doctrinal Commission*, 3.17.

ional churches. Bishops also exercised a ministry of prophetic witness. In the period after Constantine, the role of the bishop changed significantly. The bishop became part of the hierarchical administrative structure of the empire on the model of the imperial civil service. In the feudal period in the West the bishop was both spiritual and temporal lord. After the Reformation in England the relationship between church and state characteristic of the Constantinian era did not fundamentally change. The imperial and feudal models of episcopacy continued to predominate in the Church of England, and the episcopate functioned culturally and sociologically as part of the civil establishment. As Anglicanism spread around the globe, it was this style of episcopacy which tended to predominate during the period of colonialism. This model, however, was not universal, and in some places it was modified by an increased sense of the role played by the bishop in leading the mission of the church and by a heightened emphasis on the apostolic nature of the episcopate.

In the Anglican Communion today, a renewed model of episcopal leadership is emerging, one that more fully reflects the servant ministry of Jesus and the baptismal calling of the whole people of God. In this style of episcopal leadership, the ministries of all the baptised are nurtured in ways which are personal, collegial, and communal.[7]

'Every diocese in the Anglican Communion knows something of the exercise of the personal ministry of oversight of the bishop (or bishops); of collegiality in the coming together of bishops and clergy; and of the communal dimension of oversight which brings together the bishop with clergy and laity in the meeting of synods. These dimensions of the ministry of oversight are expressed in different ways in the different regions of the world and are affected by local circumstance and custom.'[8]

This vision of the episcopate ought to find expression in the ordination rite for bishops and in the way in which episcopal ministry is exercised both within the local diocese and in the collegial oversight which the episcopate exercises regionally and internationally. For example, the ordination of a bishop should affirm and celebrate the ministry of the bishop in and among the members of the Spirit-filled community in which the bishop has

7. See *BEM*, 'Ministry' 26.
8. *Virginia Report*, 3.22

been called to exercise oversight. In a similar fashion, the seating of the bishop should be a sign of the bishop's role as chief pastor and teacher of the community rather than an enthronement reminiscent of the imperial model. The bishop's leadership will foster a dynamic relationship among the parishes of the diocese grounded in the organic unity of the baptismal community with its diversity of gifts and ministries, including the ordained ministries of presbyter and deacon.

Presbyters/Priests

The calling of presbyters is 'to share with the bishops in the overseeing of the church.'[9] Just as the ministry of the bishop is rooted in Christ's self-offering, so also the ministry of the presbyter is offered in service of the whole people of God. The presbyter's distinctive pastoral and spiritual ministry in the community is expressed particularly in proclaiming the word and presiding at baptism and eucharist.

'Presbyters serve as pastoral ministers of word and sacraments in a local eucharistic community. They are preachers and teachers of the faith, exercise pastoral care, and bear responsibility for the discipline of the congregation to the end that the world may believe and that the entire membership of the church may be renewed, strengthened and equipped in ministry. Presbyters have particular responsibility for the preparation of members for Christian life and ministry.'[10]

As the bishop's representative in the local community, a distinctive feature of the presbyter's ministry is to identify and nurture the gifts of the Spirit given to the community for the work of ministry.

The New Testament uses the term *presbyteros* in reference to the 'elders' of Christian communities (Acts 15:4-6; 20:17), and the language of priesthood to speak of Christ (Hebrews 4:14-5:10) and of the whole community of the baptised (1 Peter 2:4-5; Revelation 1:6). When applied to Christ, priestly language refers to the sacrificial nature of his death (Hebrews 7:26-28) and to Christ's intercession before God on behalf of all creation (Hebrews 7:23-25; Romans 8:34). When applied to all the baptised, priestly language refers to the 'living sacrifice, holy and

---

9. *Virginia Report*, 3.18
10. *BEM*, 'Ministry' 30.

acceptable to God' (Romans 12:1) which they offer. As the ordained ministry developed, language of priesthood became increasingly applied first to the office of bishop and then derivatively to the presbyterate, and sacrificial and vicarial interpretations of this ministry were overlaid upon the earlier presbyteral understanding. At the time of the Reformation, the Anglican ordinal retained the term 'priest,' interpreting this office as one in which the minister unites the proclamation of the word, the administration of the sacraments, and the pastoral care of the community.

In the various languages used in the Anglican Communion today, different terms are used for the office, with different connotations arising from historical, cultural, and linguistic factors. Provinces that use the term 'priest' (or a translation thereof) may be guided by the interpretation of the term in *Baptism, Eucharist and Ministry:*

> 'Ordained ministers are related, as are all Christians, both to the priesthood of Christ, and to the priesthood of the church. But they may appropriately be called priests because they fulfill a particular priestly service by strengthening and building up the royal and prophetic priesthood of the faithful through word and sacraments, through their prayers of intercession, and through their pastoral guidance of the community.'[11]

For example, priests/presbyters are appointed to declare God's forgiveness and announce God's blessing in order that the whole priestly people of God may be witnesses of reconciliation and agents of blessing in the world.

Whichever term is used, ordination rites should make use of a wide range of imagery in order to bring out the multi-faceted meaning of this office. Consistent with a baptismal ecclesiology, the ordination rite should affirm the priesthood of the baptised community and the sacramental, pastoral and teaching relationship of the presbyter to the entire community.

Deacons

In the Anglican Communion today, there are various experiences and understandings of the diaconate, not only from province to province but even within provinces. It is important to learn from one another and to be sensitive to the different needs and cultural contexts in different parts of the Communion.

---

11. *BEM*, 'Ministry' 17.

Historically, deacons were often managers of the local church, holding considerable authority. They also oversaw the charitable and social work of the church. The practical and the liturgical dimensions developed hand in hand and reflected each other. During the Middle Ages, the diaconate became principally a transitional order on the way to the presbyterate, and at the time of the Reformation the Church of England retained this practice.

In some places, the diaconate is being renewed as a distinct office, drawing upon New Testament (e.g. Acts 6:1-6) and patristic evidence of the servant ministry of deacons. In this renewed understanding, the ministry of the deacon is primarily directed towards the servant mission of the church in the world and has as one of its principal aims 'to interpret to the church the needs, concerns, and hopes of the world.'[12] The liturgical role of the deacon expresses this interface between the world and the baptismal community.

Although it is sometimes asserted today that the diaconate is the basis for the servant character of all three orders, it is baptism into the life of Christ which is the basis for the servant character of all the church's ministries. The distinctive nature of the diaconate is not servant ministry in itself, but the calling of deacons to be signs and animators of the Christ-like service of the whole people of God in the world. Both the missionary, world-directed aspect and the liturgical aspect of the diaconal ministry ought to find expression in the ordination rite for deacons.

Direct Ordination
Because the three orders are viewed as distinct ministries, direct ordination to the presbyterate, and even the possibility of direct ordination to the episcopate, is being advocated by some in the Anglican Communion. There is historical precedent for both sequential and direct ordination. In the pre-Nicene church, direct ordination was commonly practised, and sequential ordination did not become universal until the eleventh century. Provinces may therefore wish to consider the possibility of direct ordination to the episcopate and to the presbyterate.

---

12. From 'The Ordination of a Deacon' in *The Book of Alternative Services of the Anglican Church of Canada*, p 655.

The Act of Ordination

The act of ordination is the liturgical expression of the church's appointment of its ministers. In the ecumenical document *Baptism, Eucharist and Ministry* the meaning of ordination is expressed in a way which is consistent with an Anglican understanding of ordination:

> Ordination denotes an action by God and the community by which the ordained are strengthened by the Spirit for their task and are upheld by the acknowledgment and prayers of the congregation.

> A long and early Christian tradition places ordination in the context of worship and especially of the eucharist. Such a place for the service of ordination preserves the understanding of ordination as an act of the whole community, and not of a certain order within it or of the individual ordained. The act of ordination by the laying on of hands of those appointed to do so is at one and the same time invocation of the Holy Spirit (*epiklesis*); sacramental sign; acknowledgment of gifts and commitment.

> (a) Ordination is an invocation to God that the new minister be given the power of the Holy Spirit in the new relation which is established between this minister and the local Christian community and, by intention, the church universal. The otherness of God's initiative, of which the ordained ministry is a sign, is here acknowledged in the act of ordination itself. 'The Spirit blows where it wills' (John 3:3): the invocation of the Spirit implies the absolute dependence on God for the outcome of the church's prayer. This means that the Spirit may set new forces in motion and open new possibilities 'far more abundantly than all that we ask or think' (Ephesians 3:20).

> (b) Ordination is a sign of the granting of this prayer by the Lord who gives the gift of the ordained ministry. Although the outcome of the church's *epiklesis* depends on the freedom of God, the church ordains in confidence that God, being faithful to his promise in Christ, enters sacramentally into contingent, historical forms of human relationship and uses these for his purpose. Ordination is a sign performed in faith that the spiritual relationship signified is present in, with and through the words spoken, the gestures made and the forms employed.

(c) Ordination is an acknowledgment by the church of the gifts of the Spirit in the one ordained, and a commitment by both the church and the ordinand to the new relationship. By receiving the new minister in the act of ordination, the congregation acknowledges the minister's gifts and commits itself to be open towards these gifts. Likewise those ordained offer their gifts to the church and commit themselves to the burden and opportunity of new authority and responsibility. At the same time, they enter into a collegial relationship with other ordained ministers.'[13]

This understanding of ordination reflects a baptismal ecclesiology. It is the community as a whole, with the bishop presiding, which recognises the divine call and the gifts of ministry of those who are to be ordained. It is the community as a whole which through prayer with the laying on of hands by the bishop as the focus of the church's unity seeks from God the necessary increase of those gifts and graces for the effective exercise of the ministry. It is the community as a whole which authorises and sends forth the ordained in God's name to lead the baptised in Christ's mission and ministry. All of these dimensions of ordination ought to find expression in the rite.

II

THE LITURGY OF ORDINATION

a. General Principles

1. Christian baptism implies a commitment to serve God through the church in and for the world. It is thus the foundation for Christian ministry, both of the church as a whole, and of each of its members, including those called to serve Jesus Christ as bishops, presbyters, or deacons. Setting ordination rites in such a theological context is an expression of what is meant by a 'baptismal ecclesiology.'

2. Ordination rites should be grounded in a baptismal ecclesiology, not only in setting ordination to particular ministries firmly within the context of the ministry of the whole people of God, but also in demonstrating the principle (from the

---

13. *BEM*, Ministry, 40-44.

Dublin Statement) that 'in, through and with Christ, the assembly is the celebrant ...'[14]

3. An ordination service is an ecclesial event in which the church's life and ministry is ordered, and so should take place in the context of a eucharist celebrated at a place and time when all its ministries may be most fully represented. (The eucharistic structure outlined in the Dublin Statement provides a sound basis within which ordination to each order may take place, during the prayer of the people of God, the 'royal priesthood').

4. The incarnational nature of the gospel calls Christians to embrace in their liturgy aspects of local culture that embody the values of the kingdom of God. Such things as dress, language and symbol in ordination rites all shape the way in which participants perceive the nature and significance of ministry, and how it is authorised and imparted (see the York Statement).[15]

5. Amid the great diversity of cultural expressions of ordination rites throughout the Communion, (a) the recognition by the church of God's call of the candidates and (b) prayer with the laying on of hands remain the central focus of the ordination rite.

6. The distinct character of each of the three ministries should be made clear. This is best seen when there is ordination to one order alone at any particular service, but all orders are represented in fulfilling their proper ministries within that service.

7. An ordination service is sometimes suggested as a suitable occasion when other clergy or authorised lay ministers may be licensed. Such a practice tends to confuse ordination and licensing, may detract from the significance of the service for the ordinands, and may be in danger of appearing to express a clericalised understanding of the ministry of the *laos*, the people of God.

---

14. *International Anglican Liturgical Consultation on the Eucharist, Dublin, 1995*, Principles and Recommendations 2. See David R Holeton (ed), *Our Thanks and Praise: The Eucharist in Anglicanism Today* (Anglican Book Centre, Toronto, 1998) p 261.

15. See 'Down to Earth Worship' in David R Holeton (ed), *Liturgical Inculturation in the Anglican Communion* (Alcuin/GROW Joint Liturgical Study JLS 15).

The above basic principles and the commentary which follows seek to set out the main elements and coherent guidelines for common patterns for ordination rites throughout the Communion, which Provinces can use according to their various cultural contexts.

b. Elements of the Rite

The Gathering of God's People

Setting ordination in the context of baptismal ecclesiology affects the service throughout. Yet the opening moments of any liturgical celebration greatly influence the way in which the entire rite will be understood by all the participants.

There are many possibilities for the gathering rite. It should not be seen as a mere preliminary to the act of ordination, but convey the sense that the whole church is coming together to order its life for ministry through ordaining some candidates in response to God's call given through that church. A fairly brief dialogue between bishop and people could constitute the assembly for this purpose, setting the context by celebrating the ministerial gifts of the whole church (see Ephesians 4:11-13), or the reaffirmation of baptismal faith (see below) might be used here.

The opening part of the service may also give recognition to the diverse relationships of the various members of the congregation both to the candidates and to the wider church (Anglican and ecumenical).

Regardless of how the candidates enter the building, they should be seated with those with whom they are closely linked, such as their family, those who have nurtured them in the community of faith, those who will present them for ordination, or those among whom they will serve. Care should be taken to ensure that the ordinands continue to sit with this supportive group until they are called forward for the Questions (see below).

The Presentation of the Candidates

The Presentation may appropriately take place within the Gathering so that the ordinands may be introduced to the community at the outset, or alternatively after the sermon, where it could also be set in the context of the reaffirmation of baptismal faith by the whole assembly and the continuing examination of the candidates (see below).

Provinces may consider the respective advantages and disadvantages of the Presentation of the candidates taking place at the door, at the font, or at a central visible place.

The particular process through which candidates have come to ordination ought to determine who will present them. For example, in some cases they may be presented by those who have discerned and nurtured the individual's call to – and preparation for – ordained ministry; in others it may be representatives of the local church among whom the new ministry is to be exercised. While the role played by family and friends may rightly be recognised at some point within an ordination service, the presenters should represent the wider community of the baptised rather than the personal choice of the candidate.

During the Presentation the presenters should affirm the candidate's call and readiness for this new and particular ordained ministry. A question concerning calling should follow and be answered by each candidate individually.

Sometimes the candidates – or others on their behalf – may tell their story, providing informal personal testimony about their experience of vocation, but in some cultures it is usually easier for personal information to be conveyed in other ways (for example, printed out or spoken about at the end or after the service).

Proclaiming and Receiving the Word of God

The liturgy of the word is a standard element in every Christian assembly. The ecclesial nature of ordination may be underscored if the eucharistic readings of the day are used, when they are appropriate, rather than those that focus more narrowly on the particular order being conferred.

The sermon should be an exposition of the word of God which has been read, in relation to the ministry of the whole church, and not be an address solely to the candidates, which belongs rather to a (set) Exhortation given by the bishop elsewhere in the rite.

Reaffirmation of Baptismal Faith

A reaffirmation of baptismal faith could be a significant feature of the rite, enabling the assembly to reaffirm God's call and its response to ministry. It is well suited to take place following the ministry of the word, as a foundation for the examination of the

candidates, and leading to the ordination prayer. Such a position is akin to its equivalent place in many rites of baptism. (By
'reaffirmation of baptismal faith' is meant declarations of faith
and repentance through recitation of the Apostles' Creed, perhaps in threefold responsive form, and expressions of commitment to a Christian lifestyle and ministry, both personal and corporate). The bishop's invitation to all Christians present to engage in this reaffirmation may well include material which is
currently part of the Exhortation to candidates in most
provinces.

Exhortation and Questions

The Exhortation and Questions may be divided into sections, so
that some introductory statement about ordination and preliminary questions may form part of the Presentation; the main exhortation and central examination may take place after hearing
God's word; and questions about the mission of the newly ordained and the 'sending forth' of them may be placed at the end
of the service. Alternatively, all of these may be combined together in the centre of the rite.

The questions put to the candidates should focus on the
specific qualities and duties required of the particular order.

This is the appropriate point, after the people have heard the
candidates' answers and expression of commitment, for the
bishop to ask the people if it is their will that the candidates be
ordained and for them to affirm their commitment to support
the candidates in their ministries. Rites which include an opportunity for the people to object to candidates should also allow
for such an affirmation.

Prayer with the Laying on of Hands

Ordination prayer involves the prayer of the whole community.
This raises the question as to how continuity between the prayer
of all the faithful and the presidential prayer with the laying on
of hands may be best achieved. Should the prayer of all the faithful be in silence or in the form of prayers of intercession led by a
deacon or lay person – or both? If the second, then it should be a
responsive form but not necessarily a standard litany, and whatever form is chosen should contain petitions for the ministry of
the whole people of God, as well as prayers for the world, for
peace, justice, reconciliation and creation. A hymn or song in-

voking the Holy Spirit and musical settings of any litany should
be suitable for singing by the whole assembly.

The presidential ordination prayer should set thanksgiving
for God's call of the ordinands to their particular ministry within
the context of praise for the diversity of ministries given to the
church by the Holy Spirit, and should make petition for the bestowal of the gifts and graces necessary for the effective exercise
of that ministry. It might well be punctuated by appropriate
congregational responses, and should culminate with a great
'Amen.'

The particular posture adopted by those involved – both the
community offering prayer and those for whom the prayer is
being offered – is significant. For example:

- if the bishop adopts the same posture as the rest of the assembly for the intercessory prayer and invocation of the Holy
  Spirit, the bishop is identified as praying with the whole
  community;
- if the candidates kneel while others stand, it is more clearly
  indicated that they are being prayed for;
- if both the presider and assembly stand for the presidential
  prayer, it is clearer that the act is that of the whole assembly
  and not just of the president alone;
- if those who are associated with the presidential imposition
  of hands (i.e. presbyters at the ordination of presbyters, and
  bishops at episcopal ordinations) join in any other manual
  gestures with the president throughout the entire prayer, its
  unity is more clearly demonstrated.

Traditional Anglican ordination rites have located the laying
on of hands after prayer and accompanied it with an imperative
formula. Recent revisions have tended to revert to the more ancient custom of locating it during the presidential prayer itself.
While this appropriately brings the two into closer association
with one another, it raises problems when more than one candidate is to be ordained. Three options for the imposition of hands
suggest themselves:

- before the prayer, in silence;
- during the epicletic (petitionary) section of the prayer, with
  part of it being repeated over each candidate (it is desirable
  for this to be a substantial portion of the section to avoid the
  impression that ordination is effected by a particular formula
  alone);

- at the end of the presidential prayer, in silence, before the doxology.

The ancient practice of the church seems to have been that usually the bishop alone laid on hands, and this continues to be the normal practice in most Eastern churches and at the ordination of a deacon in the West. In the Western tradition, however, it came to be the custom for presbyters at the ordination of presbyters, and bishops at the ordination of bishops, to join the president in laying on of hands. Nevertheless, not every one of the bishops or presbyters present needs to join in tactile contact for every candidate; the stretching out of the hands will suffice to associate others with the action and thereby help make the imposition of hands more visible to the rest of the congregation. It is also important that the way in which bishop, ordinands, and others move to and from the hand-laying should not by fussiness detract from the central act, nor should it destroy the unity of the presidential prayer.

In rites where the laying on of hands has been brought within the presidential prayer, it would be more consistent for the bishop to stand (without mitre) throughout the prayer, including the laying on of hands, rather than sit to lay on hands, as is sometimes the custom in traditional Anglican ordination rites.

Traditionally in Anglican rites the Bible has been given to those who are newly ordained immediately after the laying on of hands. However, because the ceremony fits naturally into the sending out of the newly ordained, serious consideration should be given to transferring this action to the final part of the service along with the presentation of any other secondary symbols of office. This would also help to preserve the centrality of the act of the laying on of hands, which should not be obscured by other symbolic actions, however generous and significant the role of symbols may be in the rite overall. At whichever point it takes place, because the word of God provides the basis and authority for all ministry, a copy of the whole Bible should be presented to deacons, presbyters, and bishops alike, and for the same reason its presentation should be the action of the presider rather than another minister.

The Welcome
In ancient practice, the newly ordained were greeted with a kiss by the bishop, their fellow clergy and the whole congregation, as

a sign of their acceptance. At the least, the newly ordained should be presented to the whole congregation by the bishop, and the congregation might welcome them with signs such as applause or ululation, as culturally appropriate. Care should be taken lest the welcome overshadow other parts of the rite or become an occasion for focusing too closely on individuals and their families.

In some places it has become customary for the bishop to welcome newly ordained deacons and presbyters to their 'order,' when they are then greeted by other members of their order. In the case of deacons, however, their primary relationship is to the bishop and their congregation rather than to a diaconal 'college'. In the case of presbyters and bishops, other presbyters and bishops have just taken part in the laying on of hands, so only the welcome by the congregation as a whole is necessary at this point. However, if there is to be a welcome into a particular order, care should be taken not to portray a clericalised model of the church.

Celebrating at the Lord's Table
Some believe that the newly ordained should take an appropriate part in the remainder of the service, to exercise some aspects of their ministry. Examples would include deacons 'laying the table,' assisting with the distribution of communion, or giving the dismissal, and presbyters being visibly associated with the presider during the eucharistic prayer. Such practice is more readily done when there are few candidates. Where it takes place, it should not usurp the regular ministries of others and should involve all those who have been ordained, not just selected individuals.

Others believe that the ordination service should function as a ministry to the newly ordained. Following ordination, they should have opportunity to reflect and focus on the charism they have received from God, especially after reception of the communion. The initial exercise of their new ministries is better left to be done in the context within which they will minister. Since only the eucharistic parts of the service remain, an unbalanced view of diaconal and presbyteral ministry may be presented, and the false impression may be given that ministry is primarily liturgical.

In either case, the newly ordained should remain with their new order until sent out at the end of the service.

When a bishop is ordained in his or her own cathedral, it is appropriate that he or she be seated in the *cathedra* immediately after the Welcome and then preside at the eucharist.

Going out as God's People
The focus at the end of the service should be on sending forth the newly ordained to exercise their ministry in church and world, as part of a local baptismal community. The newly ordained might therefore appropriately be 'handed over' by the bishop to representatives of those among whom they will serve. As indicated earlier, this is also a very fitting context for the presentation of the Bible to the newly ordained.

If other secondary symbols of office are also to be presented at this time, this action by might be performed by ministers other than the presider. These should be items that the newly ordained would be able to take away with them, which might fittingly limit their number. Much will depend on local custom and culture. However, two considerations are paramount: first, the giving of secondary symbols must be subordinate to the primary aim of sending the newly ordained to minister with their community; and second, only the church's symbols should be used, and not personal gifts to the newly ordained from friends and family, which are more appropriately given in another context.

The pastoral staff is the central symbol which explicates the episcopal office. It might therefore be held by the new bishop during the final blessing and carried in procession. In some provinces, there is a custom of the retiring bishop presenting the staff.

c. Other Points to be Considered
Anointing
In some parts of the Communion, anointing the hands of a newly ordained presbyter with chrism, and anointing the head of a new bishop, have been introduced into ordination practice in imitation of Old Testament and medieval Western custom. While some would view this as a valuable link with baptismal anointing, others see it as opposed to a baptismal ecclesiology. When presbyters are anointed, it might be considered whether the anointing of the head would be a more appropriate symbol of their consecration to service.

Vesting

Vesting is not part of the act of ordination, but discloses the new standing of the ordained person. Care should therefore be taken that vesting does not in any sense distract attention from the centrality of the laying on of hands. The following places might be acceptable:

- candidates are vested before the service, entering already dressed for the ministry to which they have been called by the church, a practice adopted in the ancient Roman tradition;
- the newly ordained are vested after the conclusion of the prayer of ordination and the Welcome – not during or immediately after the prayer, where it would disrupt the integrity of the rite. This vesting need not be done in a place that is highly visible.

Other Symbols of Office

For bishops, some will wish to present a mitre, ring, and pectoral cross. This may be done in silence or with appropriate words.

For presbyters, a paten and chalice (communion plate and cup) are sometimes presented. These might be the set belonging to the local church. In cases where the new presbyters join the bishop at the table, these vessels may be brought to the table with the bread and wine at the eucharist, used in the distribution of communion, and then given to the presbyters when they are sent out at the end of the service.

For deacons, there is no generally accepted appropriate symbol of office.

The Ecclesiological Implications of the Setting for an Ordination

The choice of location for an ordination will emphasise a particular understanding of church and ministry. For example, the ordination of candidates in their diocesan cathedral may accent the universal dimension of ordained ministry; ordination within the parish where they will serve earths their ministry within the local community.

Occasionally there is good cause for a candidate to be ordained in a place other than their diocesan cathedral or parish church, perhaps in a different diocese or province. In order to make more evident the link between the candidate's ordination and the ministry of his or her local church, a rite of reception should be arranged at a suitable time soon after the ordination.

There is no compelling reason why episcopal ordinations should be restricted to feast days of apostles. The important principle is that they should take place in the presence and with the involvement of abundant representatives of the whole church.

The use of the normal presidential chair as the chair for the ordaining bishop links it with the church's normal eucharistic activity, especially if it is set in a position which declares that the bishop is presiding over the whole event, and not simply the ordination. For the ordination prayers and laying on of hands, the bishop need not be at the presidential chair.

The Place of the Family

The place of the family of the candidates at ordinations will vary from one culture to another, and needs to be considered with sensitivity and care. Faith and vocation have often been nourished and encouraged by the family of the candidate, who may wish them to be involved in some way in the liturgy. On occasions, however, the family may oppose or ignore the candidate's calling.

In many societies the extended family is central to community and church life, and failure to recognise this would detract considerably from the significance of the ordination service for the whole community. But does overemphasis on the family in the ordination service detract from ordination as an ecclesial event?

Important aspects to be considered will include where the family is placed for the occasion and possible provision for each candidate's family to receive communion together. In many cases the families will welcome such initiatives. However, in some cases candidates may not have close families or may come from families without faith. In such cases an overemphasis on family ties may be embarrassing and undesirable.

APPENDIX

The statement on ordination of the sixth International Anglican
Liturgical Consultation held at the Church Divinity School of
the Pacific, Berkeley, California needs to be seen in the light of
the ecumenical movement in which liturgical renewal has
played and continues to play a significant role. The deliberations
of the Consultation were implicitly informed by the various
multilateral and bilateral conversations in which the member
provinces of the Anglican Communion have been involved. In
addition to direct quotation from the World Council of
Churches' document *Baptism, Eucharist and Ministry* of 1982, the
participants authorised an appendix containing relevant references from recent Anglican bilateral conversations.

These references are grouped around five themes that
emerge from the Berkeley Statement: (a) the primacy of a baptismal ecclesiology, (b) the ministry of the episcopate, (c) the
ministry of the presbyterate, (d) the ministry of the diaconate,
and (e) the act of ordination.

a) Baptismal Ecclesiology
In confessing the apostolic faith as a community, all baptised
and believing Christians are the apostolic church and stand in
the succession of apostolic faith. The apostolic ministry which
was instituted by God through Jesus Christ in sending of the
apostles is shared in varying ways by members of the whole
body. (*Anglican-Lutheran International Conversations: The Report of
the Conversations 1970–1972 authorized by the Lambeth Conference
and the Lutheran World Federation*, London: SPCK, 1973, para 75)

Together with other churches, Anglicans and Lutherans are
rediscovering the importance of the ministry of the whole
People of God, the general priesthood of all baptised believers.
This priesthood has its foundation in the unique priesthood of
Jesus Christ and is given through baptism. Its members are
called and sent by Christ and are equipped with the gifts of the
Holy Spirit to fulfil their priestly task in everyday life as well as
within the Christian community. They do this by offering themselves, their love and commitment in witnessing to Christ and
serving others. In our largely secularised societies this witness
and service of committed Christian lay people is more than ever
required as an essential part of the missionary vocation of the
church. (*Anglican-Lutheran European Regional Commission.*

Anglican-Lutheran Dialogue: The Report of the Anglican-Lutheran European Regional Commission, Helsinki, August-September 1982, London: SPCK, 1983, para 34)

The church lives in *koinonia* and is a community in which all members, lay or ordained, contribute their gifts to the life of the whole. (*Anglican-Lutheran Dialogue*, 1983, para 48).

The church is an embodiment of God's final purpose for all human beings and for all creation because it is a body of actual men and women chosen by God to share through the Spirit in the life of Christ and so in his ministry in the world. (Anglican-Reformed International Commission, *God's Reign and Our Unity: The Report of the Anglican-Reformed International Commission 1981–1984: Woking, England, January 1984,* London: SPCK, 1984; Edinburgh: The Saint Andrew Press, 1984, para 30)

The rediscovery of a missionary perspective has been made possible by the experience of the worldwide church during the recent centuries of missionary expansion. This has helped us to enter again into the perspective of the New Testament, where the church is a small evangelising community in a pagan society, ministry is primarily leadership in mission, baptism is commitment to that mission, and eucharist is the continued renewal of that commitment. (*God's Reign and Our Unity*, 1984, para 36)

It is to the whole church that the commission is given and it is to the whole church that the gift of the Spirit is made. The church as a whole is constituted by this act of sending and anointing ... The primary ministry is that of the risen Christ himself, and we are enabled to participate in it by the power of the Spirit ... This ministry is exercised by and through the entire membership of the church. Every member of the church, therefore, abiding in Christ, shares in this ministry. (*God's Reign and Our Unity*, 1984, para 74)

Every member of the church is an integral part of its witness and its mission; and every member has received a gift of the Holy Spirit so that the whole may flourish. (*Anglican-Lutheran International Continuation Committee, The Niagara Report: Report of the Anglican-Lutheran Consultation on Episcopé, Niagara Falls, September 1987,* London: Church House Publishing, 1988, para 17)

We believe that all members of the church are called to participate in its apostolic mission. All the baptised are therefore given various gifts and ministries by the Holy Spirit ... This is the corporate priesthood of the whole people of God and the calling to ministry and service (1 Peter 2:5). (*Together in Mission and Ministry: The Porvoo Common Statement with Essays on Church and Ministry in Northern Europe*, London: Church House Publishing, 1993, para 32.i)

Through baptism persons are initiated into the ministry of the whole church. Incumbent upon all the baptised is the exercise of *leitourgia, martyria,* and *diakonia*. (Anglican-Lutheran International Commission, *The Diaconate as Ecumenical Opportunity: The Hanover Report of the Anglican-Lutheran International Commission*, London: Anglican Communion Publications, 1996, para 24)

b) Bishops

Episcopé or oversight concerning the purity of apostolic doctrine, the ordination of ministries, and pastoral care of the church is inherent in the apostolic character of the church's life, mission, and ministry. (*Anglican-Lutheran International Conversations*, 1973, para 79)

This pastoral authority belongs primarily to the bishop, who is responsible for preserving and promoting the integrity of the *koinonia* in order to further the church's response to the Lordship of Christ and its commitment to mission … He does not, however, act alone. All those who have ministerial authority must recognise their mutual responsibility and interdependence. ('Authority in the Church I' in *Anglican-Roman Catholic International Commission, The Final Report: Windsor, September 1981* London: SPCK, 1982; London: Catholic Truth Society, 1982, para 5)

… episcopé, i.e. the function of pastoral leadership, co-ordination and oversight. (*Anglican-Lutheran Dialogue 1982*, para 40)

… The local bishop can only perform his ministry: (1) in unity with his brother bishops, especially when meeting synodically; (2) in unity with his flock, both clergy and laity. In exercising the ministry of oversight he should pay heed to the prophetic and other gifts which Christ gives his people (Romans 12:6-8; Ephesians 4:11-12). (Anglican-Orthodox Joint Doctrinal Commission, *Anglican-Orthodox Dialogue: The Dublin Agreed Statement*, London: SPCK, 1985, para 17)

It is the oversight or presiding ministry which constitutes the heart of the episcopal office, and that oversight is never to be viewed apart from the continuity of apostolic faith. (*The Niagara Report*, 1988, para 54)

Oversight of the church and its mission is the particular responsibility of the bishop. The bishop's office is one of service and communication within the community of believers and, together with the whole community, to the world. (*Together in Mission and Ministry*, 1993, para 43)

c) Presbyters/Priests

Presbyters are joined with the bishop in his oversight of the church and in the ministry of the word and the sacraments; they are given authority to preside at the eucharist and to pronounce absolution. ('Ministry and Ordination' in *ARCIC The Final Report*, para 9)

The community needs ordained ministers, because the source of its life is Word and Sacrament, because it needs to be equipped for its witness and service. (*Anglican-Lutheran Dialogue 1982*, para 37)

In their service, [ordained ministers] are related to the priesthood of Christ and accordingly also to the priesthood of all baptised believers ... which they help to strengthen and build up through Word and Sacrament, their intercession and their pastoral guidance. In this sense ordained ministers in Anglican Churches and some Lutheran Churches are called priests. (*Anglican-Lutheran Dialogue 1982*, para 37).

We recognise however that the word 'priest,' used of an ordained minister, has acquired overtones which render it unacceptable to many Christians. We would not in such circumstances expect the word to be universally used. We would, however, wish to insist that while the word may appropriately be used, other words, such as pastor, presbyter, minister, are no less appropriate. (*God's Reign and Our Unity*, 1984, para 79)

Those who may thus be called 'priests' exercise their priestly ministry neither apart from the priesthood of the whole body, nor by derivation from the priesthood of the whole body, but by virtue of their participation, in company with the whole body, in the priestly ministry of the risen Christ, and as leaders, examples and enablers for the priestly ministry of the whole body ... (*God's Reign and Our Unity*, 1984, para 80)

d) Deacons

Deacons ... are associated with bishops and presbyters in the ministry of word and sacrament, and assist in oversight. ('Ministry and Ordination' in *ARCIC The Final Report 1981*, para 9)

A general description of diaconal ministers can be given: Diaconal ministers are called to be agents of the church in interpreting and meeting needs, hopes and concerns within church and society. (*The Diaconate as Ecumenical Opportunity*, 1996, para 48)

As a specific and focal form of a task to which all Christians are called, the service of one's neighbour, diaconal ministry should foster and bring to wider recognition the ministry of others, rather than making their ministries redundant or superfluous. The diaconal minister should lead and inspire the wider church in its service. (*The Diaconate as Ecumenical Opportunity*, 1996, para 56)

e) The Act of Ordination

Because ministry is in and for the community and because ordination is an act in which the whole church of God is involved, this prayer and laying on of hands take place within the context of the eucharist. ('Ministry and Ordination' in *ARCIC The Final Report 1981*, para 14)

It is God who calls, ordains, and sends the ministers of Word and Sacrament in the church. He does this through the whole people, acting by means of those who have been given authority so to act in the name of God and of the whole church. Ordination to the ministry gives authority to preach the gospel and administer the sacraments according to Christ's command and promise, for the purpose of the continuance of the apostolic life and mission of the church. Ordination includes the prayer of all the people and the laying on of hands of other ministers, especially of those who occupy a ministry of oversight and unity in the church (*Anglican-Lutheran International Conversations 1972*, para 78).

In our traditions we hold that in the act of ordination the triune God, through the church, calls, blesses and sends the ministers of Word and Sacraments. They receive a special authority and responsibility from God in Christ and at the same time and by the same act they receive authority to minister from the whole People of God. (*Anglican-Lutheran Dialogue 1982*, para 36)

Ordination is the act which constitutes and acknowledges this special ministry of representation and leadership within the life of the church both locally and universally. In the act of ordination, the church in Christ prays to the Father to grant his Spirit to the one ordained for the office and work to which that person is called, accompanying the act with a sacramental sign which specifies by the imposition of hands the one for whom the prayer is made, and – in faith that the prayer is heard – commits to the person ordained the authority to act representatively for the universal church in the ways proper to that particular office. (*God's Reign and Our Unity: The Report of the Anglican-Reformed International Commission 1981–1984: Woking, England, January 1984*, para 80)

(Compiled by Richard G Leggett)

MEMBERS OF THE CONSULTATION

Anthony Aarons, S.S.F. (USA), Alan Barthel (Canada), Tennyson Bogar (Papua New Guinea), Molanga Botola (Congo), Paul Bradshaw (England), Perry Brohier (Sri Lanka), Robert Brooks (USA), Colin Buchanan (England), Jean Campbell (USA), Merwyn Castle (Southern Africa), Christopher Cocksworth (England), George Connor (Aotearoa, New Zealand and Polynesia), Bill Crockett (Canada), Ian D Darby (Southern Africa), Keith Denison (Wales), Carol Doran (USA), Ronald Dowling (Australia), Mark Earey (England), Richard Fabian (USA), Kevin Flynn (Canada), Alec George (England), John Gibaut (Canada), Paul Gibson (Canada), Benjamin Gordon-Taylor (England), Donald Gray (England), Robert Gribben (Ecumenical Partner – Australia), Keith Griffiths (Southern Africa), George Guiver (England), Jeremy Haselock (England), David Hebblethwaite (England), John W B Hill (Canada), David Holeton (Czech Republic), Christopher Irvine (England), Bruce Jenneker (USA), Joyce Karuri (Kenya), John Hiromichi Kato (Japan), Richard Leggett (Canada), Trevor Lloyd (England), Cynara (Tessa) Mackenzie (Aotearoa, New Zealand and Polynesia), Tomas Maddela (Philippines), Gordon Maitland (Canada), Azad Marshall (Pakistan), Richard Cornish Martin (USA), Brian Mayne (Ireland), Ruth Meyers (USA), Harold Miller (Ireland), Ronald Miller (USA), Boyd Morgan (Canada), Clayton Morris (USA), Ishmael Mukuwanda (Zimbabwe), Gilly Myers (England), Martin Blaise Nyaboho (Burundi), Nelson Nyumbe (The Sudan), Martin Nzaramba (Rwanda), Juan Oliver (USA), Sue Parks (England – SPCK), Ian Paton (Scotland), William Petersen (USA), Isaac Mar Philoxenos (Mar Thoma Church – India), Ellison Pogo (Melanesia), Alphege Rakotovao (Indian Ocean), Alfred Reid (West Indies), Anderson Saefoa (Melanesia), Vincent Shamo (West Africa), John Simalenga (Tanzania), Susan Marie Smith (USA), Bryan Spinks (England/USA), David Stancliffe (England), Gillian Varcoe (Australia), Louis Weil (USA), Carol Wilkinson (England), John Masato Yoshida (Japan), Ian Young (Jerusalem & Middle East).